Pauline Shute

FAMILY QUARTET

FAMILY QUARTET

by

John Catlin

'What might have been and what has been
Point to one end, which is always present'
Burnt Norton,
T. S. Eliot

HAMISH HAMILTON · LONDON

First published in Great Britain 1987
by Hamish Hamilton Ltd
27 Wrights Lane London W8 5TZ

Copyright © 1987 by John Catlin

British Library Cataloguing in Publication Data

Catlin, John
  Family quartet.
  1. Brittain *(Family)*   2. Catlin *(Family)*
  I. Title
  941.082'092'2   CT787.B7

ISBN 0-241-12098-5

Printed and bound in Great Britain by
Butler & Tanner, Frome and London

LIST OF ILLUSTRATIONS

FOREWORD
by MALCOLM MUGGERIDGE

THERE are many Christians in this world but only a few are able to forgive. 'True kindness is forgiving'. This statement of Mother Teresa does fully apply to John Brittain-Catlin, author of this book, whom we — my wife Kitty and I — knew as a friend and who was the personification of kindness. John died on the 29 March 1987 just as this book was sent to the publisher. What was to be a foreword has become a tribute to him.

John Catlin's courage helped him to create his unique individuality and shaped his convictions even in the face of encountering opposition sometimes from the powerful personalities in his immediate family — some of these we discussed during his visits to us. He always was his own man and sought to express himself through art in painting and writing of which this book is an example. We treasure the painting 'Garden at St Cloud' in our possession. It emanates spirituality. And we are happy that his life's art works will be on show in an exhibition to coincide with *Family Quartet*'s publication.

It was religion, or more precisely faith which we discussed more often than anything else. And here we shared deeply. John made a conscious choice of Roman Catholicism, being baptized at the age of eighteen. He stood by his belief especially at the end of his years, never faltering, facing his death with courage and affirmed faith. The prospect of dying did not appal him. He knew redemption cannot be gained through worldly pursuits. That is why, I think, the public only now will hear of his worth, after his relatively early death. Faith is what really matters and in this he enriches us immeasurably. He was one of the few men to live by his family motto: IN DEO VINCO — in God I conquer.

INTRODUCTION

I have called this book *Family Quartet* because it is primarily about the twenty-year period between the late 1920s and the late 1940s when both my sister and I were at home with our parents.

In addition to my mother, Vera Brittain, and my father, George Catlin, the journalist and writer Winifred Holtby also lived with us. However, the term 'quartet' still remains apt because by the time my sister Shirley had ceased to be a baby, Winifred was no longer with us. Shirley was born in July 1930, and by 1932 it was apparent that Winifred was suffering from Bright's disease. Although she did not die until the end of September 1935, after 1933 she no longer lived continuously with us. So effectively we were a quartet rather than a quintet. From the time I was born, at the end of 1927, until 1933, that quartet consisted of my parents, Winifred and myself. Afterwards it consisted of my parents, myself, and Shirley.

It is now over fifty years since my mother published her best-known book, *Testament of Youth*; and it is also just over fifty years since Winifred Holtby's most famous book, *South Riding*, was published, the year after her death. A sufficient period of time has elapsed to see the major achievement of both my mother and Winifred in some sort of perspective and to explain the background in both their lives to the writing of these books. It is also an appropriate time to assess the achievement of my father, less well-known, but to my mind an equally significant figure of his times.

There will be readers of this book to whom the name of my sister, Shirley Williams, is as familiar as the name of my mother was after the unexpected success of *Testament of Youth*. The number of readers who will have heard of my father, George Catlin, and who know anything about him will be smaller. To those who have only heard of him as Vera Brittain's husband he remains a shadowy figure. I hope to correct this impression. My father never achieved the public reputation of my mother, but as an academic figure with a relatively unsuccessful career in politics he was still in many ways as remarkable as my mother, or Winifred or my sister.

In his book *The Science and Method of Politics*, my father wrote: 'There is no intellectually honest reason for permitting the title of History to be usurped by one privileged section of creation, namely, mankind, for the behoof of its own record.' Perhaps this sentence, written in 1926 when my father was thirty, can be taken as his own epitaph. My father's name will not go down in history. But that does not alter the fact that he was an unusually interesting man, and I think if he had achieved the success in politics after which he hankered — had he been, for example, Foreign Secretary or even Minister for Commonwealth Affairs he would not have been able to develop the wide range of his other interests.

As current affairs become history, very few of those public figures who fifty years ago were written about almost daily in the press are remembered at all. Such literary figures of the 1920s and '30s as John Buchan and Hugh Walpole are increasingly seen as representative figures of their own age rather than as outstanding writers. Who today has heard of Philip Snowden, Chancellor of the Exchequer in 1924 and again from 1929 to 1931, or even of Sir John Simon who was Foreign Secretary for 1931 to 1935? Today they are only known to professional historians specialising in English history of the 1930s or in the origins of the Second World War.

With passing time, the interest of posterity in my mother, Winifred Holtby and my father will be found in the way they represent a way of life between the turn of the century and the end of the Second World War: the first half of the twentieth century. Only writers and statesmen of truly outstanding achievement will be regarded as rising above this level. H. G. Wells, Bernard Shaw, D. H. Lawrence, Aldous Huxley and George Orwell will perhaps be the only writers who will be seen as more than just typical representatives. Equally, Lloyd George and Winston Churchill will be the only English politicians in the same period to have risen to the rank of statesmen. The private lives of these major figures are of great fascination, but it remains secondary to their public achievement. For those of lesser stature their private lives are of more interest and, indeed, of increasing interest for the light they throw on the period in which they lived. By contrast their literary or political achievement sinks. What Lord Hervey wrote about George III, James Boswell about Dr Johnson , or Horace Walpole about politics, art and literature in the eighteenth century, helps us to understand the times in which they lived. And what they wrote is now of more social and historical interest than most of the books written by the professional writers of their time, except only the greatest.

Without wishing to minimise the literary achievement of either my mother or Winifred Holtby, the kind of lives they lived — with my father — are possibly as interesting or more so, not least because they would certainly not have been possible in England, or Europe or the United States for that matter, before the First World War. Apart from my sister, I am the only person now living who had first-hand experience of their lives, and because I am two and a half years older than Shirley I can write about Winifred Holtby from personal experience in a way that would not be possible for her, since she was only five when Winifred died.

When we are young we like to think we are quite different from our parents and that we owe them nothing. As we get older we are forced to realise that the characteristics we acquired in our childhood environment are far more influential on our feelings, thought and behaviour than we were able to see or willing to admit when we were young. It is for this reason that I have included a considerable amount of background information, not only about my parents' parents, but also about their family history. I have done the same for Winifred but I do not have so much information about the earlier Holtbys. We are not solely the product of our family environment, just as we are not exact replicas of our parents. But these parental and family influences determine us, just as much if they lead us to react against our parents and family background than if they do not.

When my mother started writing *Testament of Youth* she began by giving a description of her parents that was considerably influenced by the socialist leanings of the 1920s and partly due, also, to her experiences in the 1914–18 war. It was a somewhat misleading picture. In the same way Shirley, on her return from the United States where she was evacuated for part of the 1939–45 war, liked to give the impression to those who did not know her well that my mother's housekeeper and her husband were her parents. To support this fiction she preferred to go in and out of our house by the back door. Shirley reacted against her undoubtedly privileged background by denying its existence as far as she could, in just the same way as her mother had reacted to her own rather bourgeois but nevertheless plutocratic background. I too reacted against their ideas and values rather than the fact that my mother was exceptionally well-off, which I took for granted until I was conscripted into the RAF in 1946 — after which I regarded it as a positive advantage. But then I was not a socialist and I did not want to go into politics.

CHAPTER I

VERA

WHEN I was seven years old I had my portrait painted by an artist, Howard Lewis, who had managed to persuade firstly my grandmother and then my mother to have likenesses done of nearly all members of the family who had not so far been painted. He also painted a portrait of Winifred Holtby after her death from a photograph which now hangs in Somerville College, Oxford. Howard was taking me home on a 49 bus from his studio in Pembroke Villas, Kensington, and as we passed Kensington Gardens he told me he thought that everyone on the bus would have heard of my mother. The year was 1937 and *Testament of Youth*, which was originally published in 1933, had gone into many editions both in England and in the United States, and my mother was basking in unanticipated glory. Although never over-modest, I had acquired a fundamental cynicism from my Brittain grandmother, and I told Howard that I very much doubted whether more than two people on the bus would have heard of my mother. Thinking back, this was still quite a high proportion.

Of the people who might read my own book, how many will have heard of my mother today? And, of those who have heard of Vera Brittain, in what connection will her name ring a bell? I imagine that the majority will know of her because she wrote *Testament of Youth*. To others, and I think these would chiefly be women, I expect that she is remembered firstly as a feminist. To some, perhaps both men and women, she may be recalled as a pacifist.

When I lived at home with my parents, my nickname for my mother was 'the novelist' and when I spoke to my father or Shirley about my mother or reported something she had said I used to say 'the novelist says' or 'the novelist thinks'. Although disrespectful, this description was a projection of how my mother liked to think of herself. Later, in her final entry in *Who's Who*, she did not mention her first published book, *The*

1

Dark Tide, a novel which, after the success of *Testament of Youth*, she liked to forget in view of its critical and financial failure. And in retrospect my mother was not essentially a novelist, but a chronicler of her times. The novels she wrote were, in many ways, fact masquerading as fiction. It was the heroine of *The Dark Tide* which attracted my father to my mother in the first place, and it was this picture she presented of herself that he fell in love with. Only two of the books she lists in *Who's Who* were published as fiction: *Honourable Estate*, a fictionalised account of her own family and that of my father; and *Born 1925*, more of a work of fiction, but based on her brother Edward and an amalgam of her friend and subsequent literary executor, Paul Berry, and myself. Those of her books which are not autobiographical are expressions of her passionate pacifism — *England's Hour, Humiliation with Honour, Account Rendered* and *The Rebel Passion: A Short History of some Pioneer Peacemakers* — and her feminism — *Lady Into Woman: A History of Women from Queen Victoria to Elizabeth II*; *The Women At Oxford*; and *Radclyffe Hall: A Case of Obscenity?*

My mother had an ambition to be famous long before she was adolescent, and in an age before the First World War, when politics were not open to women as equal contenders with men, she looked on writing as a means to achieving this ambition. Writing was not an end in itself. Like my sister, my mother was a promoter of causes rather than a woman of creative imagination. She was a great organiser of her time. Not a moment was wasted, and she inherited from her forebears in the Staffordshire potteries a keen business-like sense. Apart from dealing with her own business affairs this concern for maximisation of the efficient use of time led her in later life to what can best be described as an executive role in the various causes she championed. In the period after the Second World War she became a Director of Femina Books; she was Honorary Life President of the Society of Women Writers and Journalists; President of the Married Women's Association; and Vice President of both the National Peace Council and the Women's International League for Peace and Freedom.

Had she been born twenty years later I am certain she would have made a career for herself in politics. She told me more than once that the only reason she did not embark on a political career was that when she was formulating her ambitions, say between the ages of ten and fifteen — that is, between 1903 and 1908 — such a career was not open to a woman. The reason she did not take to politics in later life was her consideration for my father. She was aware from the mid-1930s onwards that she was far better-known than he, and if father's interests had remained wholly academic, my mother would almost certainly have added party politics to her other practical interests. She possessed characteristics which would have made her an ideal politician. She had an innate pugnacity. There was nothing she liked better than pricking the bubble of pretentiousness characteristic of many of the Conservative MPs with whom she crossed swords in the 1920s. She had a very clear idea of what she stood for and a tremendous capacity to present complex issues in a way which made them seem simple. And, although she was a great believer in moral values, she was never priggish. Like two later graduates of her Oxford College, Somerville, she could bring moral fervour to almost any contest, but by two accidents, one of history, the other of marriage, she never trod the path of Margaret Thatcher or Shirley Williams.

My father once wrote, 'To know history is to control power', but what he did not add was that to know history is not enough. One also has to control the electorate. My mother had an innate understanding of history and, what is more, she knew how to put it into practice, as she did in her campaign for pacifism throughout the war of 1939–45. My father, on the other hand, may have been a student of Machiavelli, but while he knew that it is necessary in politics to appear 'compassionate, faithful to his word, kind, guileless, and devout' his disposition was such that he forgot what Machiavelli added: the successful politician knows how to be the opposite if needs be.

My mother does not reveal the date of her birth in *Testament of Youth*. She was born on December 29, 1893, and she looked young for her age at least until she was nearing fifty. In her youth she regarded this as a disadvantage when she came to address meetings of the League of Nations in the 1920s, but gradually she got used to the fact that she was usually taken to be nearer to twenty than to thirty. Not only did she have a youthful appearance, but her sufferings during the First World War never showed on her face. This may be seen from the photographs taken of her during 1914–18, like the one of her in Malta in 1916 after the death of her fiancé, Roland Leighton.

She was born in Newcastle-under-Lyme, one of Arnold Bennett's five towns, when it still retained an identity of its own. Later it became virtually inseparable from Stoke-on-Trent. Her birth took place at her parents' villa in Sidmouth Road, while her father, typically, was at a pantomime in Hanley where his family's paper-making business was located. My grandfather Brittain was nothing if not impatient and self-indulgent.

Two years later, in 1895, my grandparents moved to a more spacious house, 'Glen Bank' in Macclesfield. I can only speculate on why my grandfather made this move from Newcastle. The new house was about seventeen miles north of Hanley, where the paper works were originally situated, and about fifteen miles north of Cheddleton, where my grandfather started to build much larger factories before and after the turn of the century. It may have been because my grandfather's own grandfather, who had lived to be nearly ninety, had died five years before, and with the death of my great-grandfather in 1885, my grandfather controlled the family business and was undoubtedly better-off than he had been while his own grandfather had been alive.

My mother's mother was the daughter of an organist who was far from well-off, and when my grandfather married her, his relatives disapproved of the marriage in no uncertain terms and did not visit her or her parents. It is significant in my mother's development that, while her father was relatively rich, her mother's family was not.

From the time the Boer War started in 1899, when my mother was six, she took an increasing interest in what was going on in the outside world and began to distinguish real occurrences from fables and fancies. Nevertheless fables, and in particular the fairy stories of Andrew Lang with their endless conflicts between right and wrong, personified by dragons and evil queens on the one hand and by noble knights and virtuous princesses on the other, exerted an immense if subconscious influence on her. (Part I of *Testament of Youth* is preceded by a quotation from Andrew Lang's *The Pink Fairy Book*.) These stories were also favoured reading of my father when a child, and Shirley and I used to receive a book of Andrew Lang fairy stories for Christmas or birthday nearly every year from the time we could both read and be trusted to look after books until 1940 when we were evacuated to the United States.

My mother recalled the Relief of Ladysmith on February 2, 1900 when she was six (one of her uncles had died in the siege); she remembered the death of Queen Victoria whose Diamond Jubilee, when my mother was three, had made a great impression on her; and how the preparations which she and her brother Edward, three years younger than she, were making for the coronation of Edward VII had to be put aside due to the King's appendicitis.

My mother remembered her childhood, which coincided with

Edward's reign, as serene and uneventful. It was the recollection of the hedges and wild flowers in the Cheshire lanes which gave my mother her great love of flowers, references to which increased in her books as time went on. Flowers, particularly wild ones, represented for her the long-lost feeling of security which she associated with her childhood and which had existed for her until she was seventeen. But my mother also recalled the irrational fears she experienced in childhood: fear of thunder, sunsets, the full moon, the dark, standing under railway arches, crossing over noisy streams, the end of the world and the devil waiting to catch her. In fact all these worried her far more than the practical jokes played on her by her father's younger brothers and sisters, of whom the youngest were only about ten or fifteen years older than she. Perhaps these fears arose from her intense absorption in the works of Andrew Lang. She not only read the stories but coloured the many illustrations and painted innumerable princesses and knights in armour of her own. There is no doubt in my mind that from a very early age she positively identified with these long-haired princesses who were the embodiment of good. I do not think my mother's fears foreshadowed any great powers of imagination but they undoubtedly indicated a sensitivity to and awareness of the external world. The perpetual battle between right and wrong impinged on her in a way which led her to perceive life as a perpetual struggle. She saw herself not as the personification of good, but as one struggling on behalf of good. Whether this struggle manifested itself in her identification with feminism in the fight against masculine chauvinism, or in the struggle for peace and peaceful means as against war and violent means, the struggle remained.

My mother recalled that the one exception to her family's middle-class ordinariness in Macclesfield was their interest in music. My grandmother had a tuneful voice and played the piano well; Edward came to play the violin with increasing professionalism and started to compose; and my mother could play the piano and on occasion sang. She recalled that my grandfather was not too partial to the musical evenings which my grandmother gave, despite the fact that he had originally fancied his voice, and, as time went on he found Edward's violin practice excruciating. I do not think my mother was essentially any more musical than my grandfather, although in later years she liked to listen to recordings, particularly of the better-known violin concertos, for example Bruch and Mendelssohn, and of the symphonies of Beethoven and the works of Elgar. Listening to these records recalled to her the tranquillity of her

Edwardian childhood, when Edward, her brother, was still alive, and before the tumultuous explosion in her life which the First World War represented. There was a sadness as well as nostalgia in my mother listening to these composers, and playing their records provided a background to periodic day-dreaming about the past.

In 1904, when my mother was ten, her father moved yet again, this time to Buxton so that both she and Edward could go to day-schools there. This brought an end to her experience of Edwardian tranquillity. Her much-loved governess did not make the move, and it was from this time that my mother came to formulate her reaction to middle-class values and respectability. Nothing would have surprised her more than to learn that, eighty-one years after that move to Buxton, the Duke of Devonshire unveiled a memorial to her, despite local Conservative opposition.

In *Testament of Youth* my mother recalled an incident which took place shortly after her governess had left and she had begun to go to what she described as 'a school for the daughters of gentlemen in Buxton', and when her brother, Edward, attended a small preparatory school nearby. One day, aged eleven, she walked past the grounds of the school where Edward was and saw him in the playground. He called over one or two of his new-made friends, and they had a few moments of what my mother described as pleasant ragging across the wall. When she got home to tea she soon became aware of an atmosphere of disapproval on the part of her mother and her aunt Florence. Florence had apparently seen her talking to Edward and his friends, and my mother was taken severely to task.

At the time my mother published *Testament of Youth* her aunt Florence was still alive and so she did not mention her by name in connection with this incident. However, it is possible to identify her because my mother went on to say that at the school she went to next, a boarding school of which Florence was joint headmistress, the letters the girls wrote had to be left unsealed 'in case any of the girls should be so wicked as to write to boys'. She went on to say that a feeling of rebellious resentment was aroused in her from that moment, because the older generation thought that free and unselfconscious association between young boys and girls was improper.

It was when my mother was thirteen, in 1907, that she went to St Monica's — the school run by aunt Florence and her partner, Louise Heath Jones. The school had only recently been founded and was designed for the daughters of wealthy parents in London. At this time Florence Bervon was in her late thirties. Louise Heath Jones had been much better educated, first at Cheltenham Ladies' College, and then at Newnham College, Cambridge; and my mother said of Miss Heath Jones that she alternated between inspiring and intimidating those around her, staff and girls alike. Her religious idealism and the tempo at which she was inspired to live wore out her fragile constitution and she had a premature breakdown that led her to retire from the school shortly after my mother left in 1911 (when she was nearly eighteen). In her book my mother did not add that Louise Heath Jones was mentally ill for the last twenty years of her life until she died in 1931.

I did not know my great-aunt Florence until the early 1930s. By the time I first saw her she had a certain air of the *grande dame* about her, and even something of a church dignitary of the Italian Renaissance. She was both unmistakably formidable and at the same time slightly mysterious. I can quite believe that any association between young women and men was not to her taste. I never met Louise Heath Jones but her relationship with my aunt is an interesting one for, whereas the former was from a well-off family and highly educated by the standards of the time, Florence had no money, possessed no degree or training in education, and yet succeeded first as a partner and then on her own in making a great success of St Monica's with what my mother described as an enlightened and broad-minded régime (except of course in so far as her attitude to boys was concerned).

Florence must have had considerable business capacity. Although she started life as the eldest daughter of the five children of an organist who was far from rich, she ended up by living in a fine eighteenth-century house, Orange Grove, just outside Guildford, which stood in its own grounds with a river at the bottom of the garden. She had collected some good eighteenth- and early nineteenth-century furniture which she left to my mother, her god-daughter, in due course. I used to go and stay there occasionally, first on my own and then with Shirley. My great-aunt was not without imagination. I used to find small notes, addressed to me in minute handwriting, in my bedroom when I woke up in the morning. When I asked my great-aunt who had sent these, she said they came from the fairies who lived in the garden. Then, when I asked her where the fairies could be found, she told me they lived in the bullrushes. I spent many happy hours looking for them. I cannot say Florence was a sinister figure, but she certainly had a presence, that of an *eminence grise*.

7

She had a masculine intelligence, by which I mean that her life had clearly been ruled by her head, and from an unpromising start she achieved a great deal. In helping to start St Monica's she may have had some financial help from my grandmother but, whether this was so or not, when the school was sold she acquired some capital which she also left to my mother. Florence combined common sense and imagination, and she was motivated by considerable drive. It was these characteristics which enabled her to make a success of St Monica's, and become the ideal partner for Louise Heath Jones who had the social background and educational qualifications that look well in a private school prospectus, but whose instability would not have enabled her to start a private school single-handedly and then persevere so as to make a success of it. Florence's alliance with Louise Heath Jones was not unlike my grandmother's alliance with my grandfather. The relationship between Florence and Louise was intense.

By contrast, my mother's relationships with her brother's friends were entirely natural, even uninhibited. Later she wrote of herself that during her schooldays she was so ambitious that she was indifferent to sex in all its manifestations and thus remained innocent at heart despite the attempts of other girls at school to corrupt her.

My mother was not only ambitious but also romantic and idealistic from an early age. Nor did she lead such a protected life at home that she never came into contact with the kind of people who appealed to her. For example, a family friend of my grandfather's was Sir John Marriott, who had been born in Derbyshire. He was a Fellow of Worcester College, Oxford, author of many books on economics, history and political affairs, and later an MP firstly for Oxford and then for York. He had been to New College, Oxford and this was a decisive factor in Edward's name being put down for that college in due course. More importantly, it was due to Marriott's influence that my grandfather came to look on my mother's ambition to go to Oxford as not wholly far-fetched and ridiculous.

Louise Heath Jones had an important catalytic effect on my mother chiefly because, like her, she was at heart an idealist. She was a sympathiser with the more militant elements in the suffragette movement, and she spoke to my mother enthusiastically of Dorothea Beale and Emily Davies, both leaders of the movement. My mother was also inspired by Louise Heath Jones's history and scripture lessons.

The girls at St Monica's were allowed to read cuttings from *The Times* and the *Observer*, but they were not given the complete newspapers for fear they would read material thought to be unsuitable for young ladies. Nevertheless, what she was able to read introduced my mother to the wider world for which she was searching. It was due to Louise Heath Jones's influence too that my mother first came to read Shelley, who appealed to her principally because his poetry combined a rebellious with a romantic outlook, Mrs Humphry Ward's *Robert Elsmere*, and Olive Schreiner's *Woman and Labour*, the bible of the women's movement. Louise Heath Jones thus opened to my mother a window on the world outside the provincial life of Buxton, and it was her enthusiasm which made this other life both real and desirable. The influence she had must have been very rewarding to Miss Heath Jones for in Vera she at last found a girl who responded to her encouraging, if idiosyncratic style, and to her interests and convictions. From what my mother wrote it is clear that most of the girls responded more with alarm than with enthusiasm.

For other reasons my mother was impressed by girls at the school who came from smart homes in Belgravia. She felt somewhat inferior to them and that she was quite without standing among them because her own parents could not afford the numerous theatres and concerts to which many of the girls were taken at their parents' specific request and expense. Her clothes were either home-made or bought from undistinguished shops in Manchester or Buxton, and the presents she got at home did not compare with the many rich gifts that the other girls received. The fact is that my grandfather, like his family in this respect, was extremely careful, and although he might indulge himself he felt that to spend a lot on his family would have been an extravagance. When he shopped in London he did not stint himself, buying bespoke suits, cigars and whisky. During 1907, the first year that my mother boarded at St Monica's, he spent nearly as much at his tailor — £37 — as he did on my mother's fees for her school, which were £42 for the first term.

My mother became a feminist primarily because she felt the provincial life in which she was brought up made it virtually impossible to live in any other way than the constrained and narrow existence expected of those outside London. She was also conscious of the preferred treatment which her brother received from her parents, particularly her father, for no other reason than that he was a boy. Perhaps the key to understanding my mother's motivation is that she was inherently ambitious, but her ambition did not have a specific direction, as did that of her brother

Edward with his passion for music. And, because it was non-specific, my mother's ambition took longer to develop and to become a conscious and specifically directed aim in life. The precise detail of the positive print of my mother's later beliefs, thoughts and activities grew rather slowly out of what may be described as the negative of her provincial background. The better to overcome this background, her picture of it was, I believe, far from objective. But had she attempted to make her values coincide with those of her parents, and had she identified more with them, she would perhaps have seen her future more in terms of making a 'brilliant' marriage than in making a successful career on her own.

Although my mother was ambitious to develop a position for herself, a platform from which she could be heard on the subjects to which she devoted her time, she was not interested in well-known or 'important' people just because they were well-known or important. Without Winifred and my father she would have taken longer to move in these circles. It was through Winifred, for example, that she got in touch with Macmillan of New York, later her American publisher and through whom she met the chief editor, Harold Latham, when he came over to England in 1932. Perhaps my mother's experiences at St Monica's left her with a lingering social inferiority complex, which is why she was inhibited when she did come to meet the famous, the rich or both. But I suspect that she was never ambitious socially because she was never particularly interested in other people and what they thought of her. Increasingly, she became classless in her outlook, a difficult achievement in a country like England where microscopic differences in social status are not only a matter of fascination but provide the motivating force of social ambition. My mother always said that if my father got a title she would continue to call herself Mrs Catlin or, to be precise, Vera Brittain.

My mother's idealism was all-pervasive. The men and women who appealed to her were first and foremost the personification of an ideal, or an abstract virtue, such as truth or justice. The Arthurian legend of gallant knights was recreated for her in the men she knew best just before and during the First World War. Her pacifism was an idealist's response to the fact that during that war she lost the men she most loved: her brother, Edward; her fiancé, Roland Leighton; Geoffrey and Victor. My father did not appeal to my mother as an Arthurian figure. He was in the Army at the end of the First War, but not in any heroic capacity. However, the left-wing views which he held when he was young, and the fact that he certainly was handsome and looked romantic, presumably compensated for the fact that he was not a hero. Nor did he come from the landed families which my mother identified with provincialism.

In her diary after a dance in Buxton in 1912, just before her nineteenth birthday, my mother said that she felt dissatisfied to have met so many stupid and superficial men with whom, she noted, the other girls felt well-pleased. She added: 'I wish I could meet a good, strong, splendid man, full of force and enthusiasm, and in earnest about his life! There must *be* such!' She continued to think in this romantic vein for the rest of her life, and from my own experience one of the most daunting things about her was that she made enormous demands on the people close to her. If I wrote a poem, I must become a second Shelley. If I painted, I must become a second Leonardo da Vinci. My mother had no time for the second-rate or the shoddy, or indeed for any form of compromise. On the other hand, provided one's motives and objectives were of the highest, she could forgive any lapse or failure to achieve the greatest heights.

When I look at photographs of my mother taken in her teens I see a cheerful, attractive, rather plump girl who in nearly all the pictures is smiling and who appears to be full of life, energy and enthusiasm. Her clothes belie what she wrote in *Testament of Youth*, because she always looks well-dressed. But it is her vitality which comes across first and foremost. Her idealism and demanding nature must have been all the more disconcerting to the perhaps not very sophisticated young men she met, because from her appearance and clothes no one would suspect the unconventional approach to life she was developing. Indeed my mother's appearance was deceptive, and remained so, since in her youth she verged on the pretty-pretty as well as being smart and well-dressed. No one could have been less eccentric or unconventional in either appearance or behaviour. Her unconventionality was confined to her attitudes, beliefs, and ideas. Perhaps this was why so many people did not like her. To the avant-garde she looked too conventional. To the conventional her views appeared altogether unacceptable, if not outrageous: the fact that people could not be shocked by her appearance or behaviour perhaps made her unconventional views more disturbing. Those who heard her lecture, attended her pacifist rallies or the political meetings she attended; who read her books and articles and who may have looked forward to meeting her, could very easily have been put out to find that her life-style was far from unconventional even in the late '20s and early '30s, while by the late 1930s it verged on the discreetly opulent.

Taking tea before the Second World War at Cheyne Walk, with cake-stands, silver pot and cream jug, maid, and other paraphernalia must have been disconcerting for those who may have expected, indeed hoped for, a ménage if not exactly bohemian or revolutionary at least less obviously upper-middle class.

In the opening pages of *Testament of Youth*, my mother described herself as a provincial débutante decked out in London-bought clothes against the background 'of an unparalleled age of rich materialism and tranquil comfort'. At the beginning of the second chapter, entitled 'Provincial Young-Ladyhood', she describes in a few words what her background was really like as opposed to the picture she presented at the beginning of the book. It took my mother the best part of ten years to finish *Testament of Youth* and one interesting explanation of this discrepancy is the developing objectivity which was impossible for her at the outset.

Before 1914 my grandfather maintained an attitude of good-natured scepticism towards my mother's ambitions and outlook, and no doubt he would have been quietly amused rather than shocked if he had read the entry in her diary for April 27, 1917 in which she wondered when would come the moments of supreme emotion in which all lesser feelings are merged. Just as she saw behaviour in black and white, so equally she was geared to looking for strong and uplifting feelings, and to despising the lukewarm or tepid. This emotional nature was of course the source of her immense energy: her ability to survive emotional crises and disasters; to take on provincial society, then to fight many a good fight firstly in the name of feminism, then socialism, and finally pacifism. If one is pursuing an unpopular or even unrecognised crusade, immense vitality is required if one is to persevere. This my mother had and did. If she saw herself as a twentieth-century evangelist with the task of helping to lead the world from darkness to light, and even if she did not have the ability to laugh at herself, she was able to see her own ambition with a considerable degree of objectivity. Perhaps if she had not been so down-to-earth, her romanticism and idealism could have led her into various forms of self-deception. But she was in no sense an Isadora Duncan. She did not dramatise herself and she was not an exhibitionist. In this way she maintained an inherent stability, a strain she inherited from her dour Staffordshire forebears. Like them she just soldiered on come hell or high water. Indeed, she felt that she had to be on her guard against the tendency to instability she saw in her father. But this came late.

FAMILY QUARTET

If it was Miss Heath Jones who opened my mother's eyes to the outside world and to some of the causes for which she was to fight, it was with her brother, Edward, with whom she established her earliest important relationship. The significance of her relationship with Edward was that she was aware that, both as a boy and as a man, whatever he might suggest to their father would almost certainly be viewed with favour, whereas anything she might suggest that was even remotely unorthodox would be dismissed as a girlish whim. An explanation, at least in part, of the good relationhsip between my mother and her brother is that whilst she was assertive, he was not. My mother described him as a good listener (to her). As he was able to express himself through his absorption in the violin he did not need to have a dominating or demanding nature; nor, as I have said, did he need to be either dominating or demanding to get his own way. He combined the musical talents and skill of his mother's family with the personality of his father who, while occasionally explosive, was debonair and self-indulgent rather than over-bearing or tryannical.

My mother said that Edward meant a lot to her after the war broke out, whereas earlier on she had regarded him as someone to listen to both the stories she invented and her problems. Once he had volunteered for the Army and gone abroad to France she came to see him in an idealised light, looking on him as a knight whose military achievement lent enchantment. This was undoubtedly how many of her generation were to see those who went out to France in 1914 and 1915. However, my mother also said that she found it difficult, and as time went on increasingly difficult, to assess what sort of person Edward really was. They certainly presented a contrast in their appearance. My mother was just over five feet in height, with dark hair, which had a reddish tinge when she was younger, and hazel eyes. Edward, on the other hand, was over six feet; his eyes, eyebrows and hair were much darker than my mother's, and his complexion had an olive tone quite different from my mother's Anglo-Saxon pink skin. Although he was killed nearly ten years before I was born I can see what he was like from a three-quarter-length portrait of him painted in 1917.

My mother ascribed the charming easy-going manner of Edward to his musical grandfather Bervon, but he undoubtedly acquired much of his own father's personality too. My mother could not see this similarity between them because, to her, her father's chief characteristics were his limitations rather than his positive qualities. From my knowledge of him, and he did not die until I was nearly eight, he was certainly urbane, even if his interests were not political or intellectual. Nevertheless, he had enjoyed singing, and he liked listening to my grandmother playing the piano even if he did not like to hear Edward practising his violin.

I remember that this house in Edwardes Square, to which he moved the year before he died, was beautifully furnished and hung with many pictures. From his mother he had inherited a large round table which had been bought by her grandfather. The frame of the table was rather heavy mid-Victorian mahogany but the centre was of mosaic. Round the figures of Romulus and Remus and the wolf were views of the major buildings and ruins in Rome (the table centre had been made in the Vatican's mosaic works which had been in operation from the time of the Roman Empire). My grandfather clearly attached much importance to this table. He told me he was leaving it to me and that I must promise never to sell it — although I was only seven at the time.

When my mother published *Testament of Youth* in 1933, standards of disclosure were very different to what they are today, and both of her parents and many of her relations and friends were still alive. So, although my mother was quite outspoken in expressing her own thoughts and feelings, she was mindful of other people's feelings. Her remarks were sometimes acid, but she was seldom unkind, and she lacked the fairly common attributes of jealousy, small-mindedness and bitchiness (except as far as nearly all other women writers were concerned). For someone so outspoken, in fact, my mother was remarkably discreet, and throughout *Testament of Youth* she gives fictitious names to people and refers to others by their Christian name or even the first letter of their Christian name. In a novel she wrote entitled *Honourable Estate* she presented members of her own family and those of my father's, in which the only significant deviation from reality is that the characters are all given fictional names. Thus Vera's Staffordshire family, and more distant relations and their friends, might take exception to what she wrote, but they could not say she was being alarmingly indiscreet.

My mother told me on several occasions, when talking about her brother Edward, that she had come to the conclusion that he was basically homosexual. At least he was certainly never interested in girls. When they used to go to dances before the First World War he never danced, always preferring to play billiards with the other men. It must be borne in mind, however, as my mother herself wrote, that before 1914 (when she was twenty) she did not really know what homosexuality meant. And after 1914 Edward was with his regiment, firstly in England and then in France and Italy, only coming home for occasional short leaves or when he was wounded and hospitalised before he was killed in 1918; so my mother had very little opportunity to get to know him better when her own experience had been widened by her work as a nurse.

When referring to Edward's possible homosexuality, my mother made it clear that she was not making a moral judgment of disapproval, but merely stating what she took to be a fact on the basis of such evidence as she had. This aspect of his character did not stop Edward participating in her romantic ideal, particularly after he was awarded the MC, recommended for the VC and killed on the Asiago Plateau in the Italian campaign at the age of twenty-two. He could not qualify, perhaps, for the highest category of hero since he could not be described as a good, strong, splendid young man, full of force and enthusiasm in quite the way she meant. But he was in earnest about his life, a further requirement if her ideal was to be realised.

My mother was innately strong enough, I think, not to despise those weaker than herself. She was only concerned for me that I might have inherited the weak strains which she saw in her father and in her brother, and it was this fear, among others, that made her apprehensive. As for herself, my mother had always been strong, both physically and in most other ways, although she claimed to suffer from physical cowardice and she had experienced numerous nebulous fears in her childhood. Until about five years before her death when she fell over some scaffolding on the edge of the pavement at dusk, an accident which brought on arterio-sclerosis, I do not remember my mother ever being ill. In her later years, as she grew nervous about almost everything, Shirley and I used to lift her off the ground to cross the road, one of us on each side of her. My mother rebelled against this usurpation of her freedom of action, but in practice allowed herself to be hurried across. My mother's excessive anxiety was her only real weakness. While her highly disciplined life provided an effective structure and régime which enabled her to deal with this, it was not a remedy for anxiety. The traumas of her life, starting with her early nameless fears, followed by her experiences of the First World War, led to a lack of flexibility, a rigidity of behaviour. Had she been able to throw away the past she might have been able to live and enjoy a more relaxed life in the present. Undoubtedly, she wrote *Testament of Youth* in part to exorcise the past, but the writing of the book did not fully achieve its objective. As she got older my mother was more, rather than less, dominated by the past.

At the beginning of *Testament of Youth* my mother's references to her family and background are scarcely complimentary and hardly objective, and this was neither overlooked nor forgotten by those of her relations and friends of her family in Staffordshire who came to read the book.

In my view what she wrote was rather unfair to her family and, by inference, to herself. Many of the characteristics which made her outstanding in her generation were those of her forebears. Like her they were extrermely shrewd and practical; nor were they lacking in a certain awareness and inventiveness. Many of those born in the Potteries in Staffordshire have a distinctive individuality, whether they are rich or poor. They have had to develop these characteristics in dealing with a life that has always lacked the softer character and qualities of those living south of the Trent.

My mother was also able to express her own independence and individuality to no small extent because she could afford to do so. Her family had made a considerable amount of money in the nineteenth century. Her great-grandfather, Thomas Brittain, had, as I have said, purchased in 1855 a small paper mill from a Huguenot family of paper-machine inventors in Hanley. What my mother did not mention is that this family were the Foundriniers, inventors of the paper machine of that name. The 'Foundrinier' was one of the two paper-making machines, invented in the early nineteenth century, which revolutionised the paper industry.

In 1855, Thomas Brittain was himself in his fifties. He had given up work as a small private banker when he saw the potential in machine-made paper. The paper-making industry was in its infancy. For example, the ordinary paper envelope was not made at all until 1841; paper bags were made for the first time in 1850. Thomas Brittain exemplified the perseverance and shrewdness of the Staffordshire man of business, and of the small local banker who, as Professor Peter Mathias pointed out in *The First Industrial Revolution*, was fundamental to the success of the first industrial revolution.

Thus Thomas Brittain was a figure of some local significance before the acquisition of the paper mill in Hanley, although his real importance lay perhaps more in his foresight than in his wealth. From the photograph I have seen of him it is clear that he was a shrewd operator. He must have been careful too. In the photograph, taken when he was in his late seventies or early eighties, he is still wearing the clothes of the 1850s. He kept a firm controlling hand over the paper company until his death in 1890, that is to say for most of the second half of the nineteenth century, not least because his son, also Thomas, died at the age of forty-seven. Thomas Brittain senior may not have had the inventive genius of the Foundriniers or the marketing genius of Josiah Wedgwood, but he certainly had the ability to exploit a major innovation of the industrial revolution.

His son, the second Thomas Brittain, was born in 1838. Before he died in 1885 he had twelve children with whom he lived at Barlaston just south of Stoke-on-Trent. Thomas junior was considerably more debonair than his father. He was a handsome man with fair hair and well-tended beard; he dressed fashionably with a diamond pin in his cravat. His smile suggests a man of some charm and greater worldliness than his father. He also looks a kind man, which he must have been because in the 1870s he allowed his eldest son, my grandfather Thomas Arthur, who had been sent to Malvern School as a boarder, to leave because he did not like it there. Such indulgence is probably common today, but was hardly consistent with the outlook of his generation.

In 1863 my great-grandfather, Thomas Brittain, had married Elizabeth, the granddaughter of a local magnate, Job Meigh. Meigh had made his money out of cobalt, the blue used on colouring pottery made by the manufacturers in the area. He had been in business in Shelton-under-Harley with a firm of earthern manufacturers, Hicks, Meigh and Johnson, suppliers to the pottery industry. In 1837, he had built Ash Hall, a neo-Gothic mansion on a hill overlooking Bucknall, just outside Hanley. Constructed in the local red sandstone, the Hall is now darkened by the smoke that blew across the fields from the Potteries in Hanley until the end of the last war. It has tall, mullioned windows and a gabled façade, elaborately ornamented with stone pinnacles and miniature turrets. Inside the house there was a double-banistered staircase and ornamental ceilings with 'Elizabethan' rafters. At the time it was built Ash Hall was designed to provide every domestic comfort. Job Meigh eventually acquired over three hundred acres in the area and the

17

Hall itself was surrounded by a park laid out with islands of trees. The outer boundaries of the estate were hidden by plantations. At the main entrance there was a lodge, on which Job Meigh's crest, granted to him in 1840, was carved in stone. Meigh must have been inordinately proud of his crest because not only was it displayed on the main house, but there were even crests on the door-knobs. By the entrance lodge were impressive gates of an elaborate design in gold and black, and these were flanked by trees of ash, fir and monkey-puzzle.

Job Meigh's son William was a contemporary of Thomas Brittain's. Like his father, he was also a manufacturer of pottery colours. When he was born his father was still living in Hanley, where in due course the family owned a wharf and a weighing machine, and a street was named after them. When his father moved to Bucknall, William lived in Ash House, which had an adjoining farm. Although Job Meigh died in 1862 at the age of seventy-nine his widow lived on in Ash Hall until she herself died in 1870. Then William moved in as a widower until his own death in 1876.

It was William's eldest daughter, Elizabeth Charlotte, who married the young Thomas Brittain in 1863. When Thomas Brittain's father-in-law died in 1876 his estate was valued at £80,000. This William Meigh's son, also William, moved into Ash Hall when his mother died and lived there for forty-five years until 1922, the year of his death. By 1925, the year my mother got married, the estate had been broken up. The main house had been converted into the Ash Hall Golf Links Hotel while the park and adjoining fields had become a golf course. Ash House was like-wise rebuilt as the Ash Bank Hotel, the name referring to the fact that there had been open-cast mining on the site of Job Meigh's estate before he had bought the three hundred acres round the house.

My grandfather, who was born in 1864, had to go and live with his grandfather in Newcastle-under-Lyme when his father died in 1885. At the time he was twenty-one, and his mother found him too much of a handful. He was the eldest of twelve children and without doubt she had quite enough on her hands without him. As the eldest son of the eldest son, my grandfather was no doubt spoiled by others before he was old enough to spoil himself. Yet he was a kindly man as I recall him. One of the other things I remember about him was that neither his hair nor moustache was grey although when I first became aware of him he was in his late sixties. He was always beautifully dressed. He had a quiet voice and a gentle manner. He suffered the disadvantages of his many

18

advantages. On the whole reasonable, he was given to what my mother called 'fatigues', by which she meant that he was apt to fret impatiently when he did not get his own way. Until his own grandfather died in his nineties, by which time he was thirty-one, he did not have much say, if any, in the running of the family business. However, as soon as he became Managing Director, he developed new factories in Cheddleton, near Leek in north Staffordshire. My mother said that members of her father's family only met at weddings and funerals and they did not get on with each other. Perhaps this was because there were so many of them and they were all close together in age. My mother did not keep in touch with any of her aunts and uncles on her father's side of the family, except for his youngest sister, Muriel, who lived on Lake Windermere. She preferred her mother's relations.

Although my grandfather was perhaps not quite so handsome as his father he was nevertheless a good-looking man, just under six feet tall. His major interest was undoubtedly his business, although I would say that he was not very ambitious. He looked on the family firm as a means of providing a very comfortable living for himself and his family, rather than as a basis for building up an ever-expanding organisation. At the turn of the century the Brittains looked on the Bowaters as equals. It is possible that, if my grandfather's father had lived beyond 1885 and had the business in his hands at least until the Great War started, he might have developed Brittains to be a bigger company more quickly than my grandfather did. However, to say that my grandfather only wanted a quiet and comfortable life is not the whole story. He had some inventive capacity, and is credited with having taken part in an important development of colour printing on pottery and of producing a new printing tissue, 'Duplex' paper.

If most of the members of my grandfather's family were determined and obstinate, he could be difficult himself and no doubt that is why, when he was young, he was bullied first by his mother and then by his grandfather. After he was married he was increasingly browbeaten by my grandmother. Like myself, my grandfather was contra-suggestive and did the opposite of what his family wanted or expected. In marrying the daughter of a local organist from whom he was taking singing lessons, he did not satisfy the social ambitions of his family. My grandmother was certainly tall and attractive but she did nothing to add to such social ambitions as the Brittains may have had. Whatever his faults, my grandfather was not a snob and since he had plenty of money

19

the fact that his in-laws had none did not worry him. He may have hoped that by marrying someone in my grandmother's position, who would be more dependent on him, he would be more able to do what he liked.

Just as my grandfather was inventive in business even if not very ambitious, he was interested in the new inventions of his time. He was one of the first to buy a car in his area and he was a keen photographer. He was not in fact a very good driver and it was because of the number of mishaps he had in his cars that my mother never learnt to drive. He drove from Buxton to the works in Cheddleton twice a day when the weather was good, coming home for lunch. When the weather was bad, or snow was on the high roads, he did not go to the factory at all.

Perhaps the beauty of the Peak district appealed to my grandfather and this was one reason why he lived in Buxton. But I am equally sure that he wanted to keep away from his relations, of whom there were a great many, especially younger brothers and sisters.

In retrospect he may appear as a rather negative figure because he enjoyed what he had inherited rather than striking out into new fields. My mother said that he scarcely ever read the national newspapers, and he was certainly more interested in what went on in the Potteries than in national and international political issues. Devoted as he was to keeping Brittain a successful company, he was cautious and not too enterprising. In two words, he was deeply conservative. During the war, when in his fifties, he resigned from Brittains, because of a board-room row over whether the company should make cigarette papers — a move he was determined to oppose. Then as both my mother and her brother Edward were either serving abroad or found it difficult to get further afield than London my grandfather gave up living in Derbyshire and moved to Oakwood Court in Kensington. Had he been compelled to earn his living he would have had to find a job. As it was he had given up all his real interests and now had nothing to do except keep ever more meticulous accounts of his income and expenditure, buy clothes, and look out of the window at the flats opposite through his opera glasses. Increasingly he became introspective and neurotic: the prisoner of his fourteen-room flat. He had worked from his early twenties and could not get used to the routine of not doing so.

I have my grandfather's account books from 1905 to his death in 1935. The accounts up to 1917 give a very clear picture of how he spent his money and where the money came from. In the later accounts, that is from the time he came to London in the First World War, he provided

meticulous detail on virtually every item he bought, on every expense incurred. These details provide a fascinating insight, although it is sad to
reflect that he had so little to do that he could afford the time for this
scrupulous but trivial analysis.

In 1906 my grandfather's income was £1,291. In 1916 it was £1,627;
in 1926 virtually the same amount; and in 1934, the year before his
death, £2,168. What does that level of income mean today? From 1890
to 1910 inflation was at a rate of less than one per cent per year. With the
beginning of the First World War there was increasing inflation, and
this rose to a peak in 1920 before falling off significantly. An income in
1939 equivalent to my grandfather's income of £1,291 in 1906 was about
£2,500. By 1960 the equivalent would have been perhaps £5,750. But
from an income of £5,750 in 1960 to an equivalent in 1987 means multi-
plying by a factor of between seven and eight and a half. Now, an annual
income equivalent to £1,291 in 1906 would probably be something in the
order of £35,000 to £40,000. Taking into account the dividends from the
company and assuming that the business was thriving and profitable, as
the record suggests that it was, then by any standards my grandfather
was a rich man even if he was not the equivalent of a millionaire today.

The first mention of my mother's name in the account books is in May
1907, when she was thirteen. The occasion was his paying 'Vera's school
fees: £42' at St Monica's. Florence Bervon, the joint headmistress, was
the eldest of the four girls of whom my grandmother was the youngest.
They had two brothers, Charlie who went to New York when quite
young, and William, of whom my mother was particularly fond, who
became a manager in the Midland Bank. I never knew Charlie, and
Uncle Bill died just after the First World War; but I knew my grandmother's three sisters quite well. Florence and my grandmother had a
certain physical resemblance. Like my uncle Edward they had very dark
eyes and did not look very English. My mother told me she had no idea
where the Bervons came from originally. Sometimes she suggested they
came from France, at others that they were Rumanian Jews. Their own
grandfather Bervon was a manufacturer in Birmingham.

My grandmother was tall and attractive-looking when young, and she
did look rather Jewish to me. Florence was nearly as tall. Both of them
had heavily-lidded eyes, a characteristic inherited by Edward, but not
by Vera, although Shirley and I have them too. The two other sisters,
Isabelle and Lily, were shorter, plumper and had an English look with a
fair complexion like their mother. Isabelle, known as Belle, never

21

married. She was for many years governess to an English family in India, before she retired to Deal, where she ran a tea-shop, 'The Golden Hinde', on the front. Aunt Belle must have been as financially skilful as Florence. Possibly when she was in India she saved up most of her pay. It cannot have been much, but, nevertheless her house in Kingswood was a substantial one with a large garden. She had a car in which there was a glass partition between herself and her chauffeur and I remember there was a speaking tube through which instructions could be given. When she died during the war she left her capital, furniture and pictures to my mother, just as Florence did. Lily married a stockbroker who was a cousin of Captain Ernest Simpson, the shipbroker whom Wallis Warfield married before the Duke of Windsor. It was said in the family that Lily had pretended when she was young to be several years younger than she actually was so as not to prejudice her chances of getting married. She had a well-developed sense of humour, and I can recall her telling this story against herself on one of the occasions my grandmother took me to tea at her house in Godalming.

My mother was not interested in making money in the sense that she was much more interested in propagating her ideas than in making money out of them. She was certainly careful but not mean. Apart from travel and the clothes she had made for herself she had no expensive tastes. Unlike my father she was not particularly interested in food, although she enjoyed going to a good restaurant now and then. However, she managed to lead a life that was exactly what she wanted, perhaps due to the fact that she exercised no extravagances. Until 1935, when Winifred Holtby died and my father gave up his professorship at Cornell University he and she maintained a good standard of living. From 1935 onwards my mother inherited money firstly from her father, from aunt Florence shortly after; from aunt Belle during the war and from her mother shortly after the war. She undoubtedly acquired astuteness in handling money not only from her mother's family, none of whom started out well-provided for, but almost all of whom ended up well-off.

My grandmother was certainly an intelligent woman but by nature pessimistic and, at least by the time I knew her, cynical. She could play the piano extremely well and I remember her doing so through the 1930s, although by the time the war began she was forced to give it up due to the increasing arthritis in her fingers. I particularly recall her playing Beethoven's 'Moonlight' Sonata in which she emphasised its melancholy character by playing it extraordinarily slowly, even lugubriously. I was a great favourite of hers, perhaps because I reminded her of my uncle Edward. She was always generous to me, but she made my mother feel apprehensive and she did not like my father. She was deaf when it suited her, though she always seemed to hear any remark not intended for her, and to annoy my father she pretended not to hear what he was saying. When my father was not using his lecturing voice, he tended to speak without an edge, almost as if he was talking to himself. Thus the following ritual. My father would say something quietly. My grandmother would say she couldn't hear him. 'Speak up, Gordon,' she would say, knowing also that my father did not like to be called Gordon. My father would then lose his temper and shout. This no doubt explains why, when my mother took Shirley and me to the ritual Sunday afternoon teas, my father seldom came too.

My grandmother stayed on in Edwardes Square after the death of my grandfather, until the beginning of the war. Then she took a flat in Chelsea, in Rossetti Gardens Mansions just round the corner from our house in Cheyne Walk. My mother would not give her a key to our front door for fear she would turn up whenever it suited her, which would have been quite often as she had nothing to do. We were ever apprehensive of her visits, for she could be relied on to upset my father or the housekeeper or, worst of all, to disturb my mother's concentration while she was writing in her study: the one thing that could be guaranteed to exasperate my mother more than anything else. My mother's love of peace was not confined to the outside world; she liked peace and calm to reign at home too. The disadvantage of this attitude was that both her mother and the housekeeper knew that to avoid rows and emotional traumas she would agree to almost anything. Thus, both my grandmother and increasingly the housekeeper were able to exploit my mother by emotional blackmail.

My grandmother, though not exactly formidable like her sister, Florence, who also had the advantage of a disconcerting physical presence, was nevertheless extremely persistent. Her vein of cynicism was certainly understandable. She did not take my mother as seriously as the latter took herself and she always treated her as if she were a teenage child. Whereas my grandfather came to accept my mother's literary ambitions and socialist sympathies, and even the fact that my father was not well-off, I think my grandmother regarded my mother's interests as the foibles of someone who had always been able to afford her private whims and indulgences. Had my mother been an alcoholic or a lover of the smart life she could not have been looked upon more critically than she was by her mother. My grandmother shared my grandfather's over-riding interest in money and she also knew how generous he had been to my mother. She had not the slightest interest in causes, except perhaps that of St Martin's-in-the-Fields, where she attended religiously not so much because of her faith as because it became the centre of her social life once my grandfather had died and she could no longer entertain herself by remonstrating with him. 'Nonsense, Arthur!' I remember her saying very frequently to my grandfather whom, like my mother, she also treated like a recalcitrant child.

CHAPTER II

GEORGE

IN the extremely long entry in *Who's Who*, in which his name last appeared in 1970, my father George Catlin's first statement was that he had been concerned with Atlantic community policy since 1925, and that he was a founder of the Movement for Atlantic Union and a joint founder of the English Speaking Union.

It is odd, and at the same time typical, that my father should identify himself so strongly with Anglo-American cooperation for rather more than fifty years and yet receive almost no official recognition for his efforts. What lay behind this official ingratitude, which persisted long after it might have been redressed, was my mother's pacifism during the last war. President Roosevelt, with whom my father had been in touch at least ten years before the beginning of the Second World War, expressed severe criticism of the condemnation of obliteration bombing which was published in my mother's name in the USA just before America entered the war. My father had also developed a close relationship with Wendell Wilkie, the Republican presidential candidate during the war. When Wilkie came over to England in 1941, he had a meeting with my father while he was still in bed in his hotel. But the official invitation to my parents to attend a reception to which Wilkie had verbally invited them was vetoed by the Foreign Office.

In a worldly sense, my father was both too naïve and too scrupulous, at least as far as the furtherance of his own career was concerned. He stuck to my mother even when her pacifism effectively undermined his own political career.

George Catlin will seem an insubstantial figure to many. This is due to the fact that he was a complex man with many interests, some of them conflicting, and that he did not have the gift of simplicity which characterised my mother, whose interests were few but fundamental. The difference between my parents may be seen in their prose. My mother wrote in a direct, uncomplicated way and expressed her views and feelings with a refreshing straightforwardness. My father, on the other hand, had what might be described as a Proustian approach — except that he was not writing fiction. There is often a disconcerting ambiguity in the meaning of much of what he has to say. He could express himself pithily, for example in the quotation from his book, *The Science and Method of Politics*, which I have already given: 'To know history is to control power'. In the same book, however, a few pages further on he wrote:

> Admitting a social situation determined, among others by factors meteorological, geological, biological, by factors of natural wealth and of technical discovery, by factors of conservative tradition and established civilisation, and admitting human nature (i.e. common characteristics in human beings) of a certain, if imperfectly known constancy, as distinct from inexplicable caprice, our problem is to examine how men have discovered and elaborated a *modus vivendi* in relation to each other without making life worthless for themselves, through restrictions, or worthless, through oppression, for others.

In this sentence my father has characteristically condensed a highly complex idea which could have been better expressed with greater clarity if he had devoted three pages to what is reduced to eighty-six words.

Many philosophers have expressed themselves with as little if not greater lack of clarity than my father. Emmanuel Kant and Karl Marx spring to mind. But a philosopher who seeks to become well-known through his books must have the gift of lucidity, a rare gift among academics, but one shared by Niccolo Machiavelli and by Bertrand Russell.

One of the reasons my father has remained a shadowy figure is that only the few who knew him really well could appreciate the full range of his interests. Perhaps those who practise in more than one field of endeavour are regarded as being 'not quite serious', the most crushing of all Oxford put-downs. In order to get away with a wide range of activities in this age of specialisation it is first of all necessary to establish pre-eminence in one field. Thus, the facts that Winston Churchill could write serious biography and history as well as journalism, and he could paint well enough to be given, later on, the title of Royal Academician Extraordinary, were regarded as signs that he was not quite serious.

26

Had he not been associated with victory, more academic historians, professional journalists and painters would have given vent to the jealous hatred felt by the ambitious but small-minded.

It was my father's relative success in a number of fields which was his undoing. His capacity to enjoy life and his natural kindness and generosity on the one hand, and his vanity and tendency to deviousness on the other, did not help him towards the achievement of his ambitions. He lacked both the judicial impartiality and the opportunism necessary to put the main chance first. The fact that he was a handsome man, with a truly remarkable resemblance (in which he revelled) to the actor Leslie Howard and that he lived a life of comparative opulence, did not endear him to rivals or those who might have helped him more. When Herbert Morrison described my father as a Dorchester socialist, the acidity of his comment revealed both the shrewdness of his judgment and his jealousy and dislike of my father. Fortunately for Shirley these attitudes did not extend to her, due perhaps to Morrison's sneaking regard for my mother (he himself had been a conscientious objector in the First World War).

Between 1922, when he was twenty-six, and 1974, my father published eighteen books. Those concerned with political philosophy ranged from *Thomas Hobbes* (1922) to *Political and Social Theory and its Applications* (1964). Most of his other books dealt with Anglo-American relations and were published over a thirty-year period from *One Anglo-American Nation* in 1941 to *Atlanticism* (1972) and *Kissinger's Atlantic Charter* (1973).

My father's most unendearing qualities were his jealousy and the appearance he gave of being a frightful snob. It is certainly true that he loved great men and loved cultivating them, to use his own expression. As far as his girl-friends were concerned, and he had many, particularly during the years when he did not have full-time academic work, he preferred tall, good-looking aristocratic women who, it seems to me on reflection, bore a similarity in appearance to Winifred Holtby, with whom my father had much in common, both in character and appearance. They were both endlessly long-suffering, adaptable and temperamentally cheerful. In living with my mother they shared a further important characteristic: an ability to adapt themselves to her. For her part, my mother, whose iron will was unbending in the interest of some supposed or real moral cause if not overt self-interest, never saw nor felt the need to adapt herself to anyone. Out of consideration for my father she eschewed politics for herself, although the support she gave him in his political aspirations was lukewarm at the best.

27

My father failed to achieve all his dearest ambitions. He failed to become a Fellow of All Souls or New College, Oxford; to be elected to the House of Commons and become at least a junior minister in a Labour government; to get into the House of Lords; or, had he accepted the American citizenship he was offered, to hold public office in the United States.

Nevertheless, my father had come a long way. He was born on July 29, 1896 in Liverpool, where his father was acting as temporary Church of England incumbent while the vicar was on holiday from his parish in Stockport. The Reverend George Catlin, my grandfather, was born in March 1858 in Maidstone and started out in life as a low-church minister. He was then ordained in the Church of England and was a curate in Stourbridge in Worcestershire between 1900 and 1904, when he became perpetual curate, carrying out the duties of vicar, at St Luke's Church in Richmond, just outside Kew Gardens. Grandfather Catlin was married at Rhyl in North Wales in July 1895. His wife Kate was seventeen years younger than he.

In her book, *Honourable Estate*, my mother gives a written portrait of the Reverend Thomas Rutherstone which is a not very kind but nonetheless accurate and unflattering portrait of the Reverend Mr Catlin: 'Rather below medium height, portly, sandy brown hair receding from a high bumpy forehead; short straight nose and dreamy eyes of a watery blue-grey which looked out upon the world with a hint of defiant apprehensiveness in their shallow depths.' My mother went on to say that his long, drooping moustache concealed full lips and disguised a weak, narrow chin, and that his hands were pale and podgy with short, thick fingers and broad wrists.

My father used to read the drafts of my mother's books, and may well have thought this portrait of his father was scarcely charitable. (Before *Testament of Youth* was published she most unwillingly reduced some of her accounts about my father in the last chapter of that book.) As *Honourable Estate* was first published in November 1936 and my grandfather had died the previous month, his was perhaps a timely demise because, being of an extremely irascible nature, he would no doubt have had a fit if he had read this supposedly fictitious description of someone who was clearly himself. I was nearly nine when he died and I can remember him quite well. He was quite short and, although amiable to me, was of a disposition which veered from the peppery to the aggressive. Like many people who are small he felt the need to assert himself. Quite apart from

28

my memory of him, I have many photographs taken throughout his life and also a portrait painted in his late fifties, when he no longer had his moustache. But in all other respects he looks in the portrait as my mother described him. In later life H. G. Wells reminded me of my grandfather Brittain, but as a younger man he resembled my grandfather Catlin more.

Both my grandfathers were obstinate, but whereas grandfather Brittain was of a more passive disposition, looking only for peace and quiet away from his closest relations, grandfather Catlin was of a more positively explosive character. When my mother described his 'defiant apprehensiveness' this was not only an accurate description of how he looked but also how he was. Not long before he married my grandmother he must have begun to regret that he had taken this step. When he got married he was thirty-seven and his wife was twenty. Apparently she had developed a schoolgirl's passion for him and had determined to marry him. She was born in Atherstone, near Orton in Warwickshire in August 1875. After the wedding her feelings quickly cooled. This was not just due to their difference in age. My grandmother was of pronounced suffragette views. Whether she had had them before marriage I do not know but she was in any case of an altogether independent frame of mind. Unlike her husband, she was quite tall. Her father, Richard Harding Orton, was a jeweller who lived in Leamington Spa, where he owned some property. He also had an original and inventive mind and he took out a patent for a railway-brake in which he invested a considerable amount of his money. But, his invention was not taken up commercially, because in practice it proved uncompetitive to the Westinghouse brake which was the preferred design in the great railway expansion from the 1840s and '50s onwards.

It is an interesting coincidence that my father's grandfather should have been concerned with a significant industrial development in just the same way that my mother's great-grandfather was concerned with early innovation in the industrialisation of paper-making, which proved to be much more lucrative. Both shared in the innovative spirit of their times. It is also significant that both my father's mother and my own mother were suffragette supporters, thus supporting social rather than industrial innovation. My mother was only eighteen years younger than her mother-in-law, although she never met her as she died in 1917.

My father recalled his childhood as being permanently clouded by the rows between his parents. Being an only child he was perhaps particularly affected by these confrontations. When my father was twelve his mother left home to pursue her suffragette activities, which had been the subject of much of the family argument. My grandfather Catlin had been particularly worried that his wife might take to such illegal activities as putting burning paper into local letter-boxes, as other suffragettes had done. As a minister of the church he was, perhaps of necessity, an upholder of the conventions of his day, and while, according to my father, he was liberal in theology, his liberality did not extend to arson or sabotage.

But my grandmother Catlin had some money of her own, and so she just managed to make ends meet without recourse to her husband. After she left home much of her time was given over to good works in the East End of London as well as supporting the suffragettes. Her life, if not rough, was certainly rigorous, and when she died she was only forty-one. My father was then twenty-one.

That my grandfather could not get on with his wife did not prevent him from being a devoted father. It was largely due to his coaching that my father did so well as a boy, first at Warwick School, and then, when they moved to London, at St Paul's, from where he obtained an exhibition to New College in 1914, when he was eighteen. My father never talked about his mother, and clearly her departure was extremely traumatic, not only in emotional terms but also in the most practical sense. Although her leaving home put an end to his parents' quarrels, my grandfather quite broke down on her leaving, and from then on he was dependent on my father, both emotionally and, when my father started to earn a living at the age of eighteen, financially too. My father never forgot that between the time when his mother left home in 1908, when he was twelve, and 1914 when he was eighteen, he and his father lived on an income of £112 a year, which provided them with a diet largely of bread, milk and rice pudding. It was hardly surprising that my father was not accepted into the Army, on health grounds, when he applied; he got a job in the Civil Service instead. He and grandfather Catlin had lived on an income that was just about 10 per cent of that of my grandfather Brittain.

My father's education at home, to supplement what he learnt at school, was given in the knowledge that unless he got a scholarship or exhibition to Oxford he would not be able to go there at all. It was this experience of dire if genteel poverty that made my father lay so much stress on the importance of financial independence and led him, in due course, to suggest to me a series of possible careers which would combine distinction with security.

Although he had been a member of two Officers' Training Corps, my father was rejected by the Army on four occasions between 1914 and 1918 on health grounds: by the Artists' Rifles, the infantry, the Royal Army Medical Corps and the Service Corps. Ultimately he was called up due to the increased level of conscription following the German offensive of March 1918. On the basis of his OTC experience he applied for a commission, but at that late stage of the war the War Office did not favour those who had been conscripted being commissioned immediately.

For four years he worked in the Civil Service. Through his mother he got a job in the Control Board, because she had met the sister of Sir Edward Harding, later Permanent Under-Secretary at the Commonwealth Office, and Harding accepted my father just before he was due to leave St Paul's. My father's experience at the Board proved to be highly relevant later, when he came to be concerned with the work which preceded the repeal of the 18th Amendment, the Prohibition Amendment, to the American Constitution, the object of the Control Board (Liquor Traffic) being to reduce drunkenness among munitions workers.

When my father was ultimately allowed into the Army in late 1918, he was taken on in the Rifle Brigade. His unit was late in arriving at the front because they first of all had to make a detour for some weeks to Newport in Wales, to give a show of strength through the streets and deter a threatened strike.

In the winter of 1918 two battalions of the Rifle Brigade were in quarters at Fay-le-Franc on the Franco-Belgian border. My father heard of the Armistice as they came up to the rail-head at Soumain and marched to where the final front lines had been near Bouchain. Up at what had been the front, the Rifle Brigade defused their hand grenades, oiled their rifles and waited. My father was instructed to give the occasional Army class. It had been decided that a little education for those stationed there with nothing to do would be a good idea.

At this time he was twenty-two. While in France he spent as much time as he could do in making notes on philosophy in what had been a Civil Service ledger. Philosophy was nothing new to my father. When he was still at St Paul's and living with his father in Kew, he had become entranced by the *Discourses* of Descartes and the *Ethics* of Spinoza.

Whereas my mother regarded most of her war experience as the most

31

frightful in her life, other than the brief period she spent at a hospital in Malta, my father's experiences were quite the contrary. He later came to feel that the Army had done him a great deal of good. He certainly had more to eat than he had had before, and the exercise did him good too. Going into the Army had enabled him to get away from home, where his father was still grieving at the loss of his wife from home and then at her death from pneumonia. His military experience of the war was confined to hearing the guns at the front while he was still at Boulogne, but being able to get away from his father showed him the way towards a less claustrophobic life.

By the Easter of 1919, my father was at New College. This was the same time that my mother returned to Somerville, and was also Winifred's first term there. It was to be five years before my father met my mother, although they had begun to write to each other nearly a year earlier. My father had hoped, while still at St Paul's, to get a scholarship. In his view the reason he did not do so was because the examiner, Ernest Barker, thought my father had plagiarised his own ideas, and so demoted the proposed scholarship to an exhibition. My father admitted that he had written his St Paul's School Truro Essay Prize for the Oxford exam, so perhaps there was some foundation in Barker's decision. As it was, my father got his exhibition in part due to the good will and good offices of the High Master of St Paul's, Dr Hilliard.

Just as the Oxford years immediately after 1945 produced a galaxy of talent, so the same was true after the First War. Among those whom my father met at New College in 1919 were Maurice Bowra, later Warden of Wadham College, and David Keir, later Master of Balliol. Many others who also went on to academic achievement were to remain his lifelong friends: Ernest Jacob, later Chichele Professor of History; Dermot Morrah of *The Times*; and Henry Price, later Wykeham Professor of Metaphysics (still a Fellow of New College when I went up myself after the end of the Second War). J. B. S. Haldane, the biochemist, was already at New College when my father arrived, as was Julian Huxley. My father recalled that Haldane advised him against joining the Oxford Union. However, my father was elected to the Essay Society, the most highly regarded club in his college — at least in intellectual circles — at which a member of the Society would read a paper and have it discussed critically over mulled claret. In due course I read a paper to the Essay Society, though I never acquired a taste for mulled claret. As Edward Gibbon had pointed out two centuries before, things do not change at Oxford.

My father did not establish good relations with either of his tutors. Efforts were being made to get older undergraduates, such as my father, into the Civil Service because it was thought they would never make good Oxford men, and most unsuitable to be Fellows of the college. 'We like to mould them', one of his tutors told my father. My father was asked if he wanted to join the Civil Service for which those graduates who got a First Class Degree, as my father did, did not have to take the entrance exam. Specifically he was asked if he would like to join the Colonial Service, which did not appeal to him. He felt that his tutor's attempts to push him into the Colonial Service forced him to take his final exams prematurely. This could have been disastrous, but in fact, by the time he came to take his finals, my father had already done extraordinarily well in the competitive exams he sat during the four terms which were all that he spent at Oxford. In this period of just over one year he won the Chancellor's Essay Prize for an essay on 'Aesthetics'; the Gladstone Prize for an essay on 'The Reform of the House of Lords and other second chambers'; and the Matthew Arnold Prize for an essay on the political philosopher, Thomas Hobbes, in whom he became much interested and on whom he subsequently wrote a book in 1922.

His tutors, he felt, were sour and unhelpful men. When my father asked his professor whether he thought the study of psychology would contribute to understandng politics, the latter replied that he would find better things in Plato. This was consistent with the view in Oxford on such matters in the early 1920s. It was thought that the psyche was an entirely subjective phenomenon and, as such, an objective study of it was, by definition, impossible. The argument ran that psychology, or indeed any other study of the psyche, could not exist. One of the conclusions drawn from this was that there was no need to have a Professor of Psychology — or indeed of Sociology.

My father came to the conclusion that in the Oxford of his time there was a general tendency to brush all gropings for truth aside. It was considered that only what could be stated with the total lucidity of logic was worthy of consideration. The fact that tentative gropings for truth, as in the so-called physical sciences, might be the basis for scientific method was considered irrelevant. The fact that the basic assumptions on which the approved logical structure was built might be either inadequate or irrelevant was brushed aside with equal firmness.

33

FAMILY QUARTET

When I went up to Oxford, thirty years after my father, the study of psychology was presided over by a Professor of Experimental Psychology and there existed the recently founded Institute of Experimental Psychology. The study of psychology was largely if not entirely confined to the study of the processes of learning, memory and the like. It was part of a course which went by the initials of PPP, the other two Ps standing for physiology and philosophy. Taken with physiology, psychology could lead to a medical degree and becoming a psychiatrist; or, with philosophy, to becoming an academic. The founding fathers of what was regarded as psychology outside the university, Freud, Jung and Adler, were hardly ever mentioned. My father considered that psychology did not exist in Oxford in the early 1920s. It had not made a great deal of progress by the early 1950s.

The Warden of New College in my father's time was Dr Archibald Spooner, best remembered for his so-called Spoonerisms. Spooner was also someone who somehow attracted anecdotes about himself. My father remembered a great number of stories about him. On one occasion he was sitting outside the Warden's study, waiting to see him, when the Warden suddenly appeared and noticed him looking at the coats of arms of Spooner's predecessors which were affixed to the wall. The Warden remarked that there were thirty-nine in all, and added that recently a lady with a love of round numbers, which is not uncommon, had said: 'What a pity, Mr Warden, that there aren't forty!' To an undergraduate at New College who had succeeded in getting a scholarship to Balliol, the Warden remarked: 'Ah well, it will be Balliol's loss and our gain.' To J. D. Woodruff, an undergraduate at New College at the time, he is supposed to have remarked: 'Well, Mr Woodruff, you will no longer have to think up jokes before Union Meetings.' After lecturing on Virgil, Dr Spooner announced to a subsequent Divinity class 'Of course, whenever I said "Virgil" I meant St Paul.' The true Spoonerism is represented by such remarks as the following, to a lady sitting in a shaded spot of the College garden: 'Oh, what a nosey cook!' and he is supposed to have said to his daughter when they were both on holiday in Egypt that he had enjoyed seeing 'the minx by spoon-light'.

However, the Warden did not only make weak jokes of an academic kind and commit trivial gaffes. On another, more important occasion he said to my father, 'I don't think the College would elect another Catholic' (to a Fellowship), by which he meant that since they already had one Catholic Fellow of the College, Professor Francis de Zuluetta, they would be unlikely to elect another in the person of my father, who had not appreciated this possible consequence when he became converted to Catholicism during his year at Oxford.

On another occasion, in Oriel College, my father was being interviewed for a possible Fellowship by the Provost. After a while the table-cloth was removed from the table. He was supposed to take this as a hint that his interview was at an end and that, finishing his glass of wine, he should make a discreet departure; but he had been so engrossed in talking about the Crusades, he left without finishing his wine. Later he heard that the Provost's comment had been: 'First time I ever came across a man who did not finish his wine!' Whether on this ground alone or not, he was not not offered the Fellowship for which he had hoped. He also applied for a Fellowship at Exeter College. Then, in an excess of over-conscientiousness or anxiety, he withdrew because he had in the meantime received another offer from America, which ironically he decided shortly afterwards not to take.

My father was in the unfortunate position of being brilliant and, if not exactly naïve, unversed in the ways of the world. Perhaps if he had obtained a commission in the Army he might have acquired the sort of worldly experience which would have prompted him to finish his glass of wine at Oriel and not to withdraw prematurely from the possibility of a Fellowship at Exeter. Essentially he was alone in the world. My grandfather Catlin was certainly not the best person to advise him; he antagonised people by writing complaining and quarrelsome letters, and his bellicosity does not suggest that finesse in human relationships was his strong point.

Many years later, my father admitted to feeling jealous of his fellow undergraduates who had become heads of Oxford Colleges. Keir at Balliol; Last at Brasenose: Bowra at Wadham. That my father did not get on with his tutors, who were said to be the best in their respective fields in the Oxford of his day, was not a help, and had he established better relations with them his prospects would have been much improved.

Both my parents had a veneration for Oxford which I find hard to understand. My mother regarded it as an essential stepping-stone in her career. My father's attitude came to be ambivalent and he never learnt to compete in the type of competitive world which exists in England. He achieved far more in the United States, and briefly in India, where perhaps his originality of mind was regarded as a positive contribution rather than as a distinct disadvantage.

Later my father sat for an All Souls Fellowship and came third after the two successful candidates, of whom one committed suicide shortly after his election. No one told my father that he could have sat a second time as did, for example, his friend Ernest Jacob, who was elected to a Fellowship on the second occasion, and who told my father some time afterwards that Warden Sumner of All Souls had told him that the only defect in my father's papers was that they showed what he described as a slight shortage of undergraduate wit. Nevertheless he was right to think that religious belief was something not then overlooked in the academic world, and that his Catholicism may have put at least one college off. He recalled Maurice Bowra saying much later that Anglicanism had been established in Oxford to save it from the ravages of religion. Even J. B. S. Haldane, a confessed atheist, attended New College chapel — because it was good for his lungs, he told my father — and certainly he was a Fellow of the College from 1919 to 1922. Oxford had only changed imperceptibly from the time of Edward Gibbon, who had been summarily sent down from Magdalene College when his father had been foolish enough to reveal to the authorities there that his son had been converted to Catholicism during one of his vacations. Gibbon did not remain a practising Catholic for long, but nor did he return to Oxford.

I can only speculate whether my father would have remained as a Fellow of an Oxford College for long if he had been elected. As he got older, unlike my mother and myself, he came to care increasingly for the outward signs of establishment status. But whether he would have regarded election to a Fellowship so highly if in fact he had been elected in his twenties is difficult to say.

At Oxford, my father became increasingly interested in developing the science of politics. The question he aimed to answer was: Why war? His interest stemmed from a near-obsession, following his time in the Army, in trying to answer this one question. But, if changing one's religion was regarded as a sign that one might be tiresome or difficult, any remotely obsessive interest could also lead to that damning academic criticism of being 'not quite sound'. I doubt whether Karl Marx would ever have been elected to a Fellowship of an Oxford College. He would definitely have been regarded as not quite sound; he was definitely too much of an enthusiast, too obsessive, and he would almost certainly have forgotten to finish his glass of wine in the heat of the moment.

Following his failure to get a Fellowship at Oxford, my father accepted a post in medieval and modern history at Sheffield University. In Sheffield, in addition to his work at the university, my father also taught philosophy to a Workers' Education Association class, the members of which were mostly miners and railwaymen. On one occasion one of the men in the class arrived a few minutes late and explained that he had just come off night-duty in a signal box. My father asked him if he had had any breakfast. The signalman replied that he had not bothered about that as he wanted to be in time for the class. My father felt particularly flattered. Later on in his life he came to realise that, with his subsequent interest in the immediate political scene, he had failed to capitalise on his time in Sheffield. He had had the opportunity to dig himself in there and get a Labour Party nomination from one of the Sheffield constituences, a course of action later adopted by both Hugh Gaitskell and Richard Crossman (also New College men) in other parts of the country. But this was with the benefit of hindsight. What he might have realised at the time was that in the WEA classes he was able to put himself across to an unsophisticated audience, and this was an asset of which he did not make as much use as he might have done when he came to pursue a career in politics in the late 1920s.

My father's first published thoughts on the factors making for war and its causes, and the answer to the question put by Rousseau: 'Not why, but how?' are given in his *Thomas Hobbes*, published in 1922 by Sheffield University. In 1921, however, my father got a year's leave of absence from Sheffield to go to Cornell University, in New York State, where he had been invited to take up the White Fellowship. (He had also had a Fellowship at Harvard offered to him but decided not to take it because it had more restrictive conditions.) The offer from Cornell came from the American historian Wallace Notestein and was also due partly to the help of Ernest Jacob, who by this time had become a Fellow of All Souls.

At Cornell my father helped Robert Cushman, a constitutional lawyer, to set up the Political Science Department from scratch. My father had been asked to take over from Alfred Zimmern, himself a Fellow and Tutor of New College, as a result of a disagreement as to whether Zimmern could be totally detached in his teaching of politics. This concern had apparently arisen because, on the day that French troops poured into the Ruhr in implementation of the Treaty of Versailles, he had been heard to play the *Marseillaise* all day long. My father did not return to Sheffield because in 1924 he was offered a professorship at Cornell which he accepted. He was then twenty-eight. After he had been there for less than two years he was invited by the Rockefeller Foundation and the US Social Science Research Council to head a national study on the workings of prohibition, its consequences, and what reforms, if any, were required. The first step in this exercise was a pilot study to establish whether the expense of a national survey was justified at all. On its completion it was decided to carry out a nationwide survey with my father as national director.

1926 was, therefore, a year of great opportunity for my father. He had become professor at Cornell, and had also been offered and accepted a job of considerable standing in United States governmental circles. As a result of the national enquiry the 18th (Prohibition) Amendment was repealed. My father was offered the chance to take up American citizenship. I have no doubt that the fact that he was by this time married to my mother — they had been married for just under a year — was what decided him against, for my mother considered her career to lie in England (although in 1926 it cannot be said that her career in England had noticeably flourished).

In my view this was a serious error of judgment on my father's part. His future undoubtedly lay in the United States. Indeed, in retrospect it can be seen that anyone who had the opportunity of making a career, whether in a profession or in business, in 1926 in the United States should have done so. The United States had become the centre of the capitalist world after the First World War, and the sun had begun to set on the British Empire, a state of affairs due in no small measure to the fact that England was ruled by those who had been to Oxford and Cambridge and who were not only out of touch with the ideas of the twentieth century but were in fact determined to live in the past. My father became a great admirer of Confucius, but he appears not to have taken to heart, this time at least, one of the major pieces of advice given by the sage in his commentary on *I Ching*, the Book of Changes, to the effect that perseverance or 'following through' is of vital importance in practical affairs because, if a particular line of action is abandoned rather than persevered with, all the time, effort and concentration put into it will always be wasted.

My father spent fourteen years at Cornell, from 1921 to 1935, but as he had got leave of absence to carry out the prohibition study from 1928 he only spent half the year there, so he could hardly have hoped to be part of a more accommodating establishment. By 1935 he had become interested in taking part in active politics and he could not of course do so in America. Although he was a student of politics, and therefore of the whys and wherefores of power, he does not seem to me to have persevered sufficiently in the various opportunities that came his way. This may have been due to the fact that there were so many of these opportunities that he felt he could pick and choose to an extent which, while possible in theory, in practice was not. Possibly he tried to do too many things at the same time; or at least to retain the opportunity of doing too many things.

The problem was that although my father hoped to be invited to return to Oxford, he also longed to retain his interests in America *and* to be involved in the academic development of political science. All these ambitions might have been combined in a plan covering, say, twenty to thirty years, but to realise them all simultaneously was to attempt too much in the 1920s and '30s where there was not the exchange between academic posts in Britain and the United States that developed after 1945. Again, there is now in Britain a greater interchange between the academic and political/governmental world which was not the case before the war. My father aimed for a career that was impossible to achieve before 1939, and which has been achieved since then only by Sir Isaiah Berlin.

Nevertheless, the fact remains it was due not to consideration of his own interests but to those of my mother that my father failed to develop his career in the United States, and that he came to leave Cornell in 1935. Whether he realised at that time that Winifred Holtby had not long to live I do not know; he certainly cannot have known that my grandfather would commit suicide shortly before Winifred's death. Whatever his plans, these two events were to make my mother much more dependent on my father and may have weighted the balance in his decision to stay in England.

I should perhaps at this stage, as I have already done with my Brittain forebears, sketch in some of my father's antecedents. The family laid claim, presumably on the basis of family legend handed down from one generation to the next, to be descended from a certain Sir Robert Catlin who died in 1574. In my father's study there hung a small painting of a coat of arms in a late Victorian plain deal frame. This rather romanticised armorial display, painted by my grandfather who was a skilful artist if an indifferent cleric, exerted considerable influence on how the Catlins regarded themselves. The large if romantic claim was not of course put to the test since careful genealogical research might prove there was no foundation in fact for this supposed connection.

What is certain is that Sir Robert was the son of a certain Thomas

Catlin, the second son of another Thomas Catlin, who owned a small estate in Raunds, Northamptonshire. Although his land holdings were not large, he was entitled to the designation of gentleman. Robert Catlin's precise date of birth has not been established and why he should have been born in Beeby in Leicestershire when his father lived in Raunds is not clear, although the fact that his only sister, Anne, was married to a Thomas Bickerton whose father did live in Beeby cannot be irrelevant. There are records of earlier Catlins in Raunds: John Catlin who was living in 1458 and Henry Catlin in 1481.

Raunds today is somethimg between a large village and a small town, about sixteen miles north-east of Northampton, with a population of nearly 6,000. When credible population statistics were first available in 1801, its population was only 890. It would seem likely that in the middle of the sixteenth century the number was not much more than 500.

Although the exact date of Sir Robert's birth is not known his further progress is recorded in more detail. By 1547 he was a Reader in the Middle Temple. Eleven years later, in October 1558 in the reign of Mary Tudor, he was appointed a Justice of the Court of Common Pleas. At the end of the following year he was created Chief Justice of the Queen's Bench in the place of Sir Robert Saunders, who was removed from office because of his religious opinions. Within a year, either at the end of 1559 or the beginning of 1560, Robert Catlin was knighted. Eleven years later, he presided at the trial of the Duke of Norfolk for high treason, but he incurred the royal displeasure of Queen Elizabeth by refusing to alter what was described rather quaintly as the ancient forms of the court to suit the interests of the Earl of Leicester.

Sir Robert must have been an astute man to have survived the transition in high office from the reign of Queen Mary to that of Elizabeth, in whose reign he remained Chief Justice for more than a decade after her accession. It is clear that Sir Robert was — fortunately — more interested in the acquisition of material wealth, chiefly in the form of land, than in religious conviction, a decidedly more contentious and dangerous area.

How did Sir Robert rise so rapidly in the highest ranks of the legal profession? Who were his influential friends at Court? Another Robert Catlin, who was the uncle of Sir Robert, had a son Thomas who married Anne Chauncey. Anne, after Thomas's death, took as her second husband Edmund Brudenell, member of a much better-connected family than the Catlins. Edmund was the fourth son of Sir Robert Brudenell, who was himself a judge. On the accession of King Henry VII he had been transferred from being a Justice of the King's Bench to the Court of Common Pleas and in April 1521, at the age of sixty, he was appointed Chief Justice of this Court, a post held until his death in 1531. Sir Robert Catlin was appointed Chief Justice of the same Court in 1559, twenty-seven years after the death of Sir Robert Brudenell. The family link with the Brudenells was not established until Sir Robert Catlin was a middle-aged man. Nevertheless the connection must have been useful to a man who left no avenue or opportunity unexplored. Sir Robert Catlin could see what the law had done for the Brudenells in his own lifetime.

A true son of his generation, and while still a Reader in the Middle Temple, Robert Catlin was acquiring land, most of which had previously belonged to the monasteries. He bought manors in Leicestershire and in Dorset as well as in Northamptonshire. In the year in which he became Chief Justice he leased for his own use the priory of Newnham in Bedfordshire and there he lived until his death in September 1574. The local public house is called The Lion's Head. The inn sign still shows the face of a lion, though it looks more like a cat, identical to that which appears on Sir Robert Catlin's coat of arms.

In 1566, seven years after he had been appointed Chief Justice and eight years before he died, his daughter Mary married a John Spencer. Their son, Robert, was born in 1570 and named after his grandfather Catlin. In due course he was knighted and subsequently became the first Baron Spencer of Wormleighton, where there still stands, in the centre of the village, an arch which is all that remains of a building on which the arms of Catlin are spliced with those of Spencer. By 1603, Lord Spencer was spoken of as the richest man in England, but before he reached this estate, his father, Sir John, had experienced considerable financial difficulties and it was only owing to his wife, to his mother-in-law and indeed to other relations of hers that they were able to survive and achieve the position which only fifteen years before had seemed to be in doubt.

But, whereas the Catlins enabled the Spencers to move on to greater things towards the end of the sixteenth century, the position was reversed in the first half of the seventeenth century. In 1631 William Catlin, who had sixteen children, ran into debt to a point where his estate was put in Chancery, thus passing out of his family's hands. Two of his many sons ended up at Althorp, the Spencer's country seat.

Wingfield Catlin, the second son, became steward there, and one of his brothers became vicar of Brington, which is on the edge of the Althorp estate.

One of Wingfield's younger brothers, John, who was christened in 1611, may be the same John Catlin who moved to Tilbrook, a very small village about five miles from Raunds. He died in 1670, and his son and grandson were both church wardens at Tilbrook, which lies between Higham Ferrers and Kimbolton. In the eighteenth century John Catlin's great-grandson, also John, was baptised at Tilbrook, in 1723. He moved to Bedford where he was a lace-maker and also parish clerk. A hundred years later my great-grandfather, William Henry Catlin, born in 1823, moved to Maidstone where he became a schoolmaster.

Towards the end of his life my father had his portrait painted by Romano Steffanelli, a pupil of Annigoni. My father never liked this picture because, although impressive, it is scarcely flattering. In his portrait my father looks like an Elizabethan figure: someone in whom high principle and self-interest are curiously combined — not the debonair figure who looked like Leslie Howard, but a more powerful yet sinister image. Not Sir George Catlin, but Sir Robert.

CHAPTER III

WINIFRED

WINIFRED Holtby was the only bridesmaid at my parents' wedding at St James's, Spanish Place, London on June 27th, 1925. In the years following my parents were to become involved in all manner of activities, academc, political and literary. Winifred Holtby's contribution to their success was equal to my parents' own, and her role at their wedding became symbolic of their joint lives for the next ten years.

Winifred was born on June 23, 1896 at Rudston House in the small village of that name which lies six miles east of Bridlington Bay on the east Yorkshire coast. Winifred's father was a farmer; her mother was the daughter of a farmer who had started life as a governess and married David Holtby rather late in life. Subsequently she became the first woman alderman in the East Riding.

Winifred's best-known novel was undoubtedly *South Riding*, but this was not published until 1936, the year after her death. In her lifetime she attached greater priority to her journalism and her position as a director of *Time and Tide*, the political journal with a feminist bias started, edited and directed by Lady Rhondda whose right-hand woman Winifred became following my mother's engagement to my father in 1924. Others too, regarded her primarily as a journalist, learning her reputation as a novelist in the making, curiously, not by the publication of *South Riding*, but by the film which appeared shortly after the novel was published, featuring Ralph Richardson and Edna Best under the direction of Victor Saville for Sir Alexander Korda. Now Winifred's other books are being reprinted too, foremost among them her first book, *Anderby Wold*, and *The Land of Green Ginger* and *Mandoa Mandoa*. Her feminist and political interests may be assessed from the titles of books other than her novels, some of which she published in pamphlet form: *Eutychus or The Future of the Pulpit*, A New Voter's Guide to Party Programmes and *The Position of Women*. She also wrote a book of literary criticism, *Virginia Woolf, a*

Critical Study, and a satire called *The Astonishing Island*, of which I have a copy with one of her own illustrations which she drew in the front for me. But the major cause with which she identified herself, not directly connected with feminism or politics in Britain, was her championship of the Black African in South Africa, to which she devoted time, energy and much of her earnings, following the six months she spent there at the beginning of 1926, after my parents' departure for Cornell. What started as a tour on behalf of the League of Nations ended up as a crusade on behalf of the Industrial and Commercial Workers' Union, which she rescued from the chaotic state into which it had fallen under the leadership of Clements Kadalie, and which she helped to put on its feet with the help (in this country) of Arthur Creech Jones, a Labour MP who became Colonial Secretary in Attlee's government in 1945.

Winifred Holtby was three and a half years younger than my mother and it is doubtful that they would have met at all if the war had not interrupted my mother's time at Oxford. When Winifred went up to Somerville College in the spring of 1919, my mother was returning to Oxford at the same time. Winifred, after starting at Oxford in 1917, had spent a year in the WRAC in 1918, so she too was going up for the second time.

Winifred was twenty-one when she met my mother, and the fact that she took up journalism, writing and lecturing, rather than following the primarily academic career offered to her after she just missed taking a First, was due substantially to my mother's influence. Her novel *Anderby Wold*, however, appeared in 1923 — before my mother's first novel, *The Dark Tide* — and her journalism also achieved recognition before my mother's when she was taken under Margaret Rhondda's wing.

In *Testament of Friendship*, my mother's biography of Winifred Holtby, published in 1941, six years after her death, my mother sketched in Winifred's childhood background in Rudston. She made the point that the Northmen and the Danes had left to the Yorkshire Wolds a vigorous race; tall, golden-haired and blue-eyed. As a true representative of this race, my mother wrote, Winifred was to stride the streets of London as the Vikings strode the Roman road from York to the sea. She had the physical appearance and appeal as one from the legends of old, perhaps to my mother's eyes a Wagnerian heroine, as her fiancé Roland Leighton was a Wagnerian hero, but in appearance rather than in character because, unlike my mother, Winifred did not dramatise herself to herself or indeed to others. Along with her strong sense of humour went a fundamental Yorkshire common sense.

44

David Holtby, her father, had managed to save enough money when still quite a young man to buy a house and an estate of about 940 acres at Rudston in 1891, when they became available on the death of the previous owner. After a period of protracted courtship, he had married Alice when she was forty. They had two daughters, of whom the elder, Grace, was even taller than Winifred, who was two and a half years younger.

My mother felt that Winifred combined the spartan optimism, positive outlook and irrespressible vitality of her mother with her father's considerate kindness. David Holtby was certainly not the supposedly typical Yorkshireman of granite. He never recovered from the farm labourers' strike on his land in 1918, as a result of which he sold up and moved to the suburbs of Hull. But the Holtby connection with farming continued. The children of David's elder brother, Tom, carried on farming at Dowthorpe Hall, at Skirlaugh between Bridlington and Hull, and Alice Holtby, who had more or less looked after the village of Rudston when she lived there, did not give up when they moved to Hull. Indeed it was then that she took on the civic duties which led to her being made an alderman.

Some of the characteristics of Winifred's Yorkshire family and those of my mother's Staffordshire relations were not dissimilar. Both believed in common sense and had down-to-earth values. Both Winifred and my mother had fathers who were distinguished by their personal kindness but could not be described as strong characters. Winifred's mother was undoubtedly the more dominant partner in her marriage, just as my grandmother, although not publicly assertive, ruled my grandfather in private. Against these similar matriarchal backgrounds, essentially non-intellectual and unimaginative, both women reacted strongly, with a more conscious determination. However, by literary temperament they were quite different. My mother kept a detailed diary from the age of about twelve, while Winifred invented stories before she could properly read, and this difference continued throughout their lives. Winifred had the imagination of the 'natural' novelist; my mother was more the recorder and commentator.

Winifred attended a girls' public school, St Margaret's, in Scarborough from September 1909, when she was eleven, and when that town was bombed in December 1914 she moved with the school to Pitlochry in Perthshire, where the school took over the Atholl Palace Hotel. Winifred's health had not been good during her time on the windswept Yorkshire coast, but in Pitlochry it began to improve. Surprisingly, it was not her own idea to go on to Oxford, but her mother's. She chose Somerville because it was non-denominational, and got through the entrance exam without difficulty. (She was later told that she had been well on the way to scholarship level.) She left St Margaret's in July 1916.

While at school my mother had played the part of the Madonna in the nativity play, *Eager Heart*. In the same play at her own school, Winifred had taken the part of the young king. But my mother's attractive appearance was decidedly deceptive, as was Winifred's rather gawky look. She hardly gave the impression of someone who wrote sentimental, often religiously inspired poetry, or who, as she subsequently said herself, was quite conventional until her early twenties. Winifred was not as ambitious as my mother when young. She had a talent for original writing, but she had to be pushed into devoting enough time to writing to make a success of it. Her real strengths were in the warmth of her personality, her vitality, and her originality, whereas my mother's lay more in her determination, her idealism and her strong moral belief.

When she was seventeen, Winifred had renewed her friendship with a childhood friend, three years older than she was. This was Harry Pearson, the son of a bank manager in Driffield, about seven miles southwest of Rudston. Harry had got a scholarship to Cambridge, but at the outbreak of the war he had joined a West Yorkshire regiment. When Winifred saw him again in Yorkshire, he had been invalided back from France. Harry sent her his poems, but in my mother's view Winifred was too immature at the time to appreciate the love for her which the sending of the poems expressed. In not appreciating them and their implied message, she deeply offended Harry. Nevertheless he was to play an important, if spasmodic, part in her life right up to her death. Before the war he had been highly idealistic, but afterwards he was utterly disillusioned, like so many of his contemporaries. Except for the seven-year period from 1925 to 1932, which he spent on the north-west frontier of India, he was unable to settle down and only held a job from time to time.

My mother felt strongly that Winifred's feelings for Harry were deeper than she realised. Perhaps she was still immature, and it took time for her to appreciate and respond to Harry. But her response came too late, so that what might have blossomed did not do so. When in due course she became aware of the extent of her rebuff, she never forgave herself, particularly as it came just at the time that his war experiences had struck him so hard. Whether due to wartime disillusionment or emotional rejection, Harry became a loner (it is significant that his best friend in the RAF in India was T. E. Lawrence, another, if more spectacular, loner). This deserves explanation if only because Harry remained at the back of Winifred's mind for the rest of her life; and in considering my mother's relationship with her, it is as important to bear in mind Winifred's relationship with Harry as it is to bear in mind my mother's relationship with her fiancé who died in the war.

A few weeks after her eighteenth birthday, Winifred went to a fashionable nursing home in London to work rather than going direct to Somerville. She did this because her elder sister Grace, who had been invited to take up the post, had already started work at a military hospital in Darlington. It was no doubt her mother's idea that Winifred should take Grace's place. At the home it was originally thought that Winifred would be working as a secretary, but because of the shortage of trained nurses, due to their departure for military duties, she gradually became involved in far more than just making beds and supervising sterilisers. The traumatic tasks she had to perform developed in her a concern for human suffering and a wish to help those in need and for this help that she was willing to give the demand seemed to grow throughout the rest of her life. Those who suffered in some way felt instinctively drawn to her, perhaps because they unconsciously felt that they could draw on her immense vitality, her obvious enjoyment of life and her wholly unselfish approach. In fact she was not as physically strong as she looked, certainly not as strong as my mother. But because she was a far more outgoing person she could not resist the demands made on her. Her optimistic temperament always made her feel that she had not suffered as others had. As her youthful naïveté was replaced with increasing awareness, so her inability to overlook and reject the sufferings of others grew.

The terrible experiences of the nursing home, which included patients dying in her arms, left their toll on Winifred. After a year of nursing she had to return to Rudston, in July 1917. She was now just nineteen. From Rudston she went up to Somerville in the autumn of 1917. Within a year, however, she felt she must share the experiences of the war. Before the end of the summer term in 1918, that is to say when she was just twenty, she joined Queen Mary's Army Auxiliary Corps. Her first post was at the New Zealand Officers' Club in Mayfair, where her job was that of hostel forewoman, but within three months she was on her way to France. She was there when her father made the decision to give up his life's work on his farm, where he had spent the best part of thirty years, and move to Cottingham outside Hull. My mother felt that this removal from the only family home she had ever known had a deep and lasting effect on Winifred and that this explained in part Winifred's revisiting the East Riding of Yorkshire again and again in her books. But I think the unsatisfactory and, in a sense, never-to-be-concluded relationship with Harry was also a factor. Although Winifred's destiny led her to London three times, twice temporarily when she was nursing and when she was in the WRAC, and finally when she came to share a flat with my mother, her heart remained in Yorkshire — and so, consequently, did her books.

When Winifred got to France she was stationed at Huchenneville, not far from Abbeville on the Somme. Even here her high spirits were as prevalent as ever. During the earlier part of 1918, before Winifred appeared on the scene, Abbeville had been bombed, so the signals unit to which she had been posted had had to be moved from there to the orchard next to the Château de Huchenneville. Soon the all-British unit was joined by the Australians, whose arrival was viewed with some trepidation. A dance was organised in their honour but, as many of the Australians had not seen a woman for several months, jealous rivalry soon flared up, centred on the Women's Army Auxiliary Corps of whom Winifred was a member. Nevertheless, she rode out the storm and became friendly with an Australian, Ken, who had given her a horse to ride, and in due course he came to stay with her family in Cottingham .

A year later the war was over and Winifred returned to Oxford. In 1920 her deep friendship with my mother really began.

CHAPTER IV

JOHN

ON October 2, 1935 Winifred Holtby, aged thirty-seven, was buried at Rudston. I was not there as I was not quite eight years old. Nevertheless, her death affected me because her character, the kind of person she was, had had more influence on me than anyone else up to that time. Although I am sure I was unaware of it then, I was always looking for someone to take her place.

Winifred had kept in touch with Harry Pearson, even though she saw him only occasionally. I did not see Harry often either. Nevertheless he exerted an influence on me too. Perhaps his absences made him seem more romantic. His drifting after his First World War experiences, and his lack of apparent aim and therefore lack of success in the eyes of my parents, had their effect in other ways which I did not evaluate until much later. My mother noted in her diary that he came to dinner in November 1932, when I was nearly five, and she recorded that he was very good-looking, and that they had not seen him for seven years, that is from the time she got married. The next time my mother mentioned him was in September 1935 when she said that Harry had turned up 'in a brown tweed suit, blue-eyed bronzed and handsome like an Army major'. My mother must have regarded him with favour since her heroes were always soldierly men who were also good-looking and idealistic. By 1935 Harry was no longer in either the Army or the Air Force and he had ceased to be idealistic. Nevertheless he still somehow fitted into my mother's pattern. She saw that the war had changed him into someone who lacked integration or purpose, but still regarded him as benevolent. His physical appearance was not lost on her: 'his long brown lashes, a little deeper in colour than his bronzed cheeks, curled lazily over his blue eyes and his vivid, humorous smile creased his face into characteristic lines of benevolence'.

Harry and Winifred had patched up their relationship after her

49

original rejection, but my father thought that Harry found Winifred less responsive than she might have been because she overworked fiercely during the last years of her life. Yet Harry's absence of seven years meant that by the time he reappeared on the scene Winifred already knew she had Bright's disease, and her doctor had told her she should not have children and there was therefore no point in getting married.

It was not until 1944 when I first read Somerset Maugham's *The Razor's Edge*, that I began to think about Harry in a more objective way. I was sixteen and my ambition in life was to emulate the anti-hero of that book, Larry Daurell, rather than to be a realisation of the ambitions which my parents had for me. In fact my own ambitions were crystallised by two principal characters created by Somerset Maugham, of whom Larry was the more influential in terms of his character, while the other, Charles Strickland, the Gaugin-like hero of *The Moon and Sixpence*, was the more influential in terms of his occupation.

Just as my mother had rebelled against what she regarded as the provincial ambitions and values of her parents, so I rebelled with increasing awareness against the ambitions my parents had for me, which essentially were that I should be a worldly success at something. Harry Pearson was the original anti-hero of my experience, and although my mother undoubtedly thought him attractive and my father was impressed by the fact that he had been a close friend of T. E. Lawrence, he was not viewed as a desirable role-model for me. The fact that Winifred undoubtedly loved him was perhaps part of his appeal to me. Increasingly, my reactions became as I imagined his would be, and I regarded him as a breath of fresh air in the world I moved in at home, constantly visited by coming world figures and their satellites. I think it unlikely that I would have been so influenced by Somerset Maugham's anti-heroes if I had not come across one who was part of my life.

My mother, in appreciating my great enjoyment of painting, and later on, writing poetry, put forward major figures from the past for my emulation; but much as I came to share her admiration for Shelley (whose rebellious character appealed to me more than his poetry), and also for Leonardo, these great figures of the past were never quite real. My father, despite his own academic and literary pursuits, always regarded artistic pursuits as altogether too risky, and from time to time he would suggest that I should get a qualification in accountancy, being in his view, and no doubt correctly from a completely objective standpoint, the profession most likely to lead to having an income for life. At other times, in keeping with his own earlier ambition, he would suggest that I became a priest, because, as he said on a number of occasions, I could well become a bishop in my early forties. At other times he thought that I should go into the diplomatic service, and no doubt he hoped by persuading me to go to Oxford that I might end up in the Foreign Office or the Treasury.

The fact that I scarcely ever saw Harry Pearson was beside the point. I knew that he had been in the RAF with T. E. Lawrence in India, and Lawrence exerted a considerable fascination on me when I was at school; and when, shortly after leaving, I was conscripted into the RAF in January 1946, I decided not to apply for a commission, my sole ambition being to go abroad as soon as I could. Oddly enough providence led me to Lawrence because I ended up first in Egypt and then in Palestine, through no decision of my own.

In Somerset Maugham's book Larry, who came from Chicago, had been in the US Air Force at the end of the First War. Afterwards he did not take the opportunity of a good job that was offered to him but started his life of drifting by going to Paris.

I never thought it necessary to be so ostentatiously apart and I have always been happy to do quite conventional jobs, but I suspect that an important difference between American and English society is that whereas in England one can carry on a perfectly conventional job with a very unconventional life or attitude to life, this is not so easy, or was not so easy, in the United States, where far more emphasis used to be put on being 'a regular guy', which essentially meant doing the same thing as everyone else in the same milieu, not just at work but in the rest of one's activities as well. It was helpful to one's career in the United States, for example, to be seen going to church, something which I cannot think has been true in England for a considerable time.

In my more outspoken phases I identified rather with Charles Strickland of *The Moon and Sixpence*, not only because like myself when I first read the book he had an overwhelming urge to paint, but because he was a much more aggressive, indeed 'macho' figure than Larry, and his rebellion against his family and background gave a positive example to me. His abandonment of his English family when he left his stockbroking job and went to France filled me with admiration for what I saw as the considerable courage he must have had to take such a step. In fact it may have been more an indication of his egotism than his courage, but when I first read the book this did not occur to me. It also did not occur to

51

me that Larry and Charles Strickland are very much two sides of the same coin; indeed both escaped to Paris and while Strickland was a stockbroker Daurell was also closely involved in a stockbroking background. Later both ended up with a not too dissimilar solution to their respective problems.

Two films which I saw when they first came out, *Pygmalion* in London in 1938 and *Citizen Kane* in St Paul, Minnesota in 1940 after I had been evacuated to America, also played important parts in developing my youthful sensibility. I identified with Professor Higgins played by Leslie Howard to whom, as I have said, my father bore a remarkable resemblance which he did not fail to cultivate. He always used to take me to Leslie Howard's films and he used to study what he was wearing and copied his clothes. In fact he became so interested in Howard that he engineered a meeting through Cyril Joad who knew him quite well. For my own part, I think I wanted to see my father as being more like Professor Higgins than he actually was.

Citizen Kane appealed to me for quite opposite but not unrelated reasons. Orson Welles embodied the individual oriented to success at all costs but who, at least in his own eyes, ended up by being a complete failure. He never achieved any of the ambitions he set out to achieve. He was defeated in his political ambitions despite the fact that he had started out by marrying the daughter of a President. His second wife did not become an opera star, despite the fact that he built an opera house for her to perform in. During the Depression the circulation of his papers decreased significantly. Citizen Kane achieved what he did and failed to do what he wanted to do entirely because of his chance inheritance of a mining fortune which lay below his parents' house located above the Colorado Lode. In Citizen Kane I saw the reverse image of my father, all the characteristics I did not like. I felt that in the end my father would also have disillusion for a constant companion in the castle of his dreams. Kane had his castle, but it became a tomb for himself and his desires. I later discovered that my father did not have the self-centredness of Citizen Kane, although he very much admired those who did, including Randolph Hearst on whom Kane was based.

If Larry Durrell and Charles Strickland were the two sides to my personality, then Professor Higgins and Citizen Kane were the two sides to my father. But Larry and Strickland had something in common, whereas the two sides of my father's character were irreconcilable, and it was this conflict in himself, in his personality which was too pleasant to

52

Rev. George Catlin,
George Catlin's father.

Mrs Catlin,
George's mother.

George Catlin, aged 14.

Below: Thomas (left) and Edith (right) Brittain, Vera's parents, in cycling outfits.

Vera in 1896.

Below: Vera and
Edward with their
parents, 1898.

Edward Brittain,
aged 8.

Vera's family in
the car.

Florence Bervon and Louise
Heath Jones.

Vera at St Monica's,
aged 9.

Vera, aged 17.

Edward at the award of his
MC, 1917.

Vera as a nurse in
Malta.

Winifred Holtby in 1921.

Winifred in Hull, 1922.

achieve his far-reaching ambitions, that ultimately led to his lack of success and disillusionment.

When I was born, on December 21, 1927 I can truly say that the world was my oyster. At the time my parents and Winifred Holtby all lived in a maisonette in Nevern Place, off the Earl's Court Road in west London. Had my father been there all the time, the maisonette would have been rather cramped, but as he spent half of each year at that time in the United States we could all fit in.

I happened to be born within two days of the anniversary of the date on which Roland Leighton, my mother's First War fiancé, had died. Thus I became the reincarnation of all her earlier romantic hopes and dreams. This was reinforced by the physical resemblance I bore to her brother, Edward, also killed in the war. My mother was devoted to me, and as I was born three weeks prematurely and weighed very little, was not supposed to be strong and needed a great deal of care, this essential attention to me increased her devotion. I had a nurse with whom I spent most of my time, but when my father was away in Cornell I was the total centre of attention for my mother and Winifred, at least for the two and half years before Shirley was born, in July 1930.

This wholehearted devotion was probably bad for my character because it did not encourage me to be adaptable, but it did ensure that I would always feel self-confident, even in the face of difficulties and, whatever the circumstances, I would almost always remain cheerful and optimistic. My mother's devotion to me gave me a great sense of power over her. Fortunately I developed what could either be described as a sense of humour or as a well-developed sense of the ridiculous at a very early age, so I do not think I exploited the situation as mercilessly as I might otherwise have done. In any case I learnt remarkably early on that my mother was determined to have her own way in everything, and since she had the ability to ensure that most of the time she did get her own way it was perhaps fortunate for me that she was my devoted slave.

Winifred was not my devoted slave. She was a totally natural and generous person with the most consistently happy disposition I have ever known. Rare in an English person, she had tremendous *joie de vivre*, a capacity for enjoying life and a great sense of humour, both of which qualities my mother lacked almost entirely. I can truly say that I loved Winifred and she loved me. As she felt the same for nearly everyone there was nothing possessive about her love, but in the way that children do, I felt she had a special devotion to me and I responded in kind.

53

To say that Winifred was killed by overwork and by helping many other people too much and too often would be an over-simplification. Being the kind of person she was, the kind of life she lived was inevitable, and in a sense she encouraged the endless demands made of her. But, perhaps unconciously, I drew the conclusion from observation of her behaviour that I was not going to work so hard or be so exploited as she was. Had Winifred been able to lead a quieter, less unselfish life, she would have been able to devote more of her time to her creative work. However, she was not sufficiently egotistical to be able to spend less exclusively in her own interests and in self-promotion. Like my father, with whom she had much in common, she was also much too gregarious to remain, except for fairly short periods, in the isolation demanded by serious creative work.

From my mother I inherited the capacity for doing things my way, and the ability to develop relationships, which gave me just what I wanted when I needed it. From her I also acquired a highly emotional disposition, while from my father I gained qualities which my mother did not possess, in particular an ability to remain detached and to analyse. I suspect that my talent to annoy sprang from the same source. Temperamentally I am an optimist; but intellectually I am a pessimist. One attribute I did not inherit from either parent, as I have suggested, was their worldly ambition, chiefly because I developed no interest in trying to impress or control others. My aim has been to achieve self-satisfaction rather than fame or glory, since I am not that interested in what other people think. Shirley acquired all my parents' ambition, along with my mother's air of moral authority and her decisiveness, channelled into the political arena for which we were prepared from the time we were born. Shirley's very positive attitude to life was similar to Winifred's, even though, when Winifred died, she was only five and with the onset of the symptoms of Bright's disease — high blood-pressure and sickness — Winifred had begun to be with us much less often. The family had moved to Glebe Place, Chelsea, in 1930, but Winifred spent more and more time in a small flat nearby, off the King's Road. Winifred looked after both of us, but she looked after me for a vital two and a half years longer.

My mother was thirty-four when I was born, and as I was her first child it was expected that my birth would take some time. However, whether owing to the cold weather or some other factor, my arrival was precipitate and I appeared before the doctor did. It was not an easy birth for my mother and I was quite under-weight, so we stayed in hospital until the middle of January 1928. By the time we got back to Nevern Place, Winifred and an Irish nurse-maid were there, but my father had had to return for his half-year in Cornell.

My mother's habitual anxiety, reinforced by her own mother's pessimism, must have been relaxed by Winifred's presence and her ability to bring a touch of lightness and optimism to the situation. For several months, and indeed to only a slightly lesser extent for a much longer period, my mother was extremely apprehensive about me, whether I would survive at all and whether I would overcome my numerous ailments and physical deficiencies, real or imagined. Long before I was born, and as a result of her experiences in the First World War, she had become very fatalistic about everyone she was fond of. In her fondness for me her anxiety knew no bounds.

Subsequently my mother ascribed my survival largely to the Chelsea Babies' Club, founded by Dr Harold Waller two months after I was born. But I have no doubt myself that it was at least partly due to a natural propensity for survival, which my mother herself had, and to the presence of Winifred who helped my mother to overcome her daily fear that when she woke in the morning she would find that I had died during the night. Possibly developing a sense of humour was part of the means of my surviving.

One of my earliest memories is of my mother singing to me, and I can still distinctly remember how mournful her voice sounded: more like a dirge or crooning than singing. No doubt my mother intended some positive purpose such as getting me to go back to sleep, but I found the experience depressing although somehow I appreciated that she was doing her best. It seems to me now that I wanted to ask her to stop, though I had not yet learned to talk. If I had, I wonder whether I would have complained. Imperfect memory suggests that I did not want to hurt her feelings.

When I was two months old I only weighed seven pounds, but two months later again I weighed ten. Whether this was due to the advice my mother got from the Babies' Club I cannot say, but certainly she had great confidence in the place, which I attended regularly. That I had an optimistic disposition and was a happy baby my mother reported to my father in one of her many letters to him in America. In fact I cannot think now that I was originally in such dire straits as my mother's agitation led her to believe. By the time I was just over one year old she was writing to my father describing me as both rosy-cheeked and fat, and self-sufficient and uncomplaining. I suspect that I had soon learnt that my mother insisted on these characteristics, and that they were as much due to the influence she exerted over me as to myself. Although my mother devoted an immense amount of thought and care to me, I was not allowed to take the place of her journalism and the writing of *Testament of Youth*. I was brought up to be self-reliant just as soon as this was feasible, and my mother's own stoic nature did not encourage my feeling sorry for myself.

My father questioned my mother as to whether one had the right to bring into the world a creature so bright as myself, on the grounds that life's experiences would be bound to disillusion me. Apart from the fact that it was rather late in the day to give practical implementation to this pessimistic thought, I managed by good fortune to combine a sanguine temperament with a fairly realistic, not to say cynical assessment of human nature, perhaps acquired from my grandmother. I did not have many illusions, although I developed a romantic outlook when I got older. I think my early realism was summed up in a remark which I made when I was about three and a half or four, and which my mother faithfully recorded, along with many of my cryptic remarks: 'I don't like my wife — I'll send her away because I want another woman'. Although undoubtedly prophetic, I think this pronouncement also shows that my parents and Winifred spoke in quite an uninhibited way in front of me so that I always took in what they said, even if I could not understand what was being said.

Considering how much my mother agonised over my health and upbringing, and that my every action and remark was recorded, it is perhaps amazing that I was not daunted. At a very early age I must have sensed that the only way not to succumb to or be overwhelmed by her anxious care was to distance myself as a form of self-preservation. The self-sufficiency which I showed and which was encouraged in me developed into relatively early independence. Although my mother was so concerned for Shirley's and my welfare she also encouraged us to think for ourselves, to express our own views and to develop a sturdy individualism. It is true that in the longer term my mother came to feel that perhaps we had both become too independent, especially in adolescence. But this was a development which she herself brought about.

CHAPTER V

ROLAND AND EDWARD

THROUGH her brother Edward my mother met the man who undoubtedly made a greater emotional impact on her than any other: Roland Leighton. Roland was at Uppingham at the same time as Edward, and my mother met him briefly in 1913, but it was only in April 1914 that Roland impinged on my mother — and she on him. After devoting herself with almost superhuman will and effort, and despite the odds against her, my mother heard in March 1914 that she had been awarded the Exhibition at Somerville for which she had aimed. This represented the achievement of her intellectual ambitions and a kind of victory over those who had suggested to her that she should try for the more ladylike purlieus of Lady Margaret Hall. Her admission to Oxford depended on the result of a further examination which she was to take in the summer of 1914, when she was twenty.

A month later Edward invited Roland to stay with the family in Buxton. Up to that point my mother's awareness of him had been confined to the fact that Edward was setting to music a poem Roland had written entitled 'L'Envoi'. But Roland combined in himself all those attributes which appealed to my mother's idealism and romanticism, except perhaps the sort of facial beauty one finds in portraits of Shelley and photographs of Rupert Brooke. However while not beautiful like them, Roland's appearance included an additional degree of masculinity. When my mother met him in 1913, Roland was nineteen — about the same age as my mother, both of them being about two years older than Edward. She wrote that he looked to her older than he was, and that he had a degree of self-assurance which made him look older still. To her, therefore, he was entirely adult even though when they first met he was still at school, just about to go to Uppingham for his last term.

My mother described Roland as not as tall as Edward but of a more powerful build, with a big head and stiff, thick fair hair which made him to her a very large person. He also had large dark eyes and strongly marked dark eyebrows, features he shared with Edward. He not only wrote poetry, but could discuss with my mother literature and religion. His family background also appealed to my mother. Both his parents worked — his father wrote boys' popular stories, his mother was a writer too — and contributed to the household expenses and towards Roland's education. He was head of work at Uppingham and in his final term he got six of the school's major prizes, mostly for Greek and Latin.

To my mother, therefore, Roland combined a dominating, wholly virile and masculine appearance with sensitivity: a rare but appealing combination. In this way he was neither wholly 'macho' nor wet or soft. Perhaps to the pre-1914 girl Roland combined those qualities which to a later generation appealed in Humphrey Bogart.

Roland was also a feminist, appreciating the contribution that his mother made. He gave my mother a copy of Olive Shreiner's *African Farm*, which meant a great deal to her in view of the books of Olive Shreiner's she had already read under the guidance of Louise Heath Jones.

My mother does not speculate on the relationship between Roland and Edward, but I have pointed out that Roland was about two years older and was definitely the more dominant partner. The words of the poem which Roland wrote and Edward set to music are evidence of a strong emotional nature:

> Only a turn of the head,
> A good-bye lightly said.
> And you set out to tread
> Your manlier road.
> But our youth's paths once met
> And think not we forget
> How great a brother's debt
> To you is owed.
>
> Sweep onward and though fame
> Shall aureole your name
> Remember whence you came
> In boyhood's days,
> And in life's darkening years
> Look back on hopes and fears
> Mingled with memory's tears
> And blame and praise.

The significance of this poem is a double one: firstly, in what Roland himself meant, and secondly the meaning read into the poem by my mother. There is no conclusive proof that Edward was the individual addressed in this poem. For example, it is not dedicated to Edward. On the other hand, that Edward set the poem to music suggests strongly that he regarded it at least as having a personal meaning for him. Is it reasonable to think that the poem was addressed to Edward as an appropriate good-bye from Roland, who was shortly to leave school, while Edward in the ordinary way would stay on for another two years? As far as the relationship between Edward and Roland is concerned the phrase 'And you set out to tread Your manlier road' suggests, to me, that Edward was upset at the thought of Roland leaving both the school and him, and that Roland had been able to encourage him to take a 'manlier' attitude and to soldier on alone. In any event, come what might, Roland would not forget Edward in the years ahead. The phrase 'though fame Shall aureole your name' must be specifically addressed to Edward if one interprets it to mean that in years to come Roland thought Edward would achieve fame as a composer. The poem goes on to express the hope, on this interpretation, that he, Roland, hoped that Edward would not forget him when he had achieved this prophesied eminence.

My grandfather undoubtedly looked on Edward, his only son, to become his successor in the paper-making business in due course. It would never have occurred to him that my mother who was both more forceful and indeed interested in herself being business-like, would have made a more appropriate and indeed astute successor. (Even if such an idea had crossed his mind, it is highly unlikely that such a solution would have been acceptable to his co-directors.) Edward looked to Roland, with his literary background and as someone not brought up in the cosiness of a successful business family, to provide moral support for his dominating interests: playing the violin and composing music.

But the seeds of the dreadful irony in the reference to a 'manlier road' were very quickly sown, because by November 1914 Edward had joined the Sherwood Foresters. He was only eighteen and had been due to stay on at school the following year. The prevailing mood was one of patriotic euphoria, however, and those who were old enough to do so joined up. Edward had put Roland's words into practice, giving up his cherished violin for the time being, only to find within four years that the 'manlier' road was not only much shorter than he had envisaged, but a dead end for both Roland and himself.

The poem's significance for my mother was different. Summed up in the title, 'L'Envoi', it came to symbolise not just meeting and saying goodbye to her brother's friend, but later saying goodbye to all that was before 1914. The words 'Sweep onward and though fame Shall aureole your name, Remember whence you came' could have been recited at my mother's goodbye to the two young men, and it was she who remembered 'whence you came' in *Testament of Youth*.

One is often aware of how one differs from one's close relations, but less conscious of the great deal one has in common. My mother thought of Edward as less ambitious than herself. I would say that Edward was equally ambitious, but that he was both more tolerant and more diplomatic. Of course, he could afford to be. Being a man he undoubtedly felt, quite appropriately to the chauvinist world in which he lived, that he would be able to have his own way and that somehow he would be able to resolve the apparent contradiction between composing and playing a role in the family business. Just as Henry Green later combined the roles of businessman and novelist, so might Edward have been able to arrive at a similar solution. My grandfather was too emotionally dependent on Edward not to have agreed to some form of compromise, and despite his explosions of irritation Edward was the last person with whom my grandfather would have wanted to quarrel. It is possible that, if Edward had had to face the same obstacles as my mother, he would have become just as obstinate and single-minded. He did not have to be. He got what he wanted without really trying.

The effect Roland Leighton had on my mother lay very largely in his hold over her imagination. The occasions on which they met were few, and even when they did meet they were seldom alone. It was because of my mother's tendency to romanticise reality that Roland took hold of her, and that is why his image was never effaced. Had they spent more time together or had they lived together they would perhaps have loved each other no less, but their relationship would have had to enter a different phase, less like a story by Andrew Lang in which the maiden, meeting the prince, is transformed into a princess. In her diary for May 19, 1914 my mother said that she longed for someone strong and loving, a man in preference to a woman as most women annoyed her. She added that while she realised the importance of solitude she hoped that permanent solitude was not necessary. She desired a sympathetic companionship, and above all she wanted a sympathetic companion and 'something to worship'.

Through her ambition and idealism my mother undoubtedly isolated herself, not only from her parents, but also from most of her contemporaries in Buxton. The exceptions to this isolation were Louise Heath Jones at her boarding school, and Edward at home. Edward gave the sympathetic understanding while Miss Heath Jones offered fuel to both enthusiasm and her idealism. That Roland provided all these qualities was a major factor in my mother's falling in love with him.

My mother and Roland were only alone for one day together when they took a journey from Leicester to Oxford. At virtually all other times they were chaperoned by one or more members of either family. This does not alter the fact that their relationship achieved a real intensity. One of the most interesting aspects of their love affair is that, for the only occasion in her life, my mother felt she would have sacrificed her ambition, by far her most predominant characteristic, to be with him. He, equally, at the last minute came to regret the superhuman efforts he had made to get to the front as soon as possible. One of their mutual friends, a man named Victor, told her long afterwards what Roland had said to him at an early stage in the war, that he could wish for no better fate than to be found dead in a trench at dawn, a sentiment not out of keeping with the speech made by the Headmaster of Uppingham at the end of the 1914 summer term in which he had stated that a man who could not be useful to his country was better dead. By 1915 Roland's attitudes had changed.

In *Testament of Youth* my mother covered her earlier life in considerable detail not only because she kept a diary which she completed for virtually every day, but because she saved all the letters she received. She was a tremendous letter-writer, and the need to communicate her thoughts, what she had been thinking, saying and doing, both to those close to her and to her diary, was compulsive. I remember she used to devote hours each day to the two activities — I always found it surprising that she dealt with her correspondence before her other writing.

However, as the years of the Great War, and particularly my mother's experiences from March 1915 to the Armistice in 1918, are essential to an understanding of her and her relationships after the war, time spent on the detail of this crucial period here will not be wasted. In any response to truly gruelling events, the personality of the person who experiences them is as much a factor as the events themselves. The knower and the known are one. The responses to their parts in the war were widely divergent for Edward and my mother, divergent as the

61

responses of Roland, Geoffrey and Victor. Again, although they were both involved only in the end of the war, my father and Winifred Holtby experienced it in quite a different way, as much because their characters were different, as that the events they witnessed were quite dissimilar.

It would be difficult to imagine a more peace-loving and self-effacing individual than my uncle, with his overriding passion for music. Perhaps this explains why his efforts to make up and then get to the front in France were continually thwarted by senior officers who thought of him as not sufficiently 'war-like material'. In the event he went through campaigns in France from the end of 1915 until the middle of 1918. Then, by this time a captain, he was sent to the Asiago Plateau in northern Italy. On the night, while on trench duty, he and his men were caught in gunfire through which they were unable to get back to their headquarters on the heights above Vicenza. Seeing that the position was critical, Edward led a party of men, including a small French contingent, to drive Austrians off. Just past midnight, shortly after they gained their objective, Edward was shot through the head by a sniper.

It is clear that Edward's detachment, down to his meticulous care for his personal appearance even when in the trenches, was a dominant factor in enabling him to remain uninvolved to a greater extent than others, even though his experiences of the war were just as bad or even worse. And paradoxically it was he, out of his circle of close friends, totally un-war-like though he was, who held command and acquired a reputation for gallantry over a longer period than any of his friends — particularly Roland — who had from the beginning identified themselves in an idealistic way with the war.

Roland regarded the war as a great crusade and longed to take part in an important action at the earliest possible opportunity. Like my mother, he idealised himself and dramatised his situation as she dramatised hers. Edward's and Roland's friends had to overcome fears of their own cowardice, and fear of what they might or might not do in front of their own men, but my impression is that Roland did not feel these fears, although his experiences in the trenches changed him very rapidly. He went to the front on Wednesday in Passion Week, my mother recorded: March 31, 1915. Between that time and his death from wounds nine months later on December 23, he underwent a complete change. His undoubtedly highly intelligent and sensitive personality was only able to cope with the horrors of the trenches by making a conscious effort to become increasingly indifferent to these horrors and to the pain of others. My mother became ever more worried that the Roland who had gone idealistically to war was becoming a wholly different man from the one she had known. This change in him was apparent to her not only when he came home on leave from France, but from their almost daily correspondence.

From the time that Roland left for France my mother began to think of combining nursing with her work at Oxford. Increasingly this became important to her because she wanted to identify her life as much as possible with his by doing an arduous and disagreeable job. She also felt that in this way she could more easily understand his changing outlook. But in order to be able to identify with his outlook she had to change herself too.

But even Oxford was changing. During the Easter vacation of 1915, the buildings of Somerville were commandeered and when she returned to Oxford in the summer it was to the St Mary Hall quadrangle of Oriel College, from where most of the able-bodied undergraduates had gone to join up, that she went.

If it had not been for the importance of getting through the Pass Moderation examinations at Somerville, my mother might well have given up Oxford at this point. However, Roland had been a classical scholar at Uppingham and had he lived, would have read Classics at Oxford, and my mother felt bound by her allegiance to carry on. She found her Latin and Greek extremely hard work, but persevered. Roland, of course, underwent a baptism of fire which led him to regard his classical education as quite beside the point. In the process of her identification with Roland, my mother did give up Oxford for nursing after her examinations, but traumatic as her nursing experiences were to be, they did not produce an immediate revolution in her values. To see bleeding stumps and quivering limbs in hospital, ghastly as it must have been, could never, in her view, be quite the same as living day in, day out in the quagmire of the trenches. Her nursing came to fulfil two functions: identification with Roland by doing a job as near as his as lay open to her; and being able to stop worrying about Roland and the danger he was in, by losing herself in the discomfort and weariness of her daily tasks.

My mother was naturally aware that, apart from the changes of mood brought about by the physical degradation of life in the trenches, Roland was irreversibly becoming a different person. It was not only their being apart that she found agonising. Her anguish was also due to the fear that he might no longer be the person he had been — that he might have become someone she could no longer idealise and adore. For what she had thought him to be, whether or not he had ever been completely so, was of course the basis of her love for him.

In *Testament of Youth* my mother wrote that war makes masochists of us all. With her capacity, indeed need, for self-dramatisation, she had to be able to do and to bear as much as she could during those months. Roland's equal power of self-dramatisation is suggested by his declaration that he could think of no better end than to be found dead in a trench at dawn. Edward did not have this same theatrical streak, or perhaps it was achieved in his music rather than in himself. Whatever the reason, he was able to undergo experiences just as harrowing as Roland's, and over a much longer period, without becoming totally changed. Not, of course, that Edward remained unaltered. He soon came to look considerably older and my mother found that he could on occasion be taciturn and uncommunicative. But, always detached and never an idealist in the sense that my mother and Roland were, Edward did not have the illusions to be shattered that they had.

In the summer of 1915, when Roland had been at the front for less than three months, Edward confirmed to my mother that all those who had been to France, if only for a couple of months, had been changed by the experience. Although he did not go to the front himself until the end of 1915, he could see this change in the officers who came back to England. Perhaps Edward survived better because he had more time to prepare for the experiences his brother officers had already had, by seeing what it did to them. Those who had gone out at the beginning of the war had had no indication of what shattering events they might expect.

Edward's nickname for Roland was Tonius, short for Antonius. It indicates the enormous influence of the classical education, not only the history of Greece and Rome, but the values of the classical past. The world of ancient Greece combined with the fairy-story world of chivalrous knights: marvellous material out of which the powers that be could lead all public-school young men to think that in going to France they would be following in the traditions of Athens and Sparta, if not actually in pursuit of the Holy Grail. Many of these young men did see themselves as doing just this and perhaps some retained their idealism in the trenches — for a short time at least. Those who would never go to the trenches, because they were too old or because they were in charge of operations in England were either blind or too out of touch to see what was happening. If Asquith, Edward Grey and one or two of their colleagues were not sons of the old Adam, greed, selfishness, revenge and lust for power triumphed over all, not only during the war but afterwards when the Treaty of Versailles came to be drawn and implemented.

In June 1915 my mother got through her exams at Oxford and took the train to Buxton in the knowledge that she could move on from her first university phase to what she now wanted to do: nursing. She felt that if she had not passed these exams her whole future would have been different. I doubt it. With her determination, she would almost certainly have tried again; her experiences in nursing would merely have been postponed for a year. In fact she began her experience of full-time nursing less than a fortnight after leaving Oxford. As she wrote, her only aim was to emulate Roland's endurance. To this end she took upon herself all the most unpleasant duties in her hospital, thus extracting the approval of her fellow-nurses who were only too pleased to be spared.

Her comments on those senior to her as well as more experienced in nursing, particularly sisters and the occasional matron, have particular relevance to her future attitude to feminism. She makes the point that feminist leaders should not be those most given to shouting and ordering others about. Elsewhere, she says that women who seek to do the jobs of men often make the mistake of copying men's worst characteristics. My mother never fell into that trap or approved of those women who did.

As a result of her down-to-earth experiences in nursing my mother increasingly felt able to express her feelings for Roland in terms other than the idealised. Thus in the summer of 1915 she wrote to him in the course of one of her many long letters: 'The earthly and obvious part of me longs to see and touch you . . .'

At this time, July 1915, Edward was home on leave and my mother referred again, not for the first time, to his serene aloofness, a characteristic that appears to have had immense power to preserve his sanity and bolster his refusal to give way to disillusion. In August 1915 Roland came home on leave and my mother got permission from her matron in Buxton to go to London. Although the war had only been going on for a year social changes had taken place. For example, she was allowed to travel to London to see him on her own. By now she was twenty-one, and this was to be a one-day visit only. It would have been unheard of, at least among those whom my mother knew, for them to spend a weekend together and alone in London. Although my mother may have rebelled against 'provincialism', this rebellion was not expressed in her behaviour, which was quite conventional. When Roland at last appeared at St Pancras, my mother was petrified by what his letters had only hinted at: the changed Roland to whom three months in the trenches had given a highly disconcerting air of maturity and apparent sophistication. On an immediate level this was expressed by the general disarray of his clothes. At this early stage of the war those who had been at the front distanced themselves from brother officers who had not by appearing shabbily dressed. Later on, when nearly all officers had been to France, if not further afield, it became modish to appear perfectly dressed down to the last detail. Edward was always immaculately turned out.

My mother's fear, now that they were face to face, that Roland might be totally changed quite overwhelmed her happiness. She feared that the Roland she saw might not be the Roland she knew. Such was the constraint of the situation that they just shook hands — which indeed is what they had done when they had parted on the last occasion. When he told her that his one regret was that his regiment had not taken part in any action so far, her worst fears were reinforced. To meet and preserve the social requirements, my mother then took Roland back to Buxton, a four-hour railway journey. Then on from Buxton they went to spend a week-end with Roland's parents in Lowestoft. They were alone on the train but there was no opportunity really to relax and unwind, particularly as these lengthy journeys would inevitably lead to confrontation with close relatives. But there was no real alternative that would not have created a scandal. Buxton and Lowestoft in the same week-end was perhaps going to extremes to meet the social requirements of the situation but my mother was only twenty-one. And in this hectic schedule my mother had even included a visit to see the Matron of the First London General Hospital in Camberwell. To meet the age requirements she told the Matron she was twenty-three. Some weeks later she received confirmation that she would be able to join the hospital in the coming October.

On the train journey to Buxton, Roland suggested that it might make it easier for both of them if they now became officially engaged. They promptly had a row because my mother felt that they would only be doing so to accommodate the expectation of provincial society. They therefore said nothing about a proposed engagement to my grandparents because my mother felt that precious moments of Roland's leave would be taken up by her father's enquiries as to how he was going to keep her. Such enquiries would have been a source of anxiety if not embarrassment to them all since my grandfather already knew that Roland was not well off.

In London once again, they met Edward and their mutual friend, Victor. They offered their congratulations, but Edward added his hope that they would have a quick and secret wedding to complete the effect. When they arrived at Roland's parents' home, my mother was meeting them for the first time. What most appealed to her was the literary gossip and talk of publishers, which had all the spice of romance and was certainly far removed from what she regarded as the pedestrian conversation of her parents in Buxton.

My mother could not avoid feeling that their few days together were disappointing simply because Roland seemed so changed. She felt that he deliberately kept himself aloof, and, worse, that his experiences in France had brought out a ruthless quality which she may have vaguely suspected before and which she had chosen to overlook but which was now inescapable. But the circumstances of Roland's leave can hardly have led him to feel anything but totally strung up. The combined pressures of the situation perversely brought out just those very characteristics which he knew my mother hated most. She had previously regarded his perversity as part of his attraction. Perhaps his ruthlessness was part of that too. Now she saw another side to this same quality.

Roland's ability to disconcert my mother undoubtedly proved to him his power over her. Such remarks of his as that annihilation had a great attraction, or that if he were killed she would soon forget him do suggest a certain cruelty and some bitterness. They also appear designed to provoke and to force my mother to express her denunciation of these sentiments. I cannot but feel that if Roland had survived the war and married my mother their life would have been a perpetual battle of wills.

It was on this leave that my mother recalled telling Roland that if he were killed she would set out to marry the first reasonable person who asked her. In due course this is just what she did. I think it significant that she did not say that she would marry the first person who fell in love with her, or even the first person she fell in love with. I do not think it occurred to my mother at the time that she could ever fall in love with anyone else. And in one sense it is true that she never did, because Roland embodied her idealisation of what a man should be. Equally, her own life — going to Oxford, becoming a writer, even becoming a nurse

67

— was planned in conscious emulation of him or from a desire to be close to him not only in spirit but in her actions. Reading Latin and Greek, or confronting hideous wounds and wholesale death after a major battle, all these experiences she undertook with Roland in mind. My mother felt that by marrying the first tolerable man who proposed she would always be able to keep Roland too. Her memory of him would live with her always, as she told herself.

They returned to London from Lowestoft and spent the day shopping for equipment for Roland to take back to the front. Roland did not buy my mother an engagement ring, because she thought of this as a token of possession, and he detested the obvious. Nevertheless, I have a portrait painted of my mother about this time in which she is wearing her VAD uniform and also an engagement ring. My mother never made any mention of this portrait to me and I had never seen it until very recently. The date on it is indecipherable but I think it must have been painted in the second half of 1915.

As Roland's leave came to an end, he must have been in a contradictory state of mind. At the last moment he said he did not want to go back to the front and from this my mother concluded that he did really love her. However anxious she might become, this final remark kept her going under the most difficult circumstances.

In September 1915 my mother was still living at home in Buxton. At this time she met Edward's friend, Geoffrey, who had been at Uppingham, and who had become his inseparable friend since Roland's departure to the front. My mother described Geoffrey as a reticent idealist who saw himself as having a future as a clergyman in a slum parish once the war was ended. Geoffrey was shy and diffident — too much so, Edward thought, for him to be any good at dealing with people. My mother found in his elusive abruptness, as she described it, a certain attraction. He might have a future as a poor curate, but he undoubtedly lacked confidence in himself and the thought of going to the front created a formidable prospect. My mother judged him the most beautiful young man she had ever met.

Less than a month later my mother was posted from Buxton to the First London General Hospital at Camberwell. She arrived there on October 18, 1916. Before leaving Derbyshire she re-visited all the places which she and Roland had been to only a few weeks before. She never returned to Buxton.

Camberwell brought my mother nearer to the war in two senses. She

68

was now faced with a formidably austere régime, rising at six every morning. And the casualties at Camberwell were far more serious.

By the time my mother got to Camberwell both she and Roland had become conscious that both were changing, changing not only more quickly but also in different directions than would have been the case in peacetime. Roland wrote to say that he feared he was becoming a martinet: stiff, narrow and practical; a real barbarian and a man of the woods, as he put it. It was not until later that my mother came to feel that, under the conditions which existed for Roland and herself, adaptation was necessary in order to make survival possible. It was indeed a case of survival of the fittest, and fitness essentially meant swiftness of adaptation. Early in December 1915 and after my mother had been to stay on her own with Roland's parents, Roland wrote to her to say, 'Well, after all, your real love was just a character in a book . . . It is quite possible to love an ideal crystallised in a person . . . though it must be very trying to be the incarnation of an ideal — very trying'. Unkind as these comments were, they were particularly so because they contained a considerable amount of truth. They are of interest to me because I later found my mother's idealisation of myself quite overwhelming: what Roland said in 1915 I could myself have said, no doubt in rather different words, in 1945. My mother was not unique. Is love for someone else a projection of one's own wish-fulfilment? The problem is that the someone else then has to live up to and will fall short in either trying or not succeeding or in not even trying. My mother certainly did expect those she loved to be the incarnation of an ideal: that this is a trying experience is an understatement. Faced with being the incarnation of someone else's ideal I think there are only two courses of action open: either one wholeheartedly undertakes the achievement of the ideal or totally renounces the idealisation. Partial realisation is bound to be a disappointment.

After completing her five-week probation period my mother was told that she could sign on for six months, and at the end of this period her contract was renewable. Shortly afterwards, she heard from Roland that he would be getting leave for Christmas, and my mother was able to obtain permission to postpone her leave until then. She left the hospital on Christmas morning and went down to Brighton, where her parents were temporarily living in an hotel. This was just after my grandfather had left the family business rather precipitately, after a disagreement with the rest of the board who were in favour of making cigarette paper.

Roland's parents had moved to Keymer, near Brighton, because their house was in an exposed and increasingly dangerous position. But Roland never turned up. He died of wounds on December 23 at a Casualty Clearing Station at Louvencourt, about two miles south-east of Doullens, not far from Amiens. He had been received into the Catholic faith. He had not been killed in any heroic action, as he had so often desired, but while inspecting an area where his platoon had been ordered to repair the wire following a preliminary reconnoitre.

My mother dwelt upon the facts of his death until 'it seemed as though my mind would never contain the anguish that they brought me . . . Had it been heroism or folly I asked myself for the thousandth time, which had urged him forth to inspect the wire beneath so bright a moon?' But my mother also felt particularly distressed that he had left at the last no message specifically for her, and in *Testament of Youth* she wrote 'All through the first months of 1916, my letters and diaries emphasised again and again the grief of having no word to cherish — through the empty years'. A week later my mother had her twenty-second birthday. She had stayed on with Roland's parents until the end of her leave, and then returned to London with Edward, who once again became the centre of her life. He concealed from her at the time not only the grief he felt at his best friend's death, but also the fact that, while Roland had already been at the front for nine months, he had so far not succeeded in getting there at all. On her return to Camberwell my mother found life particularly hateful, and she realised that it had been for Roland's sake that she had endured the hardships and the awfulness of the hospital and that it was for this reason too that she had undertaken the most disagreeable tasks left to her by others.

Following Roland's death, it was with Victor, whose meningitis permitted him only to carry out light duties combined with frequent leave, that she found her chief consolation and on whom she looked as a kind of father confessor. He made no demands on her, or indeed on any of his friends, and almost encouraged them to make demands on him. At alternative weekends, when my mother was off duty, they would meet on Sunday evenings at the Trocadero for dinner. She would do the talking, and he would do the listening. In this way he fulfilled a role that Edward had performed when they were both children, and that Winifred Holtby and also my father were to carry out in the years to come.

In February 1916 a period of night duty which had occupied my mother since Roland's death came to an end. At the same time Edward finally received orders to go to France with his regiment, the 11th Sherwood Foresters. A week later he wrote to say that he realised now how easy it was to be killed while carrying out routine duties, of the kind Roland had been involved in on the moonlit night that he was shot. While he did not hold life cheap, he said, it was hard to be sufficiently brave all the time. He added that he hardly ever felt afraid, and that even when he did it was most important to keep up appearances — setting an example was at least as important as the specific duty itself.

Soon my mother saw Geoffrey's name among the wounded; he had been at the front at Ypres. He was now in hospital at the Fishmongers' Hall in the City so she was able to go and see him. He told her that he was not such a good officer as Edward because he always felt afraid in the trenches. To my mother Geoffrey and Victor had much in common. While she treated Victor as a kind of father confessor, she felt that Geoffrey had a vocation for the church and was impressed by what she described as his compelling devotional beauty. The departure of Edward for the front, the certainty that Victor would be going out again shortly, although he believed the experience would break him one way or another, and all this against the background of Roland's death, determined my mother to continue nursing rather than return to Somerville. She therefore went to see the Principal of the College in March 1916 to make her case. In view of her past experience of terrifying matrons, she was now more able to express her views without undue trepidation: she would not be returning to Oxford until the war was over.

One day in July 1916 my mother was suddenly summoned to be told that Edward himself was in the First London General Hospital in Camberwell. He had been in the battle of the Somme. He was concerned about the long-term effects: would he be able to continue to play the violin? When my mother first saw him he looked infinitely happier than Geoffrey with his much less serious wound. She felt that this was due to his having faced danger creditably. As he came later to think more deeply about the battle he began to age, seemingly more like thirty than the twenty he actually was. He had indeed acted with considerable heroism and been awarded the MC. The British offensive of July 1916 had begun on a front extending about ninety miles along the north of the river Somme. Edward was stationed at Albert near to Montaubon, Fricourt and Mametz, where the fighting was fiercest. Edward's battalion took part in the initial attack. Sections of the regiment in front of Edward's panicked and began to retreat. Edward got his men together and led them over the top; twice he had to go back to push them on. He was hit in the thigh about seventy yards from his own trench, tried to get up but could not do so and crawled into a shell hole. He was wounded a second time, in the arm, by a splinter from a shell bursting nearby. When the machine-gun offensive finally slackened he dragged himself back to his own lines.

News of this came to my grandparents just as my grandfather had decided to take the flat in Oakwood Court, where they were to live until 1934. When my mother remarked to Geoffrey how amazed she had been at Edward's gallantry, and particularly by his success in rallying his men after their moment of panic, Geoffrey said that, on the contrary, he had not been at all surprised, and that he, Edward, was 'a stout fellow'. Edward's nickname was 'the immaculate man of the trenches', not least due to his habit of always shaving even on the worst days, to bolster his own morale and that of his men. My mother reflected that Roland would have been bitter had he lived to hear of Edward's Military Cross. For it had always been Roland who sought glory.

In October my mother went on leave to Macclesfield, where her parents were staying temporarily, having given up the lease of their house in Buxton, and before moving to London. She had hardly arrived before she was notified that she was being posted abroad. She had to return to London immediately and on September 23, 1916 was at Southampton ready to sail to Malta.

My mother regarded her eight months in Malta as a welcome respite after the death of Roland. There, she came to life again, and indeed a photograph taken of her at the time shows her looking particularly cheerful. By March 1917 she felt sufficiently her old self to have what she described as agreeable teas and drinks at the officers' mess, followed by games of tennis. Fraternisation was not officially allowed but the tennis and the drinks were possible because nurses were housed at the opposite end from the Sisters' compound, but next to the medical officers.

This tranquillity was not, however, to last for long. In early April my mother received a cablegram to say that Victor had been seriously wounded at Arras. No details were given, but in reply to her anxious enquiry Edward cabled back tersely: 'Eyesight probably gone. May live.' In fact, thinking he would not survive, a matron at Rouen summoned Victor's father, but he recovered sufficiently to be sent to the London General Hospital in Chelsea. Victor's Colonel wrote to his father to say that he had recommended him for the Victoria Cross, and in fact he was awarded the MC a few weeks later. Edward also wrote to Geoffrey to give him news of Victor, but Geoffrey never got the letter. He had been killed at Monchy Le Preux a few days earlier on April 23.

These tragedies decided my mother that she could no longer stay and enjoy herself in Malta. She felt she must see Victor and discover if there was anything she could do for him, just as he had stood by her in her blackest hours after Roland's death. On May 22 she began her journey home by the overland route up through Italy, since the Mediterranean was infested with submarines. It took six days. She went via Syracuse, Messina, Rome, Pisa, Turin and, ultimately, Paris, then on to Victoria Station and her parents' new flat in Kensington. The day after her return to London my mother went over to the Second London General Hospital, next door to the present Chelsea Football Ground. There she found Victor in the garden; he was learning to read a book in braille. A fortnight later Edward arrived back on leave.

He appeared frightening to my mother — unsmilingly grim and uncommunicative. She felt that this change in him was due more to the death of Geoffrey and to the blinding of Victor than to his own experiences. He spent much of the time at the piano, playing over and over again Elgar's 'Lament for the Fallen'.

My mother had given up the enjoyable life of Malta in order to return to the fray and, specifically, to be of whatever service she could to Victor. She even intended to marry him if that was what he wanted. Victor's father, as well as my mother and Edward, were staying at my grandparents' flat and early one morning they got a message to say that Victor had died during the night. My mother's immediate reaction was that his efforts at readjustment had been cruelly wasted; but later on she came to think that, had he lived, their relationship would inevitably have been without serenity because, in her words, she had always been 'too egotistical, too ambitious, too impatient' to marry someone whom she would have to nurse for the rest of his life.

In June 1917 Edward returned to France and two months later my mother was posted to the general hospital at Etaples, just off the north French coast. Here she cared for wounded German prisoners. Although she did not like Etaples as much as Malta, there must have been something about the place as she wandered along the coast when off-duty that appealed to her because for many years, when Shirley and I were small, we used to go to this part of France for our summer holidays. A major reason for my mother trying to be posted to France was to be near

Edward — but following the Italian collapse at Caperetto at the end of October he left Ypres for Italy. Glad though she was that Edward was leaving the dreadful Salient, my mother was disappointed that he would now be far away from her. But in January 1918 Edward was able to get leave and as my mother had been in France for nearly six months she was also able to get leave at the same time.

On her return to Etaples, my mother recorded that she had been totally unaware that the Representation of the People Act, giving the vote to women aged thirty and over, had passed through the House of Lords. She would be able to vote in 1924. At the end of April, she had to return to London following repeated entreaties from her father. Her mother had had a breakdown in health and my mother found it hard to decide whether this was basically physical or psychological. Having been away in Malta and at Etaples, she only gradually appreciated the strain of the war on those at home in England. My mother felt torn between her wish to remain at the front and the apparent need to look after her parents. She had to face the fact that in France she was no longer near Edward, and she realised that, while her parents had adapted unexpectedly well to her wartime activities, they had been brought up to think that at a time of crisis it was the duty of an unmarried daughter to be at home. Through the summer of 1918, therefore, she stayed in London. Before long all the feelings of frustration which she had experienced living in Buxton reappeared. In spite of the news that the hospital at Etaples had been destroyed by German bombers during the final German offensive of March 1918 she was incapable of resigning herself to a life of enforced domestication.

Then came news of a sudden blaze-up on the Italian front. On the Asiago Plateau, where Edward was based, to the east of the river Brenta, the artillery struggle suddenly intensified. Edward was killed on June 15. My mother records that the period which followed the death of Edward, even more than the early months of 1916 after Roland had died, were the most desperate she had ever experienced. From the middle of 1918 for the better part of two years, she had no one with whom to communicate, and as the enormous volume of her letters and diaries show, communication was essential to her. She felt the loss of Edward to be greater even than the loss of Roland because they had been together for virtually the whole of their lives. Edward had always listened to my mother, even when his own experiences made him unusually reticent, for instance at the time of Roland's death, and subsequently that of Geoffrey and of Victor. Roland had been more like my mother than Edward was, but Edward, like my father, was more complementary to my mother's character.

By September 1918 my mother felt her parents' need for her was no longer an overriding claim. She had at least found them a satisfactory maid, an extremely difficult achievement in wartime. The call to action was once more uppermost in her mind. For the third time she returned to VAD Headquarters in the hope of getting abroad. But, there was now a rule that anyone who had broken their contract — and of course going home to look after her parents was just that — could no longer be sent to France. She felt that her considerable experience so close to the front was not being fully utilised; nevertheless, she had no alternative, if she were to return to nursing, but to work in a London hospital. The first one she was posted to she found so insupportable that after a month she called on the matron whom she had come to know at Etaples, and who was now at Queen Alexandra's Military Hospital in Millbank. My mother joined her staff, staying for five months until April 1919. At Millbank, she later felt, she had become the complete automaton, beyond both fear and enthusiasm, and in 'a permanent state of numb disillusion', that virtual paralysis of both the personality and the will which follows the most traumatic experiences. Never having experienced anything quite like this before, not even at the death of Roland, my mother could hardly allow for the deadening of her will and her feelings which Edward's death produced. In time this total numbness passed away, but not without leaving its effects and perhaps never quite totally.

In the end my mother went back to Oxford. She no longer had her original overwhelming desire to go there, but such a course of action was the only way of picking up the old threads again. It was all that remained of her life that was important to her from the days, both so recent and yet so long ago, when Roland and Edward, Geoffrey and Victor, had still been alive.

CHAPTER VI

VERA AND WINIFRED

WHEN my mother returned to Oxford in 1919 she decided to read history. She was coached in modern history by the Dean of Hertford College, and her tutor told her that a Miss Holtby, also of Somerville, wanted equally to study the nineteenth century. My mother described her reaction as 'unaccountably antagonistic'. On the day in question, she waited with the Dean for Winifred to turn up, and at last she did. My mother described her as 'superbly tall, and vigorous as the young Diana with her long straight limbs and her golden hair, her vitality smote with the effect of a blow upon my jaded nerves'. She also confessed that, in her resentment of the newcomer, she was overjoyed to find that Winifred did not appear to have read any of the books which the Dean had previously said were an indispensable introduction.

Although my mother and Winifred continued to see each other it was not until the following Easter term that their friendship blossomed. Indeed it really began on an occasion when my mother was in bed with a cold, feeling sorry for herself. Winifred suddenly appeared with a bunch of grapes and immediately disappeared, only to return the next day. Winifred was to prove the ideal companion to my mother because of this outgoing and generous personality: sympathetic, understanding and enthusiastic. Her vitality was a balm to my mother even though at their first meeting she had found Winifred so overwhelming.

Winifred lacked the total ambition and self-discipline which characterised my mother, and I think it was her communication of these two qualities to Winifred which provided the impetus the latter needed in order to become a writer. If my mother needed a sympathetic companion Winifred equally neeeded a mentor to guide her. When they first met my mother was very nearly twenty-six while Winifred was only twenty-one. My mother therefore provided that guiding influence which, previously, Winifred had found in her mother. The personality of the one did, in fact, constitute a near-perfect counter-balance to that of the other. In time my mother came to feel that she owed everything to Winifred because it was through her that she was able once more to lift her head. In her natural response to suffering, Winifred appreciated the need of my mother for understanding and comfort. A therapeutic result was achieved as both were great talkers and letter-writers. To be able to communicate with someone else close and personally involved was essential. Both looked to Oxford to provide a key to a future the shape of which was far from clear at the time of their meeting.

My mother wrote to Winifred as having been something of a tomboy as a child and she remained so. She would run along the Isis tow-path, shouting, while boat races were taking place. She enjoyed parties on the men's barges. In her academic life she missed getting a First in the Modern History Honours School due to her ribald replies in the Viva. However, the examiners could see that, despite her very poor spelling, immature hand-writing and lack of dedication to the academic life, she did have definite originality.

My mother suggested that Winifred was torn between a social con-science and her desire to write, but I think that this conflict applied more to my mother than to Winifred, who had a natural magnanimity of spirit which was incapable of resisting the demands made on her. Her passion for social justice was based on her generous spirit rather than on a detached or intellectual foundation. She may have been torn between her magnanimity and her writing, which like any creative pursuit is essentially a solitary and rather self-centred one, but the fact remains that her books were inspired by her concern for people and their prob-lems. If she had been a different sort of person, her books too would have been different. At Oxford, Winifred's solicitude was aroused by any fellow student suffering from a problem. Indeed one of the scholarships she would fund at Somerville was for the benefit of those who had to earn their own living before going up to Oxford. To some extent my mother resented Winifred's omnipresent generosity, but it was my mother's clear need of love, sympathy and affection which found a response in that generosity of Winifred's and from which she undoubtedly benefited beyond all others.

Those who are perpetually giving of themselves, as Winifred was, suffer from a kind of emotional claustrophobia and from time to time they have to get away. When Winifred was able to do this she pressed on with her writing. While it could be said that my mother exploited

Winifred's endless goodwill, it is also true that my mother did prevent Winifred from being exploited by others to a point where she would have become too exhausted to write at all. My mother admitted that she envied Winifred her popularity at Oxford, but then my mother never aimed to be socially successful. Although dependent on those very close to her, she was indifferent to most people. As she grew older she would fall asleep at dinner parties, even those in her own house, and at cocktail parties she often could not remember the names of the people who had been invited. I recall on one occasion, in the 1960s, she went up to one of her guests and, apologising profusely, said: 'I know your face, but I simply can't remember your name.' 'Not at all', replied the guest, 'I am Mary Wilson'. Her husband was Prime Minister at the time.

The last hundred and sixty pages of *Testament of Youth* cover the time from when my mother returned to Oxford and met Winifred until she married my father in 1925. When she came to write *Testament of Friendship*, which was published eight years later, she covers the same period in rather less than half the number of pages. Comparison of these two portraits, one written in 1930–31 and the other rather less than ten years later, is instructive. By the time she wrote the second book my mother had achieved her ambition of becoming a well-known writer, whereas at the time of writing *Testament of Youth* she was largely unknown. In *Testament of Youth* my mother said that for a short period Winifred suffered from a feeling of moral obligation to become a schoolteacher, 'which she had inherited from the example-setting tradition of her hostel-forewoman days in the WRAC, but the project soon collapsed before the more congenial notion of sharing a tiny flat with me in London and trying to write, while my own intentions were too long established to be shaken by the flattering tutorial encouragement to take up research'. In *Testament of Friendship* my mother treated this rather differently. She wrote: 'Long before we actually started to look for a modest flat suited to our limited incomes, Winifred had agreed to share with me the adventurous, experimental life on which we proposed to launch ourselves the following January.' She went on to say: 'It was probably fortunate for Winifred that she did just miss getting a First, for had she achieved one the pressures upon her to take up academic work would have been vigorously renewed . . .' Although my mother wrote that it was fortunate for Winifred, in fact it was fortunate for my mother. She needed Winifred's support and this would almost certainly not have been forthcoming had Winifred got a First, and remained at Oxford as a don.

In *Testament of Friendship* my mother fully indicates the debt she owed to Winifred. Her influence over Winifred is not emphasised, though it is quite clear from a careful study of *Testament of Youth*, written nearer in time to the early 1920s and while Winifred was still alive. My mother persuaded Winifred to agree to her own plans for what she describes as their joint future. My mother's powerful personality motivated a simple determination to achieve success as a writer. Winifred had the capacity to be extremely good at a number of alternative careers, and it is true that my mother channelled these gifts in the direction she was going herself and in what she conceived also to be Winifred's best interests. But is it academic to ask: Would Winifred have done better to have stayed on at Oxford? She would undoubtedly have done more than most dons for those undergraduates in her care. And, though it is true that time was against her in that she did not live long enough to be considered as a potential Principal of her College, no one could have known that in 1921. It also cannot be said with certainty that if Winifred had stayed in Oxford she would not have written her novels. But it is likely that she would have been less involved with journalism, an occupation which she took up really in emulation of my mother.

In their final exams in the summer of 1921 both my mother and Winifred took Second Class Honours. They were among the first women at Oxford to take part in the matriculation ceremony which up to that time had been reserved for men. Even though she only got a Second, Winifred was in fact offered a History tutorship at St Hugh's College. This suggests not only that she was thought to have a first-class mind, but also that she was consideded to be the right kind of woman to be a tutor to others. My mother was offered a lectureship at Westfield College, Hampstead, not quite the same thing. I find it in the highest degree paradoxical that it was Winifred, who had never thought of going to Oxford, who was offered the opportunity to be tutor in an Oxford College, whereas neither of my parents whose ambition to get to Oxford was so strong and who had a positive reverence for the place, succeeded similarly.

Not only did Winifred fit in with my mother's programme for the years ahead as far as work was concerned, but for their joint holidays too. In September 1921 my mother made a pilgrimage to see the grave of her brother Edward, in the cemetery at Granezza, high up on the Asiago Plateau. They then moved across Italy from east to west, via Rome and Florence, to France where they visited Amiens and that area of the

Somme between Bapaume and Albert where Roland's grave was, at Louvencourt. They did not, however, go on to Huchenneville, the other side of Amiens, where Winifred herself had been stationed. My mother wrote that they both looked forward to their return to England to an existence of novel-writing and journalism, combined with part-time teaching, to which lecturing and political speaking were added in due course. Finally, she said Winifred agreed to launch their joint life together in London in January 1922.

The great strength of my mother, like that of Shirley, was, as I have said, her implacable will and inspired practicality. I have always been fascinated by the personality of Queen Victoria and the considerable amount I have read about her suggests that the three women have much in common. Each of them could have said, as the Queen did on ascending the throne: 'I will be good.' There is nothing like moral fervour combined with shrewd awareness. In practical terms these are more advantageous than being brilliant, creative, imaginative or intellectual, qualities shared in some degree by my father and Winifred Holtby but not, significantly, by my mother. All those who were close to my mother and lived with her, with the exception, in my view, of myself, came to fit in with her life-style and with her outlook, if not on every issue then certainly overall. Over a period of time she influenced her father, whose values had been so diametrically opposed to hers. He came to accept that she should go to Oxford and that she should take up nursing; he even accepted her socialism, though he himself remained conservative to the end of his life. The revealing incident of how mother got Roland to meet her in Leicester during the war, under the pretence to his commanding officer that he was going for an official interview, although slight in itself, is also indicative because Roland was far from being adaptable or willing to accede to my mother. Winifred came to fit into my mother's way of life before they had even left Oxford. My father, too, had to follow suit, having more or less agreed in principle to my mother's freedom in order to persuade her to marry him.

When my mother and Winifred first arrived in London in January 1922 they took a flat in Doughty Street in Bloomsbury, where they stayed until the autumn of 1923, when they moved to a fairly large mansion flat in Maida Vale. At this time Winifred received from her father an allowance of slightly less than £200 a year, perhaps equivalent to £2,000 a year today. My mother does not say whether she got an allowance from her father. My grandfather had given her £100 in 1919;

but she did not receive anything between 1920 and 1922. In February he gave her £28, which he noted down as being for housekeeping and wages; they now employed Winifred's old nurse, who came down from Yorkshire to do the cooking, washing and ironing, leaving my mother and Winifred free to get on with their work. I do not know what my mother's earnings were from the various jobs, and it may be that she had been allocated some shares in the family paper-making business by my grandfather. What is apparent is that, before my mother was thirty, she had formulated a plan which she was to follow for the rest of her life and which emphatically excluded all domestic chores and cooking. Vera and Winifred's joint financial position seems to have improved by the end of 1922. When they first arrived in Doughty Street, their weekly rent was thirty-two shillings and sixpence (£1.65p) which my mother thought on the steep side. She said they had to lead a very economical life even if it was not exactly a penurious one. In *Testament of Friendship* she wrote: 'Rents in Bloomsbury were then so high that the bed-sitting room standards of college were beyond our means; even garrets in the house to which our chilly habitation was attached fetched 32s. 6d a week without food.'

My mother regarded the real luxury of this kind of life that they led, a twentieth-century young ladies' London equivalent of *La Vie Bohème*, as being its freedom from disturbing responsibilities, an asset which she said, in *Testament of Youth*, they had both lost by the end of the 1920s; by then she had married, had one child, and was expecting another. Indeed one thing that both my parents undoubtedly had in common was a love of freedom from disturbing responsibilities.

If Winifred's life was divided between the demands made on it from the outside and her literary ambitions, my mother was not entirely the garret-loving and solitary writer she had imagined herself becoming while still at Oxford. Once based in London she did some teaching for a school in South Kensington and also for her old school near Reigate, St Monica's; all of this contributed to paying the rent. She wrote to the recently-established headquarters of the League of Nations, and gradually, although the progress was slow, became increasingly in demand as a platform speaker.

In September 1921 she took part in a bazaar in aid of Somerville College. The book-stall was under the supervision of Rose Macaulay, whom my mother and Winifred assisted with what my mother described as jubilant eagerness; she felt that the opportunity to help 'offered that prospect of a temporary acquaintanceship with a really famous writer which had hitherto seemed utterly unattainable by a struggling journalist whose persistent onslaughts on London newspapers remained lamentably fruitless'. It is also interesting to read of my mother's response to meeting John Buchan and Hugh Walpole at this function: they clearly appeared to her, in their capacity as successful novelists, almost as if they were stars from outer space. She wrote of the bazaar: 'I stood entranced and watched Rose Macaulay . . . casually conversing with the half-legendary gods of literary London. John Buchan was there, brisk and unpretentious, and the bluff and cordial Hugh Walpole . . .' My mother expressed the veneration she felt for them in the early 1920s in a wrily humorous way in the early 1930s when she was coming to the end of writing *Testament of Youth*. But, by the later 1930s, she had begun to regard successful writers more as equals or competitors, particularly if they were women. To my mother distance definitely lent enchantment.

Between 1922 and 1925 my mother spent as much as four days a week making speeches or leading discussion for the League of Nations. For example, in the summer of 1922 she took part in a League of Nations Summer School, and in September 1923 appeared at a United Nations assembly, attending as the official representative of *Time and Tide*. Gradually my mother came in touch with political events, and in particular with those people concerned with the preservation of peace. Her work for the League enabled her to meet influential if not world-famous figures. For example, one of those who acted as Chairman at one of her meetings was Percy Harris, a member of the London County Council, who would shortly afterwards become Liberal MP for South-West Bethnal Green. In preparation for the General Election of 1922 she helped in his campaign, and in the General Election in December of the following year, she worked for him to an even greater extent. My mother had had no specific political party affiliation but both she and Winifred now briefly became members of the National Liberal Club after the enfranchisement of women permitted the admittance of a few women. They did not remain members long. My mother soon came to regard the National Liberal Club as a masculine stronghold, where women might be seen but not heard. And her experiences while canvassing during the run-up to the General Elections of 1922 and 1923 led her to abandon the Liberal Party altogether. Many of those living in Bethnal Green had fought in the recent war. My mother had come across them in their hundreds in hospital. She felt that the Tommies had been abandoned by the state for which they had fought, been wounded and of course in many cases died, only to be forgotten. In her view this was treachery and equivalent to the enforcement of the articles of the Treaty of Versailles which poisoned the political scene in Europe following the Armistice.

During this period, Winifred supplemented her allowance from home with small teaching jobs. She gave a course of lectures on six major characters of medieval and Renaissance Italy at my mother's old school, St Monica's, and she coached some girls for Somerville at a school in Notting Hill High Street. In late 1923 she gave courses in Kendal, Seascale and Windermere under the auspices of the Oxford University Extension Delegacy. A wide variety of employment was part of my mother's philosophy for living since, in her view, one thereby remained free and was not at a single employer's beck and call. A major appeal to my mother of being a writer was the fact that she could be her own master. To someone less unselfish than Winifred it might have seemed that coaching girls to get into Oxford and lecturing for the Oxford University Extension Delegacy was a poor substitute for the prestige and security of a lectureship at St Hilda's, a post which would reasonably be expected to lead to a fellowship, in those days a job for life.

During the General Elections of 1922 and 1923 much space was given in the newspapers to the recent enfranchisement of women. There was considerable discussion on the so-called 'problems of women', largely due to the fact that after the war there were far more women than men. Such women were often referred to as 'superfluous'. It was generally held, by most men at least, that the objective of women was to get married. Those who did not marry were, therefore, superfluous. There were many women, mostly unmarried, but some who were married, who were civil servants, doctors, nurses and teachers. Nevertheless, there was a campaign to persuade unmarried women to emigrate. Taking the opposite point of view, my mother said that it was the individual's contribution to the community in which he or she lived which was important, and that marriage in itself was irrelevant. She conceded that a happy and successful marriage could help in the achievement of this contribution to the community, but that was all. As far as my mother was concerned, both before and after she got married, marriage was never an end in itself. She regarded the concept of marriage as the be-all-and-end-all as an inherent part of the provincial outlook. She also declared that the idea of marriage without love had never attracted her, although she went on to say that the overwhelming passion she had once felt for

83

Roland had burnt itself out, as far as she was concerned, by the early 1920s. What she visualised, at least in the cool atmosphere of her study, was a more companionable relationship in which 'mutually respectful equals of opposite sex' were devoted to some worthwhile end.

For herself, my mother felt that the intense emotional experiences which she had undergone during the war, but which had ended in death, had left an emptiness which even the most intimate friendship could not fill, and that such sensations or experiences were gone for ever. This indicates that, close as my mother's relationship with Winifred was, she did not place it in the same category as her relationship with Roland. On the basis of what my mother felt during the early 1920s, she concluded that with the death of so many of her contemporaries she was unlikely to be get married. She would not marry without love and, leaving aside the fact that there were so few of her eligible contemporaries left alive, she felt incapable of such depths of feeling even being rekindled. She wrote in *Testament of Youth*: 'Very deliberately, with an aching regret that I had been born physiologically so normal, I pushed into the deepest recesses of my mind the old haunting memories, the once confident dreams, the sweet anticipated comfort of warm responsive flesh, the visionary children for whom during strange dark nights in Camberwell I had planned to work and achieve, and resolutely turned upon this too poignantly equipped storehouse the firm key of purposeful ambition.' However, my mother overlooked the fact that she had felt 'purposeful ambition' long before the outbreak of the First World War. While in the immediate post-war years her capacity for feeling was numbed, it did not follow that this would remain so for the rest of her life, as she undoubtedly and rather gloomily forecast.

After 1918 the first opportunity arose in Britain for the position of women in society to be radically transformed. My mother, ever alive to practical opportunities, meant to make the most of this by becoming in- volved in the process of change. It was, therefore, in the early 1920s that my mother came in touch with those women who were involved both inside and outside Parliament with female emancipation which would stretch far beyond merely having the vote: Lady Astor, Lady Rhondda (who was prevented from taking her seat in the House of Lords), Mrs Pethick-Lawrence, and those organisations fighting for the liberation of women. Among these were the Society for Constructive Birth Control, started by Dr Marie Stopes; and the Six Point Group, of whom Lady Rhondda was a leading light. The latter's objectives were pensions for widows; equal rights of guardianship for married parents; changes in the law covering assault of children; the status of unmarried mothers; equal pay for teachers and equal opportunities for men and women in the Civil Service. It is worth noting that, over sixty years ago, Lady Rhondda, speaking on child assault and its increase, claimed that this was due to what she described as the mental and moral instability which had followed the war. Today the ravages of unemployment, with social repercussions similar to those caused by war, are also held by many in a position of public responsibility to be a factor in the same 'mental and moral instability'.

My mother's involvement in public causes, from the days when she caught the enthusiasm of Louise Heath Jones for the suffragette movement before the First World War, and her love of speaking in the 1920s on issues of national or international importance, raises the question of whether she would not have found more fulfilment as a politician than as a writer. As I have said, she would speak for the League of Nations, before she became disillusioned with it, as often as four times a week. Her interest in such legislation before Parliament as the Criminal Law Amendment Bill; the Guardianship of Infants Bill; and the Illegitimacy and Bastardy Bill, to all of which she gave considerable space in *Testament of Youth*, suggest the interest of the reformer and the politician rather than of the novelist; of someone who feels a compulsion to influence other people's attitudes and behaviour. If my mother had not married someone with political ambitions of his own I cannot see how she could have failed to take an active part in the politics of the left to the point of standing for Parliament. Her pacifism would not have been an electoral disadvantage, except during the Second World War. Undoubtedly her feminism would have secured important support from career-minded as well as unmarried women.

I think my mother built up the idea of becoming a writer while she was still a child, well before the concept of votes for women became a practical reality. Of course the suffragette movement started before the turn of the century, indeed Bertrand Russell records that his mother, Lady Amberley, was looked on with considerable disfavour by her smart friends in the 1880s for soiling her hands with such riff-raff. But before 1914 it would have been a bold spectator with prophetic powers who could have forecast not only votes for women after the end of the war but other rights granted through legislation, and women taking their seats in the House of Commons. In the years of my mother's adolescence before the First World War, when she was forming her views, the occupation of writer was, however, a realistic and attainable one as it had been from the days of George Eliot and Mrs Gaskell. Being a writer provided an opportunity for being independent, which was extremely important to my mother, and something that even in politics is difficult to achieve until one is Prime Minister. Being essentially practical, my mother did not, I believe, seriously consider going into politics before the war because to do so would have seemed unrealistic. By the time the war was over my mother had embraced the idea of herself as a writer and therefore did not think of herself as a prospective politician.

Nevertheless, not only was my mother committed in serious matters of the day by the early 1920s but she also had the belligerence of the successful fighter of elections. In her description of her verbal encounters with, for example, Sir Dennis Herbert, Conservative MP for the Watford Division of Hertfordshire, she portrays him as one who passionately advocated policies appropriate to the Britain of fifty if not a hundred years before. Perhaps my mother did not appreciate that a significant proportion of the British electorate likes to think that the Britain of the past, which exists only in their imagination, should remain untouched.

My mother's absorption in issues which were explicitly political explains why in the summer of 1922 Winifred Holtby found a publisher for her first book, *Anderby Wold*, prepared to pay her a royalty, whereas my mother's debut with *The Dark Tide*, also a novel, did not come until a year later, in July 1923, on far less satisfactory terms from the publisher. Winifred published her first novel when she was just twenty-four. My mother was nearly thirty before her first book appeared. It must have been an ironic, not to say disconcerting experience for my mother, as indeed she admitted in *Testament of Youth*. Later on, she admitted that *Anderby Wold* was a better book than *The Dark Tide*, although this must have cost her a considerable loss of pride. In a letter to Winifred, she made two interesting points: that the world seemed subtly changed by Winifred's book having been accepted (first); and that those who have crossed the gulf between aspiration and achievement are never quite the same again. *The Dark Tide* did, however, have sufficient success on publication for Grant Richards to accept my mother's next book, *Not Without Honour*. She looked back on this vital step in her career as moving from amateur to professional status. She now saw herself as achieving the ambition which she had formulated perhaps twenty years before: the independent woman living the independent life and free to do as she wished.

Winifred was not ambitious in the same relentless way as my mother. She was the first to agree that she had only gone to Oxford because her mother wanted her to. But Winifred, unlike my mother, did not dramatise herself. For example, her experiences towards the end of the war did not seem to her traumatic. She had an extraordinarily magnanimous personality and always felt that it was others who were suffering not she, and that it was others who needed her help. The spotlight of her ego was not focused continuously on herself. She was, in two words, supremely unselfish. To this characteristic she added both keen observation and a sense of humour. Against the background of a larger charity to mankind these two qualities are the key to her writing. It is true that to the end of her life she could never make up her mind whether she was basically a reformer or a writer but gradually she came to trust herself as the latter and in doing so came to enjoy writing more. My mother wondered whether Winifred was bascially a Brontë, writing about the countryside she knew, or a Josephine Butler, an eloquent humanitarian. In my opinion, Winifred was basically an artist who kept in touch with the movements of her time, especially those affecting the status of women in Britain. My mother was essentially a catalyst to social change who preferred the independence of someone who can earn their living by writing. The difference between the two can be summed up by saying that while Winifred was a humanitarian with a small 'h', my mother was one with a capital 'H'.

The publishing of *Anderby Wold* in the summer of 1922 must be regarded as a critical date in the relationship between my mother and Winifred, as I have already implied. By this time they had known each other for very nearly three years. The success of Winifred's novel made it clear to my mother that Winifred could no longer be regarded as the junior partner in their relationship or indeed in their team devoted to the writing of novels, journalism, and in participation in the political aftermath of the emancipation of women.

When my father first wrote to my mother, *The Dark Tide* had not been published, and with her usual anxiety I have no doubt that my mother was quite reconciled to the idea that she would never be a writer, except of journalism. Perhaps she was becoming reconciled to the idea that a complete change of course might be on the cards. Not that my mother ever gave anything up once she had undertaken it. I am not saying that she wanted to reject Winifred just because she was the first to publish a book, but that at this point their relationship altered, to that of two equals rather than a senior and junior partner. This change and its cause may have led my mother to reconsider the idea of getting married — if only in principle.

It is significant too, I think, that it was just about the time my parents became engaged, in July 1924, that Winifred first met and had lunch with Lady Rhondda in her capcity as owner of *Time and Tide*, the first women's paper of its kind. My mother wrote that Winifred had that instantaneous magnetic attraction which the warm-hearted extrovert has for the shy and diffident. She undoubtedly had precisely this attraction for Lady Rhondda. Winifred became more and more involved in *Time and Tide* and, within two years, was the youngest director of the paper, acting increasingly as the captain's executive officer, a job which she carried out until her death.

In her copy of *St Joan*, Winifred wrote 'Ave atque vale' in the margin, with the date of my parents' engagement underneath: 5 July, 1924. This event was by no means farewell to Winifred but, just as the publication of Winifred's *Anderby Wold* had been a traumatic experience for my mother, so my mother's engagement two years later must have been a similarly traumatic experience for Winifred.

My father had to return to Cornell in September 1924, and on the very same day my mother and Winifred set out on a protracted tour of Europe. Their first stop was Geneva, where they attended the Assembly of the League of Nations on behalf of *Time and Tide*.

They wished to visit those parts of Europe which still showed the ravages of war. So, leaving Geneva, they travelled via Basle to the Ruhr, which was under French control, and then on to Essen. By the middle of October they had reached Berlin, and from there they went to Czechoslovakia, Austria and Hungary. My mother's experience of this tour confirmed her view that the courage and generosity of the dead had been in vain and that the peace was being lost by the absence of these qualities in the survivors. The fact that those who had died had done so for a false dawn and for a hope which was betrayed confirmed my mother in her pacifism. The war had destroyed so much to so little purpose. Although the death of millions had indeed achieved nothing, mother was inclined to ignore the fact that the destruction of Germany ensured the survival of Britain as a major industrial nation for another twenty years and also led to the emergence of the United States as leading nation of the West, both industrially and financially.

While my mother and Winifred were away there had been a General Election. Stanley Baldwin replaced Ramsay MacDonald as Prime Minister with a majority of nearly two hundred and fifty seats in the House of Commons. It was then that my mother joined the Labour Party, taking this step partly under the influence of my father, but more, I think, as a reaction against Baldwin's majority.

The opening months of 1925 were auspicious for Winifred and my mother. They both found they were able to exploit the situation created by the publication of their first books, even if neither had been a spectacular success. Winifred wrote increasingly for *Time and Tide*, and my mother for the *Nation and Athenaeum*. She rationalised her approaching marriage, the prospect of which combined the opposite emotions of pleasant anticipation with a certain deep-seated dread. My mother had become fatalistic. Even if she was driven by ambition, one reason for her feeling of foreboding was that the closest personal relations she had established had all ended in early death and she undoubtedly felt the same would continue to be the case. In fact her premonitions were not misleading although they did not happen to apply to my father. On a more positive note, my mother came to feel that by marrying she would be living more in the present and for the future and that she would no longer be exclusively preoccupied with the past, a past, she reflected, which to her children would be as remote as the Napoleonic Wars were to her.

At the beginning of 1926, when my parents had been at Cornell for three months, Winifred made an extensive tour of South Africa under the auspices of the United Nations. This was really the first occasion on which she had set off entirely on her own, without either the guidance or direction of someone else. Winifred was now nearly twenty-eight. While she was in South Africa Winifred found a cause which she made exclusively her own, and identified with until her death: that of the South African negro.

As a consequence, she of necessity devoted less time to her creative writing, her novels. In South Africa she received a good deal of publicity. She was temporarily overwhelmed, especially as she was asked to give far more talks and interviews to the press than she had ever expected. This notoriety neither went to her head nor diverted her; she had the capacity to carry such a situation off. Winifred had not travelled to South Africa with the specific purpose of investigating the plight of the blacks, she merely became acutely aware of the situation during a very extensive tour. She travelled from Cape Town to Kimberley, where she was particularly appalled by the conditions under which diamonds were mined, then on to Durban, Natal, Maritzburg, and Pretoria, where she came across Margaret Huxley, sister of Julian and Aldous, who was on the staff of the Pretoria High School, and finally to Johannesburg.

There, Winifred felt that she had identified four wholly separate and distinct, indeed exclusive societies: the intelligentsia; the leisured women who spent their time at the Country Club and the Automobile Club; the businessmen who supported the second group; and by far the largest group, the blacks. What might be described as the coloured underworld of Johannesburg and the memory of the native compounds in Kimberley provided the stimulus to Winifred's indignation, and above all, her compassion. My mother thought that in the plight of the black people Winifred could see that suppression which had until comparatively recently existed for women in Britain. It is true that their legal status had had until recently much in common, and, undoubtedly, women were also regarded as inferior. But, while many in Britain lived in poverty, few did so in total squalor. Winifred was nevertheless able to transfer directly her concern for the rights of women under the law in Britain, to her concern for South Africa's black people.

While in Durban, Winifred went as an observer to the Indian Congress at the Town Hall. When she came to address the audience about the League of Nations she realised that she must be not only the first person to lecture them on this subject, but also the first white person — and a woman. She recalled how astounded people were in the street to see her, a white woman walking with an Indian. This incident, unimportant perhaps in itself, is however symbolic of how both my parents and Winifred although each extremely independent individuals, nevertheless thought and acted in some ways in a quite similar fashion. Winifred's tour of South Africa in 1926 acted as a significant introduction to the part played by my parents, particularly my father, in the campaign for the independence of India some ten years after Winifred's death.

Today, it is interesting to note that what most impressed Winifred in South Africa in 1926, now more than sixty years ago, was the atmosphere of nervous tension which she believed was due to the complete separation of the black people from even such moderate white opinion as existed. It was this segregation, she felt, which allowed a form of communism to have considerable influence over uneducated blacks. She met Clements Kadalie, self-styled leader of the Zulu Bolshevists, at the offices of the Industrial and Commercial Workers' Union. Quite apart from the importance of the ICWU in the political history of South Africa, Winifred's relationship with and sponsorship of this union exemplifies an important part of her personality and her work.

By the time she returned to England in June 1926 after her six-month tour Winifred realised that the high standard of living enjoyed by the whites in South Africa was achieved almost entirely at the expense of the blacks. She also realised that the whites would not hesitate to fight for this advantage which they had achieved and maintained. On the way home, when she had time to reflect on her experience of life in South Africa, she decided she would do her best to arouse interest and support from those who she felt would share her concern. Winifred immediately engineered an introduction to Arthur Creech Jones from Mrs Mabel Palmer. Mabel Palmer was a member of the Fabian Society and a lecturer at Durban Technical College, and it was she who had brought home to Winifred the seriousness of the racial antagonism in South Africa. Creech Jones, subsequently Colonial Secretary in Attlee's first government, was a trade union official as well as Labour Member of Parliament for Shipley in Yorkshire. He knew nothing about the ICWU, but under Winifred's persuasive enthusiasm he started to take an interest.

In the summer of 1927 Clements Kadalie came to Europe. It was arranged that he would appear at that year's International Labour Conference in Geneva, where he would also be unofficial spokesman for the black people of South Africa. While he was in England, Creech Jones spent much time explaining trade union structure and practice; he produced policy statements, and even drafted a constitution for the ICWU. How much of this made any impression on Kadalie is hard to say. He was essentially an effective demagogue who had the support of many fellow black Africans. What is clear is that Kadalie realised the effect he was having on these white people in England, and with his lack of sophistication this success went to his head. Creech Jones did his best to persuade Kadalie to look at the problem of the South African coloured worker in a way that would be most likely to receive support from European sympathisers. But this was not the primary message which Kadalie took away with him. Back in 1919, without either money or relevant experience, he had built up the ICWU; but by 1927 he had developed a flamboyant life-style which impressed his totally naïve followers. As the

ICWU was an unrecognised organisation in South Africa its funds could not be banked. The substantial sums collected were kept at the Union's local offices and there was no proper supervision of the money. It became clear that Kadalie was being supported by these funds. Complaints were made against him. The flashy clothes and high living had, after all, to be paid for. He had become seduced by his own power and the more successful he became the more he lost touch with reality.

Both Creech Jones and Winifred realised that if the ICWU were to develop into a truly effective organisation it must start to have a coherent structure in which some form of discipline was imposed. An organiser who would go out to South Africa was found in the person of William Ballinger. Although he did not have the level of trade union experience Creech Jones had been seeking he had at least been Honorary Secretary of the Trades Union Council in the Scottish town of Motherwell and local secretary of his own trade union branch. Ballinger was a Scottish insurance agent and it was felt that this experience would be relevant in dealing with the chaotic state of the ICWU's finances.

Following Creech Jones's interview with William Ballinger it was decided that the sooner he arrived in South Africa the better, not least because by this time the financial problems of the ICWU had become something of a scandal. In fact Winifred Holtby paid out of her journalistic earnings for William Ballinger's passage to South Africa, when he left England in June 1928. From that time on and for the next seven years, Winifred was the major contributor to Ballinger's expenses. His financial position was not improved when he married Margaret Hodgson, a lecturer at the University of Witwatersrand. She was dismissed from her post, supposedly because she had married but in fact because the University was financed by interests wholly opposed to the ICWU and the efficient activities of her husband. Characteristically Winifred, who had received a much larger cheque than she had expected from the United States, £750 for royalties on her book *Mandoa Mandoa*, spent £200 of this on a car which she gave the Ballingers as a wedding present. But Ballinger's problems increased because Clements Kadalie was no longer accepted by black South African workers. He was regarded by some as an 'Uncle Tom', someone who had sold out to the whites in Europe. Even those who did not go this far felt that he had been seduced by Europe and had spent too lavishly on himself. They had not minded his haphazard behaviour and extravagance when he had confined himself to South Africa, but it was now seen that the money contributed by his followers had not been spent on the organisation and officials of the Union itself.

Ballinger felt, not for the first time, that he was facing a nearly hopeless situation, but Winifred was never one to give up in the face of odds however apparently overwhelming. She canvassed financial help from sympathisers in England such as Bernard Shaw and H. G. Wells; also from Colonel Josiah Wedgwood. She herself contributed whenever she could, and indeed when she could not really afford to do so. Creech Jones was also successful in getting some financial support from the British Trades Union Congress.

Towards the end of her life, Winifred came to feel that all the journalism she had written in support of Ballinger and for what the ICWU was doing in South Africa was worth more than the achievement of her novels. (In fairness, it has to be remembered that her best-known and best-selling novel, *South Riding*, did not in fact appear until after her death.) In June 1937, Margaret Ballinger was elected to the House of Assembly as one of the first representatives of the natives of Cape Province. At the same time a library for the use of black people was founded in Winifred's name in Johannesburg.

Winifred arrived back in England in July 1926 and two months later both she and my mother made their annual pilgrimage to Geneva; returning to their flat in Maida Vale, which my father had once again left in order to go to Cornell. Although my mother missed my father's company, she also enjoyed regaining the route which she and Winifred had developed together. The absence of my father in the United States and that of Winifred in South Africa seem to have stimulated the demand for their journalism. It was at this time that Margaret Rhondda asked Winifred to join the board of *Time and Tide*, an invitation which totally astonished Winifred. She was now twenty-nine and her new commitment to Lady Rhondda and to *Time and Tide* was to keep her increasingly, not to say frantically, busy. Harry Pearson was still, interestingly, in her thoughts. *The Land of Green Ginger* was dedicated to him.

Winifred's joining *Time and Tide* was the beginning of a new chapter for her. But my mother's relationship with her did not come to an end in 1925 – 6, it merely occupied a very important place in a wider context.

In the prologue to *Testament of Youth*, my mother wrote that, whereas the friendships of men have enjoyed glory and acclamation, the friendships of women have not only been unsung but also misinterpreted. She went on to say that she hoped to show that loyalty and affection between women is a noble relationship, and one which far from impoverishing actually enhances the love of a girl for her lover — wife for husband, and mother for her children. In the context of these comments it is interesting to see that, although my mother wrote *Testament of Friendship* as an account of Winifred's life and their life together, *Testament of Youth* is also the story of the friendship of four men: her brother, Edward; her fiancé, Roland; Geoffrey and Victor: and of her relationship with them.

My mother went on to consider how much of the truth about Winifred she could tell, and how she had turned to the *Life of Charlotte Brontë* by Mrs Gaskell for guidance. She quotes Mrs Gaskell, who had made the decision to withhold nothing, with a proviso that some things could not be spoken of as fully as others. She adds that Mrs Gaskell was criticised for telling the whole truth as she saw it. Both Mrs Gaskell in writing about Charlotte Brontë, and my mother in writing about Winifred Holtby told the full truth as they saw it. They both believed that only by doing so could they enhance the reputation of their respective subjects. My mother may have been romantic at heart and she was certainly idealistic. Nevertheless, she was often a disconcerting apostle of the truth as she saw it. She was inherently outspoken. She had inherited a nononsense approach to the facts, and she would no more have scrupled to call a spade a spade than would her equally down-to-earth forebears. On the whole she told the truth in a way that was not unkind, but I would not say she went out of her way to spare anyone's feelings, certainly not the feelings of those she knew best. Paradoxically, it was because her motivation was of the highest that she felt able to speak a great deal more frankly than if she had been spurred on by a desire to create publicity through scandalous revelation.

CHAPTER VII

GEORGE AND VERA

BY the end of 1923 my mother had discussed with Winifred the disconcerting possibility that a man might be about to intrude on her life. The fact that my father had been to Oxford; that he had been in the Army, albeit only at the end of the war, and that, like Roland, he had been converted to Catholicism, all these factors told in his favour with my mother — as indeed did his socialist leanings. By Easter 1924 they had exchanged photographs after writing to each other for the past nine months. So far they had never met. My mother continued to express her alarm to Winifred, who held the view that life was either agitation or stagnation, and that of these two the former was at least life.

At the time of his conversion to Catholicism while he was still at Oxford, my father had given serious thought to becoming a priest. One of his friends at this time was the Jesuit, Father C. C. Martindale. By the time my father started writing to my mother he had definitely abandoned such an idea; as he decided in favour of secular life so the idea of getting married also occurred to him. By the time their correspondence had lasted until the spring of 1924 my father had come to realise that Virginia Dennison in *The Dark Tide* was probably a reasonably accurate self-portrait of my mother, who shared the attitudes and outlook of the book's heroine who had so greatly appealed to him in the first place. The views expressed by my mother were also close to those of his own mother which had led her to support the suffragettes and work in the East End of London until her death seven years earlier.

When my father returned to England in June 1924 my mother arranged to meet him, but at the last minute deliberately made an appointment to see Lady Rhondda at the same time. Anyone less determined than my father might well have been put off, but he was not deterred. He overlooked the snub, inviting my mother to tea, after which they went to see Bernard Shaw's play, *St Joan*. Then followed a weekend in which they

95

walked in Richmond Park and Kew Gardens, close to which he had spent much of his youth. He invited her to Oxford and, as my mother expressed it, rather against her better judgment, got engaged on July 5. Perhaps it was being in Oxford which disposed my mother in his favour; that he had been to New College, where Edward would have gone had he survived the war, was a further recommendation. My father was more importantly similar to Edward in that he also was prepared to listen, and she was also to regard him as a kind of sounding board much as she had previously regarded Edward.

When Winifred heard of the engagement she accepted the fact with equanimity, although she must have thought that the life she had shared with my mother would now be at an end.

My mother's parents, particularly her father, had regarded the fact that Roland's family were relatively poor as a considerable obstacle, but since 1915 my grandfather's attitudes had either changed or at least he did not express them so forcefully, and he accepted my father although he had no money. At least he had a good job. My grandfather could not have forgotten that he himself did not marry for money.

In resolution of my mother's extremely ambivalent attitude to getting married at all, my parents agreed to postpone the event for a year; this decision, which my mother regarded as being too 'sensible' to be typical of her approach to men in general, did have the advantage of providing a let-out if she were to change her mind in the meantime. At this stage in their relationship it naturally occurs to ask whether my mother loved my father or whether he loved her. My own view is that my father was attracted to the idea of my mother by reading *The Dark Tide*, that through correspondence he came to realise that my mother closely resembled Virginia Dennison, and that he fell in love with my mother as represented by that character, who was not of course a precise mirror-image. As far as my mother was concerned I suspect she was physically attracted to my father once she had actually met him as well as being flattered by his persevering interest. But I do not think she was drawn to him as she had been to Roland; before meeting him she made up her mind that marriage was not for her, even though she was subsequently talked out of remaining a spinster by my father. My mother's relationship to my father was much closer to the one she had had with Edward, or so it came to be; and such a relationship was both close and important to her, though it could not be said that it was based on the non-intellectual chemistry of love. In his own biography, written after the death of my mother, my father wrote that his life with her was so completely covered by her own books that there was nothing more to add. This is slightly disingenuous if only because what my mother wrote, she wrote from her own point of view and not from his. After the death of Winifred, my mother came to rely more on my father than she had previously, but reliance is not the same as love. I recall my father's advice to me, that it was better if someone fell in love with you than if you fell in love with them, and in due course I drew the conclusion that my father was speaking from his own experience, and that after his original experience with my mother it was not his intention to be the dependent partner, emotionally speaking, in any other relationship that might come his way.

My mother used to say that my father first wrote to her as an admiring reader of *The Dark Tide*, and indeed this is what she repeated in *Testament of Friendship*; but in *Testament of Youth* she makes it clear that the first postcard which my mother ever received from him arrived just before the publication of the book. The later version suggests that my father originally contacted her as a fan of her book, but in fact this was not so. In his own biography my father wrote that he had thought he had seen my mother in Oxford on the day he sent the card. He wrote to her at Somerville and the College forwarded the card to her in London. In it he said that, although she would probably not remember him, he had seen her at debates in Somerville. My mother did not reply, but two months later, in August 1923, by which time *The Dark Tide* had been published, she received a small book entitled *Thomas Hobbes*, which my father had published in the previous year, and with it a short note to say that he had read *The Dark Tide* with real pleasure. My mother was pleased to get a flattering letter about her book because most of the reviews had been far from good. After some indecision as to whether to respond or not she did at last do so. By the time my father replied to this, my mother's first letter, he was on the way to the United States, passing the coast of Labrador aboard the s.s. *Regina*.

I am not sure whether my mother was ever aware that my father had also sent a copy of *Thomas Hobbes* to Edna St Vincent Millay, the American poet, from whom he equally received a reply. Perhaps his move to Cornell had given him a feeling of security on the basis of which he could now undertake new interests, and perhaps marriage was one of these. He was nearly twenty-seven, two years younger than my mother. He claimed that he sent copies to the two women as a result of reading Conrad's *Nostromo*, identifying himself with one of the characters in that novel. In any case he felt sufficiently adventurous and romantic to write to them both.

Just as my mother was probably unaware of my father's tenuous connection with Edna St Vincent Millay, so my father was unaware that my mother's initial response to his overtures had been hardly flattering. My mother reflected at the time that the men she had come across since the end of the war had only made her feel even more certain that the best of her generation had been killed off. But it was not only that the men she cared for were dead, she had also come to prize her hard-won independence above all else. She did not regard children as part of her scheme of things. Nevertheless, she did reply to my father's second communication because it was not only an appreciative letter from a prospective admirer but it also contained some constructive criticism of her first book. My father felt that the heroine expressed a new attitude to women which was both gay and courageous. No doubt my mother's curiosity was aroused by these comments and she was therefore keen to establish the identity of this unknown admirer. In any case, letter-writing was one of my mother's favourite activities and before long they had embarked on a prolonged discussion, entirely through the medium of letters, on such subjects as marriage for the independent post-war woman. Rather in spite of herself, she kept up this correspondence during the later part of 1923, wondering occasionally whether her admirer was perhaps really only poking fun at her, or whether he really did mean what he said in his letters.

In their continuing and indeed continuous correspondence my mother and father agreed that for them love and marriage must be subordinated to work. In retrospect I think this was an idea of my mother's with which my father felt compelled to agree. While my mother's reasons for taking up this position were different from those of her predecessors the end result was curiously similar. For the previous three generations the Brittains had subordinated everything to building up their paper-making firm and to making money. My mother was not interested in making money as such, except in so far as it was essential to maintaining her own independence, but she was in fact just as much a slave to work and to making a success of it as ever her great-grandfather was. In establishing her position quite clearly — the sort of life she wanted and the degree of independence this would involve — my mother may have thought she was making it equally clear to my father, if only by inference, that at least in principle he would retain a considerable degree of independence too in what she was to describe as 'semi-detached' marriage: a perhaps unfortunate phrase since it conjures up a suburban ideal of life which was the very opposite of what my mother had in mind then or at any other time.

In the long run, my mother had the better part of the bargain through her initial insistence on her own independence and right to her own point of view, and her own way of doing things, in the realms of feminism and in due course pacifism, but also, and more relevantly, in her own life and in her own home. But, whereas my mother had carefully worked out how her career should develop, my father had not. He could not foresee, in 1923 or 1924, that his developing political ambitions would be severely inhibited and ultimately stultified by my mother's pacifism, particularly as expressed by her in the Second World War. But in the much shorter term he could not have known in advance that, after one year in Cornell, my mother would decide that her place was in England not the United States. It clearly did not occur to him that, in marrying my mother, he was entering a rather one-sided contract which, for all that the arrangement was verbal, was in practice enforceable, not of course legally but, more subtly, in its actual influence on their day-to-day lives.

My mother, in the first instance, thought in terms of such practical matters as how to retain a household in England even though my father spent initially all year and then six months of the year in the United States. From the moment that my parents got married they established a sort of ménage à trois with Winifred Holtby which lasted for the best part of ten years. While these arrangements caused some to be scandalised and others to regard both my parents as far more avant-garde than they really were, they were in fact extremely practical. The more subtle, less easily detectable drawback to the rather one-sided 'independence' which my parents enjoyed was that, slowly but surely, my father was put in the position where, to put it bluntly, he either had to give in or get out. This issue raised itself not in terms of my father's academic career but of his political ambitions and perhaps in the conflict that existed in his own mind between the two. When my mother met my father he did not have any obvious and immediate plans for a wife in politics. He had not exploited his time at Sheffield University to establish himself in a Labour-orientated constituency in that area. Even as far as his academic career was concerned, however, my mother's lack of keenness, to say the least, to spend all her time at Cornell, cannot have been without its difficulties.

My mother got my father's agreement that she would keep and use her own name after marriage. Indeed my mother always called herself Vera

Brittain, even when signing cheques or drawing up her will, a situation which often gave rise to the far from uncommon suspicion that my parents were not married at all. My mother not only did not like being called Mrs Catlin, she even said that in the event of my father ever receiving a title she would continue to call herself Vera Brittain. She used to recount the story of her aunt Muriel, about the only one of her father's brothers and sisters with whom she was on speaking terms. Muriel's husband had been offered a knighthood because, as well as being Sheriff of Westmoreland, he had bought Lake Windermere from Lord Lonsdale's estate and presented it to the nation. His wife's reaction was brisk: 'Nonsense, Leigh, it wouldn't be good for you!'

My mother said that, as an example of her willingness to be reasonable, she had decided to spend the first year of her marriage in the United States, and that this would be symbolic of the breaking away from the old and the beginning of a new life. During the year of their engagement my father had become a professor and co-founder of the Department of Political Science at Cornell. No doubt his impending marriage was regarded as a positive sign of stability which academic institutions like to see not only in their under-graduates but also in their staff. If, having just got married, my father had returned to Cornell two months later without his wife, senior members of the university, even if not privately scandalised, would undoubtedly in 1925 have regarded such behaviour as highly unorthodox.

From the beginning of their married life my father accepted, not so much unwisely as unrealistically, that my mother would have to spend much, if not most, of her life in England where her real work lay; although, at the time, while she was building up her journalistic work, it cannot be said that she was setting the Thames on fire. I have said that my mother described her marriage as 'semi-detached', not only in conversation but in her writing. Possibly to underline this approach, she arranged with Winifred, who was amused but also surprised, that they should both take their MA degrees at a ceremony to take place two days before she got married. Needless to say, my grandmother expressed incredulity.

Winifred had already planned to make her extended tour of South Africa; the timing was not only an example of her tact, but enabled her to find a cause of her own which was quite independent of my mother and to which she could give the same devotion, in the face of opposition, that my mother devoted to pacifism. At this crucial juncture in both their

100

lives, my mother emphasised to Winifred that they would never be parted for long. She anticipated that, when what she described as the passion was spent, and the adventure over, she and Winifred would be able to take up their less emotionally demanding life where it had left off. In fact, the outcome, less dramatic if less conventional, was the ménage à trois that lasted until 1935.

After their wedding in the summer of 1925, my parents travelled on their honeymoon to Vienna, which Winifred and my mother had visited only a few years earlier on one of their League of Nations tours. As a contribution to the honeymoon expenses, my mother had with her a cheque for £18, which represented the total amount in royalties earned by her second novel, *Not Without Honour*, for which she had originally intended the title *The Man on the Crucifix*. Three months before her wedding, she had received £25 from her father, which sum he entered into his account book as 'ex my bonus from Brittains Ltd'.

From Vienna they went on to Budapest and were on their way back to spend the second half of their honeymoon in the French Alps when they received a telegram summoning them home: my mother's aunt Edith, her father's eldest sister, had committed suicide in the Welsh mountains. At the age of fifty-eight she could bear her husband no longer.

From the time of their return, my mother, father and Winifred continued to live in the flat which my mother and Winifred had previously shared in Elgin Avenue, Maida Vale, just north of the Grand Union Canal, near the Paddington Recreation Ground.

On the day my parents set off from Euston, in September 1925 for Ithaca, New York State, Winifred left Victoria on her way to Geneva. There, she covered the proceedings of the League of Nations, as she had done with my mother the year before, for *Time and Tide*. On her return and finding life in the Maida Vale flat lonely, she went to stay with my mother's parents in Oakwood Court; the flat in Elgin Avenue was let to a Russian family for six months. My father appreciated Winifred being part of the household after he married my mother, just as he had done while they were engaged, because, as he himself said, this enabled them to afford to live in London as well as maintain the apartment in Ithaca. In fact it made possible the extensive amount of travel which my father always liked. Winifred contributed her one-third share of the household expenses to the flat and subsequently to the house my parents lived in after their marriage.

In order to show my mother the beauties of the St Lawrence River in the autumn, with the maple trees at their scarlet best, my father had chosen this particular route to the United States. However, my mother's initial reaction to such scenic beauties was merely that she was travelling to some distant backwater, to the back-of-beyond, a phrase she often used to describe the sort of place she had been trying to escape from since her childhood. The sight of New York temporarily restored her equanimity, but as they travelled north she was increasingly reminded of Derbyshire, partly because of the similarity of the countryside, for in both cases the terrain had the characteristics of a mountainous spa — but also because after a week or two the wealth of the United States made her think uncomfortably of the business community in North Staffordshire. My mother was flattered by all the attention she got on arriving in Ithaca, presents from my father's colleagues and their wives at Cornell, flowers, fruit and chocolates, but she also felt somewhat overwhelmed. She began to feel that she was regarded only as the wife of the young and brilliant professor and not as herself, Vera Brittain, who had slowly but nevertheless surely begun to make a name for herself in England. My mother liked New York but, whereas the dreaded Buxton had been at the most a four hour train journey from London, Ithaca was four hundred miles away. My parents' combined annual income was only about £750, so visits to New York were rare.

In these early months my mother, following up an idea of my father's, wrote a story under the title of *A Honeymoon in Two Worlds* but this failed to find a publisher because of the unconventional views my mother expressed about marriage. Indeed no American magazine would publish her articles, and the experience increased her determination to get back to England. In addition to writing articles for which she could find no publisher, she also typed out and polished the style of my father's *The Science and Method of Politics*. And it was at this time that the finalised idea of what ultimately became *Testament of Youth* occurred to her; although it was not completed over a comparatively short period of time as she originally planned and was not indeed published for another seven years.

As it turned out, my mother was not destined to stay long in Ithaca. In March 1926 the Social Science Research Council summoned my father to New York and offered him, as has already been mentioned, the post of project director to carry out the initial research programme for what was to become a national investigation into the effects of prohibition. It was felt that, as an Englishman, he would be impartial, and had already gained some relevant preliminary experience in his wartime job on the British Liquor Control Board.

My father had only very recently been appointed assistant professor, so the authorities at Cornell were being exceptionally magnanimous in giving him leave of absence. My parents could now move to New York, where the new job was based, and stay in a small hotel near Columbia University. My father had to be away from time to time, but my mother did not feel as lonely as she had in Ithaca, partly because they established a close relationship with some American cousins of my mother's, Standish Chard and his wife. Not that my mother always stayed behind when my father was on his travels. For example, in April 1926 she was present at a White House reception, where President Coolidge shook her hand even if he did not know who she was. It was at least twenty years before either of my parents attended any remotely similar official government function in Britain.

In August 1926 my father's work for the Research Council was due to come to an end, and my mother feared that this might mean her being more or less confined to Ithaca from then on. There was still no demand for her writing, while my father by this time was contributing to *The New Republic*, *Harper's*, and *Current History*, among other magazines and periodicals. She felt that leading the retired and relatively cosy life of a faculty wife in prosperous Ithaca was somehow morally wrong. Not only was she not fulfilling herself personally but she was betraying a trust: to carry on the good work for which her time at Oxford and her experiences in the war had prepared her. She longed to return to England and to her crusade. Had my mother by this time become quite indifferent to my father, the situation would have been simpler: she could just have left. She felt that she had to reconcile what was in practice virtually irreconcilable: to remain with my father and at the same time pursue her own career in England. So, when my father returned to Ithaca after the summer vacation of 1926, he returned on his own and remained until March 1927, while my mother stayed on in London. My mother was too conscientious not to be aware of this conflict of interest. Nevertheless she was able to achieve all her own ambitions, by embarking on their 'semi-detached marriage'. While this had its drawbacks for both of them in the longer term it enabled my mother to do exactly what she wanted. My father was increasingly put in a position where he had to sacrifice his own obvious hopes, the satisfaction of which lay far more in the United States than in England. It could be argued that if he had been a more determined or ruthless character things might have turned out as he would have liked. But this is an entirely unrealistic speculation. If my father had not been the accommodating sort of person he was my mother would never have married him in the first place.

By September 1926 my father was back at Cornell, and my mother and Winifred had reverted to sharing their flat in Elgin Avenue. Shortly after my mother's return to England both of them went again to Geneva for the proceedings of the League of Nations, of which the United States was not a member. My mother was unsuccessful in arousing much interest in the League's activities when she was in America. While Winifred and she were in Geneva, my father returned to England for a few weeks' holiday before the beginning of the following term.

From her own point of view, my mother was extremely fortunate, in her exercise of a shrewd, if subconscious, judgment in choosing such an adaptable husband, and also, let it be said, in having such an understanding friend in Winifred. My mother's decision not to return to Ithaca did not, I think, prejudice my father's career, the basis of which had been established in Cornell before my mother appeared on the scene. In the longer term, he was put in a situation where he had to make a choice which essentially involved deciding to make his career exclusively in the United States or to pursue married life in England. In fact he made a compromise, the terms of which were not really in his own interests. My mother scarcely compromised at all after her original year in America.

My father's personality and outlook fitted him far more for a career in the United States, certainly in the 1920s and 1930s, than in Britain at the same period. His very characteristics which made him an outsider to the closed academic life of Oxford were precisely those that commended him to America, where he was both more at home and much more highly regarded. My mother did not really feel comfortable in the United States until the success there of *Testament of Youth* created a demand for her to give lecture tours; in other words when there was a demand for her as herself and not as the wife of my father.

On my mother's return to England from Geneva with Winifred in 1926, she received a letter from my father in which he said that he thought theirs was a perfect marriage and my mother the ideal companion. Certainly their marriage involved an amount of separation which guaranteed a more adventurous atmosphere than that of a permanent home in one place, where an atmosphere of domestic ennui could be produced to the satisfaction of all except themselves. As long as the sensation of a perpetual honeymoon lasted all was well; but, on Darwinian or Marxist analysis, it might be said that marriage is a relationship of mutual exploitation with the survival of the fittest partner ultimately exploiting the other. In this struggle, my father started by holding the better hand but in acquiescing to my mother he allowed her to exploit him.

From August 1926 my mother found that her articles were increasingly being accepted. She added the *Manchester Guardian* and the *Yorkshire Post* to her quiver, though she said that she most enjoyed contributing to *The Nation*, which was under the chairmanship of Maynard Keynes and the editorship of Hubert Henderson, subsequently Warden of All Souls.

Like my sister Shirley, my mother always had a well-developed capacity for giving moral force to whatever she wanted to do. In the late 1920s she expressed the view that it had always been women who were compelled to make a choice between the demands of personal relationships and the demands of work, whereas men had been able to have the best of both worlds from time immemorial. What my mother said could not be denied. Up to that period only a handful of women had been able to travel extensively. There were exceptions, for instance the wife of the explorer, Sir Richard Burton, and the wives of travelling actor-managers or impresarios. The novelty of my mother's situation was that she felt compelled by her own career to live largely apart from her husband. Such arrangements became more commonplace only after the Second World War. And any frustrations which my parents may have experienced were more than compensated for by the greater excitement of being together again after some months apart.

My father's ideas on political science had been maturing ever since 1918. He felt that, if there were to be any valid examination of the causes of war and peace, an effective science of politics must be created. He also took the view that it is power, even more than an expanding population or wealth, which is the fundamental issue that must be grappled with and understood. He felt that Marx's examination was not sufficiently objective, because Marx was far more a propagandist for communism than an objective and detached student of the political scene. The nineteenth-century Utilitarian school of philosophy, borrowing from Machiavelli, Spinoza and Hobbes, maintained that there could be a science of politics; some would include Aristotle in the list. If philosophy is concerned with the continuing discussion of human goals and objectives — and of course there are many philosophers today who regard this as hopelessly out-of-date not to say unfashionable — then the science of politics is concerned with answering the question: how are these goals to be achieved? And, secondly, what are the means of their achivement? We all say we want peace, but we must also answer the subsidiary questions: do we *really* want peace and, if we do not, why do we pay lip-service to the idea? Do we only do so in order to gain the advantage over our neighbour or competitor without having to go to the trouble, expense and unpopularity of open conflict? Ultimately, we will have to give careful consideration to answering the question: how is peace to be achieved? With the cult of the individual and the craving for the unobtainable which urban society creates, is peace possible? Buddha thought and taught otherwise.

My father maintained that political science is not, or should not, be confined to the somewhat narrow field covered by Machiavelli's *The Prince*, which is essentially concerned with how a particular prince's highly egotistical aims could be best achieved. The limitation of Machiavelli is, as my father pointed out, that, where effective means are too shocking, necessary popular support for their achievement is either much more difficult or impossible to maintain. This is the practical barrier to the implementation of the theory that the ends justify the means, a standpoint taken by or attributed to, for example, the Jesuits, who have therefore come to be regarded as distasteful because Machiavellian. Lenin and Gandhi could visualise such limitations; Hitler and Stalin and perhaps Napoleon before them, were not deterred.

My father felt that Hobbes overstated the case when he said that politics consists of certain rules, of the kind found in arithmetic and in geometry. His approach, understandable as an application of seventeenth-century developments in the natural sciences and astronomy, for example, is too simplistic, too unimaginative, and too closely tied to the mechanistic outlook prevailing in his time. But while Hobbes's projected solution was too rigid, it did not and does not make the reverse proposition true: that there can be no science of politics or that there can be no scientific selection of data and examination of them. Even Harry Truman, most pragmatic of Presidents, admitted, in addressing the American Political Science Association, that there could be a science of politics which should be able to provide an objective commentary on political practice. As in economics, my father held that in the study of

106

politics it should be possible to achieve at least some consensus on what would be agreed by all serious students of political science, just as there is a modicum of agreement even among economists. He emphasised the importance of the distinction between the philosophy of politics — determining the goals of endeavour — and the science of politics, determining how the agreed goals are to be achieved. My father felt that this essential distinction was not fully appreciated by English writers on the subject, except by Isaiah Berlin. At the end of March 1927 my mother returned to Cornell to join my father, and a month later she wrote to Winifred to say she thought she would be having a baby at the end of the year. This was one of the factors which influenced my father to arrange with Cornell to spend only half his time there from 1928 onwards. Winifred herself suggested that she should join the shortly-to-be-expanded household, and in September of that year they moved from Maida Vale to Nevern Place.

True to form, my mother finished an article the night before I was born in St Mary's Hospital in Marloes Road. My arrival represented an important event in the lives of both my parents and Winifred and I do not say this out of sheer egotism. My mother was just thirty-four; my father twenty-nine; and Winifred also twenty-nine. If my mother had not had any children, I think it highly likely that sooner or later my parents would have separated. It was due to my arrival that my father decided to set about finding an academic post in England and to start a political career there.

In January 1928 my father returned to Cornell for the spring term. In August my mother was surprised and delighted by a telephoned commission from the *Yorkshire Post* to write a leader on President Coolidge's delphic announcement: 'I do not choose to run for President.' It was a breakthrough for her to be invited by a Conservative newspaper.

My mother later recalled one of my first utterances, in 1929, when I addressed a figure from New Ireland, which Bronislaw Malinowski had given my father, as 'Daddy'. This figure, carved out of very brittle chalk, and just under two feet high, stood on a wall-stand in my father's study. This mistaken identity was not wholly inappropriate, I now think, since the image's face had a rather disarming smile, no more scratched on the surface than carved, which resembled that of my father. Subsequently it was dusted too fervently and 'fell off' its stand. Its body was totally smashed, except for the head.

In May 1929 there was a General Election in which Ramsay

MacDonald became Prime Minister of a minority Labour government. It was the first occasion in Britain that party political broadcasts were made over the air. In South Kensington, Rayner Goddard KC, subsequently Lord Chief Justice, contested the seat as a Liberal and Independent Conservative candidate. My mother was a member of a deputation which went to see him. They were received with approval, to my mother's surprise, because they had apparently prepared their brief in a competent way. My father had been stimulated to found *The Realist*. He was particularly interested in the likely future, under a Labour government, of both Harold Laski and Oswald Mosley. I think it says much for my father's charity that he remained on good terms with Harold Laski, who must have exercised considerable fascination for him. He even invited him on to the board of *The Realist*. Whether his benevolent attitude had useful political repercussions, I very much doubt. Laski's future in the higher ranks of the Labour Party was thought to be limited because of his background as an academic. Mosley, on the other hand, was talked of as a possible future Foreign Secretary. My father met him on the introduction of the Quaker politician, Charles Roden Buxton, who was aware that my father and Mosley had a common interest in political research. Buxton spoke about Mosley as a young and brilliant Member of Parliament who had the added advantage of being married to a daughter of Lord Curzon. Mosley wrote to my father inviting him to lunch to discuss the possibility and practicality of carrying out research on behalf of the Labour Party. My father was flattered. The others present at the meeting were Maynard Keynes, Wedgwood Benn (later the first Lord Stansgate) and G. D. H. Cole. It was agreed that there was a total lack of centrally collected information on the basis of which government policy could be considered.

My father was now only spending January to June in Ithaca. The second half of each year was taken up in travelling and keeping in touch with current political affairs. My father liked to be able to study political events at first hand and his travels were supposed to provide the data on which his more theoretical deliberations on the development of political science were to be based. Although he had been invited to help organise political research for the Labour Party, he did not take any practical steps that could have helped him to get selected as a Labour Party candidate at the next election, in May 1929. He came to see that he should have struck while the iron was hot, in other words while Mosley remained an important force in the Labour Party. He thought he had plenty of time, and did not consider the practical implications of the adage: it is later than you think. In due course my father became tarred with the Mosley brush, although he never followed him out of the Labour Party.

By the middle of 1929 my mother had resigned herself to the fact that she might not be able to have another baby because of the complications she had experienced when I was born. Instead, she took up again the preparation of what was to become *Testament of Youth*. The undertaking was formidable not so much in the concept but because the writing involved careful examination of and taking of notes from her voluminous diaries and correspondence, so much of what she had saved meticulously from 1914 onwards and from earlier on in a less systematic way.

No sooner had my mother begun this great undertaking, however, than she realised that she was pregnant after all. She was filled with consternation. Not only had she hoped to give all her energy and attention to the book's preparation but, unlike Winifred, she liked her life to be well planned and planned well ahead. She even admitted to what she felt to be an unreasonable resentment against the child to be. Perhaps this has been a factor in Shirley wanting to prove that she could achieve as much as if not more than my mother.

CHAPTER VIII

THE THIRTIES

IN April 1930, we moved to what my mother described as the tall, ugly house at 19 Glebe Place, off King's Road, Chelsea; Shirley was born there in July. It is true that the Victorian detail on the front elevation must have plumbed the depths of unfashionableness in the early 1930s. Nevertheless, the first place a child remembers always remains home, acquiring as it does a kind of nostalgic glamour after the child becomes an adult. My first memories, like those of Shirley, are of Glebe Place. Although my mother described the house as tall, it was in fact built on only three floors plus a basement and an attic.

I do not recall the rooms of our house clearly, with the exception of the first-floor sitting-room, which had bookshelves from floor to ceiling but was otherwise sparsely furnished. On the ground floor next to the front door and with a window looking out on the street was our nursery. Except for the cupboards which held our toys and books I cannot remember there being any other furniture at all. Nevertheless, all the toys scattered about the floor had to be put away every night before we went to bed. Shirley was not indoctrinated into the importance of tidying up, and it was nearly always I who carried out this task. It might be supposed that I was the more obsessional of the two but I could rationalise this by saying that I liked order. It is also true that in due course I actually came to enjoy the process of tidying up.

The other room on the ground floor was the dining-room overlooking the garden at the back, which could be reached through french windows and down some outside steps. In one corner of the room was a lift which went down to the kitchen in the basement, and was so well disguised that on at least one occasion a guest was so alarmed by the floor rising that he rushed from the table to try to hold it down. The lift was also a great joy to Shirley, when she was old enough to get into it, and she used to travel up and down at high speed since her weight was just sufficient to drive the lift downwards without the handle in the kitchen having to be turned. I did not share this extremely claustrophobic pleasure, and I believe I only went down in it once to prove that I was not afraid to do so. I was certainly in every way more cautious than Shirley.

Shirley and I did not eat in the dining-room except on special occasions, but we did eat with our parents, Winifred and their friends when they came to lunch from about 1933 onwards when Shirley was three and I was six. Shirley and I had our own routine. When Winifred was alive we saw more of her than of my mother, and we saw very little of my father who was away so often at Cornell.

In 1932 Shirley and I began to go to nursery school which was almost immediately opposite the house. When Shirley started there she was only eighteen months old, but my mother thought she would prefer to be with me rather than remain at home on her own. One of Shirley's most repeated phrases was 'Me too!' and I believe these were the first words she ever uttered. My mother was probably pleased to have us out of the house where we would have been a potential distraction from her writing, a sacred rite, around which everything had to revolve.

The first-floor sitting-room was where Winifred lived when she was with us; the sofa converted into a bed. The walls were covered from floor to ceiling with bookshelves, which provided Shirley with a challenge. I was reluctant to climb much above the first four or five shelves, but she would go right up to the top. There was a gas fire in the sitting-room round which the convertible sofa and two armchairs were placed. Above the fireplace hung Margaret Bourke-White's black and white photograph of the Woolworth Building in New York, which my father had bought from the photographer herself in 1929. Although a straightforward, objective picture it had a curiously surrealist quality. If de Chirico had painted a skyscraper in New York I feel sure it would have born a close resemblance to the building in the photograph.

The smaller room at the back on the first floor was my mother's study. I can remember sitting on the floor in front of the gas fire as my mother used to read to us every day for half an hour. Again, the room was sparsely furnished with just sufficient room for my mother's quite small desk and chair and her own books. On the second floor was my parents' bedroom, containing two single beds bought from Peter Jones, and which looked over the garden. At the front of the house was a single room which had been split up between me and Shirley, each of us having one of the two windows. Partitioned in this way a quite reasonably sized

111

room provided two rather cell-like areas, with scarcely space for more than a small bed, chair and chest of drawers. On the windows there were iron bars to prevent us, particularly Shirley, from climbing out. On one occasion she got her head stuck between the bars and the fire brigade had to be called. In my bedroom I had two more photographs of Margaret Bourke-White: one of the AG Farben works in Germany and another of oil-storage tankers.

At the top of the house was an attic which ran across the whole house and which had been converted into a study for my father. He spent hardly any time there even when he was in England. It was rather a dark room since all the wood had been painted with creosote. It held most of my father's books, by 1930 a considerable collection, and fulfilled the function of a library rather than a study. By 1930 Winifred spent most of the working day at the office of *Time and Tide*, so when my father was in London he used the sitting-room for his writing. The best feature of the attic was the wide window running the whole width of the house and from which you could step on to a parapet. There was a wonderful view of the tops of the various museums in South Kensington: the green-topped tower of Imperial College; the gothic cathedral-like towers of the Natural History Museum, and the crown-like structure above the Victoria and Albert. The sky-line of these museums continued to hold a far greater fascination for me than the contents.

My chief recollection of Glebe Place is the austerity of its contents, disguised by the fact that there were a tremendous number of books belonging equally to my mother, Winifred and my father. Otherwise it would have looked extremely bare. But the rooms were full of sunlight, and in winter I remember the reassuring flame and hiss of the numerous open gas fires with their asbestos elements.

My mother enjoyed the garden at Glebe Place although she acknowledged that it was not possible to make it beautiful. This was in part due to the fact that the rockery at the end disguised a large and varied assortment of rubbish buried just below the surface, and Shirley and I spent much time over a number of years digging it up. It was seemingly inexhaustible. As I got older I found even more enjoyable than the rubbish dump was a small wooden garden shed, hardly ever used by adults. There, I kept numerous match-boxes filled with caterpillars, and in due course jam-jars filled with leaves for the butterflies and moths' eggs.

Go, said the bird, for the leaves were full of children.
Hidden excitedly, containing laughter.

Part I of *Burn Norton* conveys to me my recollection of our garden at Glebe Place except that my memory of it is not one of emptiness. I spent many of my happiest hours in the shed, and my greatest pleasure was either smoking tea in a pipe I had found, or smoking cigar butts, when my father was at home, or cigars cut into pieces when he was away. At least this early indoctrination gave me the capacity to smoke cigars immediately after breakfast without ill-effect. Such are the lessons of childhood.

Shirley and I led our own life. We saw my mother after tea. Her routine, and indeed that of Winifred and my father, was quite separate from ours, except that in the summer she would take us to the seaside; sometimes Winifred would be there too, but in any case, even on holiday, first a nanny and then a governess came too. My father seldom if ever joined us; the seaside did not appeal to him.

In 1930, my father helped to start a new journal, *The Realist*, which was begun under the guidance of Arnold Bennett, something of an arbiter of taste and a maker and breaker of reputations. Bennett had been responsible for the appointment of Kingsley Martin as editor of the *New Statesman*. He also owned a yacht called *Success* which in one word summed up a remark of Malcolm Muggeridge to my father. 'It was brass he wanted from the beginning; brass he got; and brass he became.' Bennett involved himself with the *New Statesman* at the same time as *The Realist*, so that according to my father, he could widen the sphere of his influence. He hoped to have the best of both worlds, though it is doubtful whether he achieved this. On his death-bed he is supposed to have said: 'Posterity wants too much and will pay nowt for it', adding: 'It's all gone wrong, my girl.'

Both Arnold Bennett and my mother had their background in the Staffordshire potteries and both ended up in the centre of London, Bennett in Cadogan Square and my mother eventually in Whitehall Court, with a view of the Thames and within sound of Big Ben. Both had the same determination: Arnold Bennett to make money; my mother in her promotion of feminism and pacifism.

Bennett only contributed one article to *The Realist*, dying shortly after it was founded. His place was taken by H. G. Wells, whom I remember chiefly because he looked to me like my grandfather Brittain. Wells was considerably shorter than my grandfather but he had a similar moustache and a certain facial resemblance. Although he became the doyen of *The Realist* group, Wells did not contribute anything. He stipulated at the outset that he would only write an article — on the economic future of Britain — if Lord Melchett, who was financing the paper, replied. Melchett was unwilling and so H.G. never wrote.

J. B. S. Haldane, another influence on *The Realist*, was four years older than my father and, as I have said, had been a Fellow of New College from 1919 to 1922. My father always admired aristocratic figures with intellectual interests who had the courage not to become members of the Establishment. He would have liked to be sufficiently aristocratic to cock a snook at them too, but he lacked the courage or even the self-confidence. My father described Haldane as a genius, after the Leonardo–Goethe model, the well-rounded man quite unsuited to what he described as our 'mediocre bourgeois-departmental-computerised civilisation'. He wrote: 'Haldane could begin an argument in the field of philosophy with obvious brilliance; make an excursus into theology, which would show unexpected erudition; illustrate the points with an accurate quotation or two from Homer; and then end up in that field of biology where he was now an acknowledged master.' It was a matter of regret to Haldane that he made no memorable discoveries in biology.

Discussions at *The Realist* were usually serious, but the dinners not always so. On one occasions, Wells entered with Haldane in a charade as Antony and Cleopatra: Haldane, tall, aristocratic and intellectual; Wells, short, rubicund and, while a man of great intelligence, not an intellectual in the sense that this term is understood at Oxford. My father felt Wells was underestimated if only because though he came from the same middle- or lower middle-class background as many Oxford men they had become superficially transformed by a lifetime in the groves of academe. Unlike them, Wells had an extraordinary ability not only to foresee but actually to describe the future.

Since Shirley and I were allowed from a very early age to stay and listen when our parents' visitors came to lunch or tea, we heard the most intellectual conversation well before we understood what was said or before we knew the names of those who were present. We came to take the famous for granted. There had to be something intrinsically interesting about the visitor; their appearance, their expression or their way of talking had to be memorable in itself. H. G. Wells made an impact on me, as I have said, not because he was a famous writer but because he

114

reminded me of my grandfather. I remember Margaret Rhondda because when she came to a meal she always brought an enormous number of medicine bottles with her which she put on the table. And of the many Africans who visited Winifred I remember particularly Paul Robeson, though simply because he looked very large and he had a winning smile.

Another of my father's colleagues on *The Realist* was Julian Huxley. According to my father, Huxley had been persuaded to give up being a Professor of Biology at King's College, London in order to cooperate on Wells's encyclopaedic *Science of Life* series. However, what appealed to him were Huxley's risqué stories, though the only reference that my father made to these of which I am aware concerned the phallic qualities of Nelson's statue in Trafalgar Square, if seen from the right angle. Bronislaw Malinowski, the anthropologist, had a similar collection of stories and, according to my father, had not been offered an important post at Harvard because, under pressure of his interview, he only succeeded in shocking his questioners by telling a few. It proved to be Harvard's loss and Yale's gain.

Another member of the board of *The Realist* was Harold Laski, who said of Kingsley Martin that he was the luckiest man in Britain to have been sacked from the *Manchester Guardian* and immediately appointed as editor of the *New Statesman*. However, Laski was jealous of nearly everyone whom he could even remotely regard as a rival. He treated Bertrand Russell as a lightweight, and even with some contempt, because in the late 1920s Russell was very short of money. My father's relationship with Laski was distinctly ambivalent. While he always found him stimulating to talk to — indeed there was no one whose company he enjoyed more — he also became aware, somewhat belatedly, I think, that Laski was a far from loyal friend.

Laski had many far-fetched characteristics. One of these was his tendency to elaborate on his contacts with the great. One of his topics was supposed conversations with George V, in which the King and Laski would discuss various matters of importance. The King would subsequently be quoted by Laski as saying, for example: 'Let me see, Mr Laski, what university are you at — Oxford?' In describing how he had gone to see the novelist Henry James, Laski called him the great bore of Rye. Malinowski warned my father of Laski while my father was still at Cornell, saying that Laski was no friend in life's competition. Indeed, in a lecture which Laski gave at Cornell at my father's invitation, he told his audience that the world was not big enough for both my father and himself and that they had both divided the globe between them. My father felt that in Laski's view both halves were his. Once, my father had gone back through the file of correspondence between Laski and the Department of Political Science at Cornell to discover that, while Laski was calling my father by his Christian name and walking arm in arm with him, he was at the same time writing damning letters about my father to the chairman of his Department.

No doubt Laski was motivated by jealousy. On one occasion he read out to the Common Room at Yale letters my father had written to him and in which he had expressed his private hopes and fears. One must admit that, though Laski may have been motivated by jealousy, my father was indiscreet and naïve in trusting Laski with private information.

However, Laski may not have been driven purely by jealousy, because he was fearful for his position at the London School of Economics. My father had wrongly assumed that Laski was strongly entrenched there. In fact he only had a part-time appointment. William Beveridge was Director of the Department and he and Laski did not see eye to eye. My father subsequently regretted that he had not exploited this situation in his own favour since his own views were similar to those of the Webbs, of whom Beveridge was a supporter, and he might have been able to move from Cornell to a full-time position at the LSE.

In my father's view Laski's political philosophy of the state was much influenced by Laski's own relationship with his father; in referring to the overbearing state he was really referring to his overbearing father, Nathan Laski. Laski did not get on well with the British Communist Party but he aimed to establish a high regard for himself in Moscow by taking the line that there was much good in Stalin which had been overlooked and that he, Stalin, was the great and good champion of the world's workers. In his footnotes, Laski discreetly hinted at how the Soviet régime could benefit from his advice. He was looked upon with favour in Russia, and was a welcome guest in Moscow. His book on communism led to his being regarded by such people as Stanley Baldwin as the major intellectual influence on the Labour Party.

When he became Chairman of the Labour Party, it was said of Laski that he would now be meeting some of the people about whom he had been telling everyone for so long. In a supposed conversation with Poincaré, the French Prime Minister is reputed to have asked, 'Now that

Above: Winifred
and John with
Nanny.

Vera with John
and Shirley.

John and Shirley with Vera's mother.

John and Shirley at their grandparents' house.

John, aged 13.

No. 2 Cheyne Walk.

Shirley, aged 10.

Ruth Colby,
1951, in
New York
City.

Shirley at 15.

The family in 1945.

John in the RAF, Port Said.

Shirley, aged 19.

John at Oxford.

John in 1951.

Shirley in 1952.

we have gone into the Ruhr, Mr Laski, tell me, what are we to do?' H. G. Wells also found Laski infuriating and told my father of how on one occasion, following an incident which Laski had related to him, Wells had rung up Lady Sybil Colefax, who knew all the people involved. She had telephoned back to say that there wasn't a word of truth in the story. Wells made the point that, while you might be able to get away with this kind of thing in America, a large country, it was not possible to do so in a small country like England where everyone knew everyone. My father said that Clement Attlee had written to him to say Laski was an intriguer, and the one-time High Master of St Paul's School commented on Laski that he was strangely uninterested in truth. Attlee can hardly have cared greatly for Laski, particularly after he had the audacity to suggest to Attlee that he ought to resign as Prime Minister.

Nevertheless, my father thought highly of Laski as an intellectual force, and also admitted that he was generous to his students, particularly those who were poor. Overall, my father took a charitable view. It was high praise for him to describe Laski as the most brilliant conversationalist he knew, since my father was a great collector of both talkers and distinguished letter-writers. He regarded Laski as a remarkable thinker and a stimulating teacher. He even went so far as to say that there was no single person to whom he would rather entrust his own reputation; it is open to doubt, however, whether Laski could be entirely objective about his rivals.

My father did, I think, learn a few tricks from Laski, except that he did not have the courage, even if he had wished, to adopt his rather Machiavellian and maybe unscrupulous techniques. In fact Laski and my father had a lot in common. They were both outsiders operating simultaneously in the academic and political worlds. They preferred to paddle their own canoes rather than play safe by boarding a larger and in the long run surer ship. Consequently, they felt quite ready to give the world's captains good advice — prime ministers, presidents, East and West.

The Realist came to an untimely end because Lord Melchett decided, as a result of financial losses made early in the Depression, that he could no longer afford to continue to support it. When it closed my father rationalised the event with the comment that he himself had always preferred action to words. Indeed he became so keen on 'action' that he got involved in everything: fighting elections, assisting Mosley in his

Labour Party years; making journeys to Russia, to Spain during the Civil War, and to Germany immediately after Hitler rose to power, both as an observer and often as a journalist too. But he was essentially an observer and analyst, and not a man of action. He merely liked to be where the action was. He did not find sitting alone in his study sufficiently stimulating. By nature he was a vicarious man. He loved conversation and talking about the great issues of the day, and perhaps he was closer to the reality of life than Karl Marx ever was. If, however, my father hoped to make a similar contribution to political philosophy to Marx's, he would have had to spend a great deal more time in the equivalent of the Reading Room of the British Museum than in the stimulating atmosphere of discussions and dinners at *The Realist*.

By 1931 and 1932, the circle of my father's friends and acquaintances, and those of Winifred Holtby, had widened considerably. My mother was less dependent on other people. Before the publication and subsequent success of *Testament of Youth*, her friends and associates were mostly, although not entirely, those of my father in the academic and political world and those of Winifred in the literary and journalistic world. But, while my mother was perhaps the most ambitious of the three, by 1931 both my father and Winifred had achieved more than my mother.

The relationship between my parents and Winifred was established as a household of three though perhaps not quite in the sense of a ménage à trois. My mother was considerably influenced by Winifred with whom she either discussed everything in conversation or communicated in her letters. They had certainly discussed my mother's developing relationship with my father. Winifred was not a jealous person, but had she either disliked my father or had not wanted my mother to be involved with him it would have been extremely easy for her to bring the relationship to an end.

My father's spheres of interest and those of Winifred coincided and undoubtedly Winifred's literary friends became his too. For example, it was in Nevern Place that Rebecca West, who knew Winifred, first met her husband to be, Henry Andrews, whom my father had known when they were both up at Oxford. Winifred was also a contributor to *The Realist*. Like my father, she looked forward to meeting those she described as important people, just as my father relished those he classified as 'the great'. Harold Nicolson referred to Winifred as that girl who cared so much about second-rate celebrities, and my mother subsequently agreed when she said that you can waste a lot of time if you meet too many 'interesting people'; but Winifred had not been brought up among either interesting or important people and she therefore did not approach the world of those who get things done with quite the same degree of complacency which Harold Nicolson could exercise.

My mother was quite aware of the gossip to which our household gave rise as a result of my father only being in Glebe Place intermittently and to Winifred living there with us. The gossip increased after Winifred's visit to South Africa, after which a steady stream of black South Africans visited us. The effect on me was that I increasingly preferred gollywogs to all other dolls. Shirley had few dolls; she always preferred animals.

According to my mother I was critical, intuitive and self-possessed and had the knack of making disconcerting and occasionally cynical remarks. But it was largely due to my mother that I was so critical. Shirley and I were brought up to be observant and independent. I must have succeeded in keeping my mother amused because I was permitted occasionally to play in her study, from the time when I was three or four years old. Later, it became entirely out of bounds. At her desk my mother was able to conjure up a degree of concentration that was not allowed to be broken by any interruption — least of all by childish prattle.

I discovered that the way round my mother was to amuse her — not an easy task. I also found that it was the slightly bizarre which entertained her most as she could never see anything humorous in an ordinary story or joke. She recorded some of my early remarks. These suggest a certain surreal quality of imagination but also indicate that I intuitively realised, when very young, that this was the kind of thing that appealed to my mother. Thus I pretended to be a naughty lobster, making the terrible faces I felt appropriate to this role. This kind of play-acting occurred to me as a means of attracting my mother's attention in her study and was 'allowed' in a way that talking was not. It broke the ice, and then, when my mother smiled or laughed, I could start to talk. 'My wife's got a photograph of his mother,' I said. 'I'll show it to you after tea if you like. She's rather like you. She's quite old but very pretty. Well, not very old, but quite pretty. But never mind. When you're better and I'm better, we'll take ourselves away.'

The urge to re-create people, especially if they are strong and apparently fairly successful, may of course have results which the creator had not foreseen. Insofar as my father may have hoped to mould my mother's character when he first started writing to her, or my mother hoped to mould mine from the very beginning, both must have become disconcerted if not disillusioned by the result. In bringing me up from the very earliest age to be independent, to develop and express my own intelligent comment, my parents may have thought that this process might lead me to arrive, as it were separately, at the same point of view as their own. Perhaps my early, rather surreal remarks were an early expression of independence, for what surrealism, rather like Zen Buddhism, has is a totally non-logical relating element. So, if one is brought up 'to be oneself' and is not indoctrinated with the conventional wisdom of the society in which one happens to live, one does not inevitably develop into a model of abstract high-mindedness, which is, I suspect, what my parents hoped I would become. Nor does one necessarily reflect the values and beliefs of those by whom one is brought up. It is true that we grew up in a politically orientated household of the left, but we were not instructed in left-wing doctrinaire views. Shirley acquired these but I did not.

My personality developed in reaction against my mother. This development meant to me, but not to my mother, being independent of her just as much as being independent of those bourgeois values of which she had been most critical and against which she herself reacted most strongly. In this way I was able to remain to some extent free of my immediate environment's influences. This remained true long after I had left my parents' home. Of course, this floating 'free' independence is to some extent like living in a vacuum. If I was brought up to be untouched by every influence, I equally found it hard to identify with the objectives and beliefs of my parents; and almost equally hard to do so with the aims of my contemporaries, whether their objectives were religious, political, social or financial. In being influenced not to accept the conventional wisdom, I found it hard to know and find out what to put in its place. To be detached, to the extent that I was brought up to be, protects one from the longer-term effects of life's disappointments. Learning to be independent is a training in detachment both from close relationships, which are apt in due course to seem extremely claustrophobic, and from generally accepted objectives which do not appear worth the necessary dedication in time and effort. I came to have a considerable regard for Bertrand Russell, whom my father greatly admired, though it may not have occurred to him that I might be influenced by some of Russell's less endearing characteristics. In fact my father felt that Russell's auto-

biography revealed an inhuman callousness, even if his heart did bleed
for mankind in the abstract. He felt that Russell had too much in
common with Rousseau who had proclaimed similar generalised views
while at the same time placing his own children in a home for foundlings.

Like Bertrand Russell my father believed in the importance of the
individual but also in the value of relationships. As a husband he lived up
to this belief and was extremely self-sacrificing. He was also a good
father, not that I saw much of him until I was nearly eight and he left
Cornell. Even when he gave up spending half the year in the United
States he would be away much of the time: during the 1930s in Europe
and the Soviet Union; after the war, further afield in China and India as
well as the United States and Canada. However, when he was at home
he used to take me to the cinema frequently; not only to see films of
Leslie Howard but George Arliss as Disraeli and in other historical roles.

Since my mother was not really aware of the true seriousness of
Winifred's illness until virtually the end, she and my father had felt quite
able to go away together or separately on various foreign tours, during
which time Shirley and I were left in Winifred's care. After her death it
was no longer possible for my mother to carry on her writing and lecture
tours and for my father to make frequent excursions abroad, leaving
Shirley and myself at home. So first I and then Shirley had to go to
boarding schools.

From the time my father attended the Reichstag fire trial firstly in
Leipzig in September 1933 and then in Berlin, he spent an increasing
amount of time travelling in Europe up to the outbreak of war. He went
to Russia in 1935 and he was in Spain during the Spanish Civil War. It
was during his tour in Russia which lasted from March to May 1935 that
he made the decision finally to leave Cornell.

He felt the need to see what was happening in Europe and to take part
in real-life politics. Early in his academic career, if not before, my father
had decided that there could be a real science of politics, just as there was
a science of economics. He thought that the basic law of political action
involved the relationship between authority and freedom: the authority
of the state or leader; the freedom of the individual or the liberal state,
and that this was the equivalent in politics to the law of supply and demand in economics. My father was certainly best suited to thinking
about political action rather than taking part in it. But he became so
enthusiastic about going to see for himself as the storm clouds gathered
over Europe, and becoming involved on the fringe of so many crucial

events, that he devoted his time wholly to these rather than to developing his own ideas about political science.

On my grandfather's death, my mother was left a considerable inheritance so that within a space of two years, from the beginning of 1934 to the end of 1935, her financial position was quite transformed. She had always been careful both by upbringing and temperament, now she could live extremely well in a quiet way. With Winifred's death, my mother's position relative to her had also undergone a drastic change. Fond as my mother was of Winifred she was undoubtedly to some extent jealous of her too, not least because Winifred's earlier success had been in part due to the way of life she had adopted under my mother's influence. Had Winifred not died at the age of thirty-seven, it is reasonable to expect that *South Riding* would not have been her only distinguished novel. Because she did die, because my mother was now quite well-off, and because from 1935 on my father did not have a permanent job, my mother by a combination of circumstances, luck and through her own ambition and determination was transformed from being a not particularly successful journalist with a definite commitment to feminism and pacifism, to a well-known writer able to exploit her success in the interests of those causes to which she had always dedicated herself.

1935 was a year of significant change for the whole family. My grandfather spent an increasing amount of time in nursing homes and then threw himself into the Thames at Twickenham in August. In January Winifred had gone to Hornsea, on the Yorkshire coast, because despite her always considerable vitality the ravages of Bright's disease had made it necessary for her to get away from London in order to concentrate completely on finishing *South Riding*. In February, my father came back from Ithaca and within a month was on his way to Moscow. He returned to London after an extensive tour just before King George V's Silver Jubilee in May. Shirley and I saw the procession on May 6, 1933 from a large ground-floor window of the Midland Bank in Queen Victoria Street. It was nearly the end of the King's reign, just as for us too it was nearly the end of a significant period.

My mother did not condemn her father for 'giving in to himself', as she called it. Pity, however, she did not feel. She was critical of any form of weakness and, whenever I was ill or feeling sorry for myself, her invariable comment was that I must not give in to myself or I might turn out like my grandfather whom she constantly presented as a warning. Equally, she did not criticise my uncle's apparent homosexuality (she

122

even chose my third name, Jocelyn, in case I too turned out to be homosexual; and gave Vivian, used for boys as well as girls, to Shirley as her
second name). She would have regarded it as a failure to live up to her
masculine ideal rather than as innately bad.

She certainly had broad-minded views on sex. When I used to look at
the shelves in my mother's study I came across the various books which
she had been given to review. Among these was *How Babies are Born*,
perpetually fascinating to me. I used to get it out of my mother's room
when she was away, and read it on several occasions when I was eleven
or twelve. She also had several of the works of Havelock Ellis, including
one volume of his collected works which contained a number of case
histories. The only one I remember clearly described how women
workers in a factory which used leg-operated sewing-machines could use
these to provide a form of masturbation. The detailed written study
provided a bizarre stimulus to my imagination.

In adolescence I was rather puritanical, or perhaps priggish, and I was
quite shocked when my mother said that she would pose for me so that I
could draw her leg, for example. On another occasion I remember going
into my mother's bedroom without knocking and found her standing
naked in front of the gasfire. The only comment she made was that
perhaps I could knock in future before coming in. I was much more em-
barrassed than my mother. She prided herself on not being shocked by
anything.

In June 1935 my mother wrote in her diary that Winifred and my
father were in touch with another world where desires and worldly
achievement counted for nothing. She compared them both to T. E.
Lawrence. For herself she felt, on the contrary, that she had only trivial
ambitions: 'earthly desires for love, fame, beauty and success and for
position in society.' She was trying to explain to Winifred her being attracted to George P. Brett of the Macmillan Company of New York; she
had been attempting to get at the larger morality by flouting the lesser.
This seems to me something of a rationalisation.

My mother first met George Brett and his wife, Isabel, when she
arrived in New York off the *Berengaria* in September 1934. That my
mother found him immediately attractive is confirmed in a diary entry
for September 23, following a long walk with Brett at his home in Con-
necticut: 'then discussed Phyllis (Bentley) with George Brett, whom I
find attractive.' Brett bore a significant resemblance to my mother's
fiancé, Roland Leighton, partly in appearance but perhaps more so in

personality. He had been with the American forces in France at the end of the war. George had the same short, bristly hair as Roland; he was of a similar muscular build, only slightly above average height. He also had the same rather macho personality: the dominating male with more than a certain touch of ruthlessness.

George must have been aware of my mother's response to him and from her diary it is possible to see that he had an uplifting effect on her. They only met when my mother was on one of her lecture tours in America or when George had to come to England on business, but of course George's fascination for my mother did not depend on the frequency of their meetings.

George did much to promote the success of *Testament of Youth* in America and the relevant lecture tours she made; but then, as he was her publisher, it was very much in his interests to do so. He was, I think, quite aware of his attraction for my mother and he was able to exploit this to their mutual advantage. He may have been in love with my mother, but I feel confident that his relationship with her had, at least in part, a business motivation.

The Bretts came to England in June 1935. They dined at Glebe Place on the 11th, only a few days after their arrival, and my mother saw them on several occasions. It so happened that my father was spending a considerable amount of time in Sunderland where he secured the Labour Party nomination. However, the moment of truth as far as George Brett and my mother were concerned appears to have taken place on June 19. The evening before my mother and the Bretts had dined at the Savoy when, as my mother noted, George danced with her three times, and only once each with the other women present in the party. On the 19th my mother and George met for tea, possibly at the flat in Chesterfield Court where the Bretts were staying. All my mother says in her diary is: '3.00 – 3.30 pm, "when that which is perfect is come, that which is in part shall be done away".' The quotation has to be read in context. I think that when my mother ten days later spoke to Winifred about her experience with George Brett getting 'at the larger morality by flouting the lesser' I cannot help but feel that it was somewhat portentous rationalisation of George having made love to her.

But, whether he in fact did so or not, it is clear that from that time on my mother hoped to arrange another 'tea', though without success. While George no doubt flirted with more than one of his women writers he may have been alarmed to discover the depths of my mother's feeling for him, and perhaps felt that while mild flirtation was good for business a more serious relationship might have more serious and perhaps tiresome repercussions.

My mother continued to feel elated by his presence. For example, a year later she wrote in her diary for June 22, 1936: 'It will again be a year, I suppose, before I see him — but I recollect Olive Schreiner's words: "Sometimes such a sudden gladness seizes me when I remember you are living and working."' The quotation is particularly illuminating because Olive Schreiner was one of Roland Leighton's favourite writers.

My father detested George Brett, and it is perhaps not hard to see why. Oddly enough, or perhaps significantly when I knew him in the mid 1930s, when I was seven or eight, I did not like him either. I found his forceful manner overwhelming. My own assessment of his personality is underwritten by no less an authority on human nature than Harold Macmillan who in the 1930s was a successful publisher. At a dinner given in February 1937 for the Booksellers' Provident Institution, my mother sat next to Macmillan and she recorded what he said about Brett whom he obviously knew extremely well: 'He said he had read *Honourable Estate* while in bed with 'flu and much admired it — especially the reconstruction of war part. He said it was quite ridiculous of George to say it had not done well enough in America when it had been in the best-seller list for so many weeks — but that George was never satisfied with the way any book did because he always pictured to himself how much better it might do. Harold Macmillan said he was going out to the USA in three weeks and therefore George might not come over this year.'

In September of the same year my mother was in the United States on another lecture tour. George Brett's father had died. In her diary for September 27 my mother noted: 'George came back late and seemed vexed with life and overpowered by his family, which is certainly too numerous and very trying.' However a few days later George and my mother had tea 'in my sitting room and he was perfectly charming to me'. He stayed until about seven, when he had to go out to dinner. My mother 'had supper at the little café [in the Fifth Avenue Hotel where she was staying] in the state of keen exhilaration to which his society always lifts me'. Just as Roland Leighton had looked forward to a hero's death, George Brett anticipated ever greater success, and to this end everything was grist to his mill. Like Roland he was never satisfied. Perhaps this perpetual restlessness gave him the vitality to which my mother responded.

Two years before my mother's meeting with George Brett an important misunderstanding arose between my parents. She had received a letter from my father at the end of 1932, after he had read the typescript of *Testament of Youth*, in which he said that he had always accepted that she really belonged to Roland. She was not well at the time and did not read the letter or so she said; in any case she did not reply. My father wrote again, a rather similar letter. Unfortunately, he never posted it.

My father did not do himself justice, as I am sure my mother would have pointed out if she had read the first letter. She was quite aware of what he had done for her, particularly after the death of Winifred. But, as a result of the unanswered letter, my father came to think that the sacrifices he had made for my mother — and they were considerable — had been in vain. This misunderstanding was not cleared up for many years — not indeed until my mother came across the letter when she was reading through the file of his correspondence for this period, possibly when she was preparing material for *Testament of Experience*.

In the emotional vacuum that occurred as a result of my mother not confirming the importance of their relationship, it is possible that the ground was created for George Brett to make the impression that he did.

After the completion of *Testament of Youth*, my mother began work on *Honourable Estate*, supposedly a novel, but really a fictionalised account of her own family and that of my father. In the course of her research my parents visited The Cloughs, the house near Newcastle-under-Lyme, where my grandfather had been born in 1864. They found it in a state of total decay and just about to be demolished. My father took one of the stones away with him as a memento and gave it to my grandfather shortly afterwards — in fact on Shirley's fifth birthday in July 1935. Grandfather accepted the stone in good grace and showed my parents the photographs which he had kept of The Cloughs. My parents no doubt told him what a dilapidated state the house was in, and perhaps this had a particularly depressing effect on my grandfather, bearing in mind his neurasthenic condition.

Shortly after Shirley's birthday, my mother took us to Wimereux on the north coast of France for our summer holiday. We had hardly arrived when Winifred suddenly appeared to tell my mother that her father had committed suicide. Winifred immediately returned to London with my mother, while Shirley and I remained behind with friends. It was a difficult time, as my father was seriously ill with an obscure form of glandular fever.

If my grandfather's suicide at the beginning of August was a serious blow to my mother, Winifred's death, less than two months later, was even more overwhelming. In her last weeks Harry Pearson reappeared on the scene at her specific request and spent much time sitting alone with her by her bedside. Her doctor told her that she was having too many visitors for her own good and that she must restrict the number to three. The three she chose were her own mother, Harry and my mother. In the last months of her life she returned to the idea of marrying Harry; indeed she said that there could not be many women in love with the same man for thirty years who did not marry him in the end. After some prompting from my father Harry went to Winifred's nursing home and proposed to her. The effect was to make her so excited that her doctor had to give her a morphia injection to calm her; indeed he feared that violent convulsions might follow accompanied by both physical pain and mental anguish. He thought it best that this moment of happiness should be her last; before, indeed, she understood that what she was hoping for could never be realised.

After Winifred's death my parents went for a short holiday to Cornwall. It was not a success. My mother had suffered two traumatic experiences, similar to those she had experienced during the war, but this time almost simultaneously. When she ascribed my father's unusual touchiness to the efforts of his glandular fever I think she did the situation less than justice. My father had a great capacity for being conciliatory, but those who possess this gift are often well aware when it is being abused. She had failed to reassure my father at the time of the famous letter, and she had not really taken much interest until the very last moment in his political campaign in Sunderland. For the first time in ten years or more their relationship had broken down. Perhaps an important factor in its strength had been the presence of Winifred. As my mother reflected at the time, Winifred had identified herself with our family not least because her own relationship with the only man she really loved, Harry Pearson, had not developed satisfactorily. And, as she had been told quite early on in her own illness that she could never have children of her own, Shirley and I had become her substitutes.

My parents' holiday ended abruptly when my father left my mother in Fowey so that he could go and inspect the hunger-stricken coal fields in South Wales in preparation for the election campaign in Sunderland.

In September 1935 the Labour Party annual conference had taken place with the majority of the delegates endorsing the Government's policy. As a result both George Lansbury, leader in the House of Commons, and Lord Ponsonby, leader in the Lords, both pacifists, resigned. The senior men in the party, Stafford Cripps and Hugh Dalton among them, could not agree between themselves, so the leadership fell to Clement Attlee who was less outspoken and quarrelsome than the others.

The next month Parliament was dissolved. My father went up to Sunderland accompanied by my mother. She threw herself into the election, perhaps out of guilt that she had not taken more interest at an earlier stage. The situation facing my father was considerably less satisfactory than they had previously thought, due in large measure to the fact that one of the two candidates opposing him was also the proprietor of the *Sunderland Echo*. Although Labour increased their number of seats in Parliament by 100, the election still remained a triumph for Stanley Baldwin. My father was not elected.

It proved to be disastrous for my father that there would be no General Election for ten years. The contest in Sunderland demonstrated a point that he himself had appreciated, but had not acted on, either in Sheffield in the early 1920s, or in the Brentford and Chiswick campaign before the General Election of 1931. In order to win a marginal seat it is necessary to put in a year or two's preparatory work in the constituency. Getting to know the electorate and the local situation and on the basis of this knowledge to build up local support, was essential. Neither in Sunderland nor previously in Brentford and Chiswick did my father allow himself a real chance of success — except perhaps by a fluke of exceptional luck, which was not forthcoming. He had had to contend with a great deal in 1935, with problems at home as well as with his own illness. It is possibly true that he might just have had a chance at Sunderland, seen against the overall increase in Labour support indicated by their gain of 100 seats, if he had devoted virtually every moment to the constituency from the moment he was selected in June 1935, even though this allowed only four months of preparation before the election actually took place. The odds were not in his favour: in both 1931 and 1935, Labour support was near rock-bottom. Some Labour candidates were elected but not from marginal seats like Brentford and Chiswick in 1931 and Sunderland in 1935. My father had many assets for fighting an election. He had a good presence and a fine speaking voice and he was accustomed to addressing an audience. His personality was pleasant and he had sufficient practical intelligence to grasp the significant local factors in any given constituency.

But the democratic process involves bringing round the majority of the electors to vote for you and your party. This cannot be done at short notice except possibly by a candidate who is already well-known in a constituency, where the constituency is reasonably safe, or where there is a strong national trend in support of the party for which you are standing. My father had decided in March 1935 to give up Cornell; but this did not really allow enough time, particularly when the tide was running strongly against the Labour Party, to nurse a constituency before the next election which turned out to be only six months away. The Parliament elected in 1935 would become the longest sitting in English history. It is interesting to speculate that, if my father had got in in 1935, he would have been in a strong position in the Labour Party. It was the first Parliament in which Clement Attlee was leader of the Labour Party, a position he would retain for twenty years. In October 1935 my father was not yet forty, not too old to enter the House of Commons for the first time; by the time of the next election he was nearly fifty — rather a different story.

In fact by early 1936 my father had become involved in more obviously exciting activities. At the suggestion of Philip Kerr, Marquess of Lothian, until recently Under-Secretary of State for India and whom my father first got to know at Oxford, my parents invited a group of younger but rising stars in the Labour Party to meet Pandit Nehru, President of the Indian Congress who had just come out of prison. Nehru told my mother that one of the last books that had been sent to him while he was still in prison was *Testament of Youth*. Among those he met at Glebe Place were Arthur Creech Jones, a future Colonial Secretary in Attlee's first administration, and also Hugh Gaitskell, future leader of the Labour Party. The tea party took place on the afternoon of the funeral of George V. Ten years later Nehru was undisputed leader in India and the sun had begun to set on the British Empire.

At the beginning of 1936 I started at Gibbs', a day school in Sloane Street. My parents gave serious consideration to the choice of school. They apparently chose Gibbs' because they thought it was not too conventional (I remember that when I first went there one of the older boys was Peter Ustinov). Maybe I went there also because the deputy headmaster was a particularly charming man whom my parents liked. Mr Gibbs, the founder of the school, was still alive. He had the unpleasant habit of twisting your ear while he talked to you in order to ensure your full attention. While pulling your ear, he would smile.

On my journeys to Gibbs' I passed Peter Jones, the department store. On one occasion I was briskly asked to move on because I had been making disparaging remarks about the window displays to passers-by. I do not think that my parents ever made the point to me that while free speech was encouraged at home the expression of all one's uninhibited views would not always be favourably regarded elsewhere. In the summer terms we used to have what seemed an interminable journey by school bus to Barnes to play cricket. I did not enjoy this game and gave expression to my dislike by trying to throw the cricket ball at the face of the master in charge in the vain hope that I would break his glasses.

I had acquired my mother's rebellious feelings, and I gave expression to my own both in speech and action; though, under the care and guidance first of nannies and then of a German governess, I did acquire some social graces. Although my parents espoused left-wing political views which were distinctly non-conforming, neither of them approved of unconventional dress or uncontrolled behaviour in public. My father was always well turned out and my mother, particularly after the publication of *Testament of Youth*, aimed not only to be smart but fashionably dressed. Intellectual rebellion was encouraged but only in conjunction with conventional dress and behaviour. The advantage of this combination, although I did not appreciate it at the time, was that I did not appear to be the outsider I was essentially brought up to be. As a Polish architect subsequently pointed out to me, the two most hypocritical people in Europe are the Russians and the British. The schizophrenic combination in my upbringing had certain practical advantages, since it is those who look bizarre, rather than those whose outlook is bizarre, who chiefly attract unfavourable responses.

My mother was also obsessed with cleanliness and tidiness. She was particularly keen on supervising the washing of our clothes and I remember many an outburst from our emotional housekeeper who had not met my mother's exacting standards. Shirley was more of a ragamuffin than I; perhaps this was part of her more extrovert temperament. Nevertheless when the occasion required, as for example when Nehru came to tea, we had to be clean, suitably dressed and brushed so that we might sit in silence and take in everything that was going on — which Shirley and I would discuss privately later on. Unlike Orson

130

Welles as a child we were not called upon to entertain the guests. We only had to listen intelligently and provide a respectful audience.

By March 1936 political events were moving towards a critical point. Mosley held his monster rally at the Albert Hall. Hitler staged the German reoccupation of the Rhineland; Mussolini bombed Abyssinia. Both my parents went to Germany that month. They heard Göring in Berlin, and Hitler in Cologne. The object of their visit was to find out for themselves what lay behind the news in the papers and at the same time obtain first-hand material for their own journalism and other writing. My mother drew a distinction between the mass-audience techniques adopted by Göring and Hitler. She said that Göring adopted a macho approach from the start, whereas Hitler began his speeches with clarity and restraint and then, when he assessed that his audience was suitably hypnotised, there would be a sudden change. He would slip into what might be described as oratorical over-drive and gave vent to loud verbal terrorisation. My father was no admirer of Hitler but he noted his success in Europe using a process of bluff and decisive action on a small scale, thus leading his opponents to believe that Germany's position at the beginning of the Second World War was much stronger than in reality. In his political and philosophical tenets my father was a supporter of the rights of the individual and he believed in the rule of reason. He could not fail to note that Hitler was a devotee of the irrational and that his appeal was to force. In his *History of the Political Philosophers*, published in 1939, my father expanded his views on Hitler and the Nazis. My father, somewhat incongruously, brought us back from Germany some small models of Hitler with a handful of stormtroopers. I have no idea what my mother thought of these mementoes as she did not approve of Shirley and me playing soldiers, although it was one of our favourite occupations. We used to spend hours setting up the serried ranks in preparation for battles between our respective armies, in which the cavalry was preponderant, and for which our toy bricks provided fortifications. I enjoyed drawing pictures of field-marshals and generals on both sides. What I liked best was adding to their resplendent uniform an array of medals, the models for which I found in an old pre-1860 stamp-album which included the still-independent German kingdoms and grand-duchies.

My mother had not completely worked out her views on pacifism. She attended an enormous demonstration staged by the Peace Pledge Union in Dorchester, and dominated by the charismatic personality of Canon Dick Sheppard; but shortly afterwards she gave a lecture for the League of Nations — it proved to be her last one — at which she was heckled by representatives of the PPU.

Dick Sheppard invited my mother to become a supporter and sponsor of the Peace Pledge Union after the Dorchester demonstration, but she did not immediately agree. It was finally due to Sheppard's influence, the combination of his personal charm with Christian attitudes and behaviour, that she decided that the PPU's view of the League of Nations was right: it was a French-dominated organisation, the real object of which was to see the terms of the Treaty of Versailles enforced at Germany's expense. My mother's initial hesitation in joining Dick Sheppard was that, unlike him, her experiences, particularly of the First World War, led her to doubt whether a God who was good could exist. By temperament she liked positive action rather than resignation to the 'will of God'. She responded to individuals rather than to creeds. Because the success of *Testament of Youth* had more than exceeded her expectations, she now had the platform which she had been seeking. As far as feminism was concerned, the women's movement had made great strides at the end of the First War. My mother was now ready for the next crusade.

At the time of the outbreak of the Spanish Civil War, my mother was definitely moving towards total disillusion with politicians. This was underlined by my father's experience in Spain. He had been there at the beginning of 1937 in order to help set up an International Commission for Spanish Relief, an intention thwarted by the Spanish government who regarded the basic idea as good propaganda, but had no intention of doing anything practical about it.

In May 1937 we left Glebe Place, not least because my mother found the memories of Winifred too overwhelming. I think she hoped to find an equally unpretentious house, but in the end my parents moved to 2 Cheyne Walk. It was the Cheyne Walk house which led Herbert Morrison in due course to label my father 'a Dorchester socialist', an effective barb because, while unkind, it had a considerable measure of truth overtones well beyond the fact that my father liked eating at the Dorchester and other expensive hotels and restaurants. Cheyne Walk had a certain *folie de grandeur* unsuitable, I think, for an aspiring politician in the Labour Party. Had my father been Liberal or, even more appropriately, a prospective Conservative Member of Parliament, no doubt the powers that be would have excused his intellectual interests and academic occupation on the grounds that someone who lived in Cheyne Walk was either 'sound' or at least wished to appear so.

My mother would become more outspoken and determined in the promotion of unpopular causes, but my father moved slowly but surely from left to right in the political spectrum. Whatever he may or may not have learnt from the study of political science he came to admire authoritarian régimes more and more and liberal and 'permissive' ones less and less. Although a Catholic he even admired the Soviet no-nonsense style of government. In the conflict between freedom and authority he increasingly made out a better case for the latter.

It was generally thought that my father was a man of means, even rich. In fact it was my mother's financial position which had improved significantly before the move to Cheyne Walk. Not only had *Testament of Youth* provided unexpected royalties, but following the death of her father in the summer of 1935 she inherited a considerable amount of capital. Her aunt, Florence Bervon, also left my mother all her money and some valuable furniture.

In September my mother made a second successful lecture tour in America, even though she found that her audiences were more interested in hearing about the abdication of Edward VIII than the subjects she had come to talk about (there was a supposed similarity in appearance between my mother and Wallis Simpson). She also met President Roosevelt, with whom my father had been in touch for nearly ten years. Roosevelt wanted to hear a first-hand account of sentiment in England from someone with whom he felt sufficiently closely in touch to expect an objective view.

My father meanwhile was working on his *History of Political Philosophers*. Although in the late 1930s he became increasingly interested in studying at first hand the current political situation in Western Europe he was still concerned to answer some of the academic questions posed by political science and to answer the immediately relevant conundrum: 'Why war?' (subsequently, I saw a painting on the back of *Time* magazine which purported to show a Chinese philosopher working out a mathematical proof of why war could not re-occur. Behind him stood a sinister figure with dagger raised to assassinate the philosopher. My father had a great penchant for all things Chinese, porcelain and ivory figures as well as philosophy; and the picture in this advertisement reminded me irresistibly of him). But he was so engrossed in what was happening that he found it increasingly impossible either to remain sufficiently detached or to have the time to deal objectively with the basic issues of political science. Later he would claim that political science was only one of the three key issues with which he had been most concerned, the other two being Anglo-American unity and the independence of India. But neither of these issues owed much to his interest and intervention, although both had claimed a considerable amount of his time over a long period. Profound and original thought in political science was something he had been able to provide and which was uniquely his own.

Before my mother returned from her lecture tour in the States she heard the news of the death of Dick Sheppard. She had only known him for a year but his life — and death — left an indelible impression on her. Knowing Sheppard was undoubtedly a crucial factor in her decision to stay in England in the event of war, and in her determination to preach pacifism, war or no war. She did not acquire religious faith from Dick Sheppard, but his example was supremely important to her. After his death she became relatively less concerned with being the successful writer and more concerned with propagating pacifism. Certainly to my mother pacifism was not so much a political expedient or pragmatic way of dealing with international affairs as a form of religious faith.

In March 1938 Hitler marched into Austria. My parents gave much agonised consideration to whether they should accompany Shirley and me to the United States or whether we should go on our own. In fact Shirley and I went with them to New York in the autumn of 1937 but we only stayed for six weeks; then we all came back. The immediate result was that Shirley and I did not go back to our school in London, but she went to one in Swanage and I on to The Downs School in Colwall, near Malvern. My own recollection of the period between 1937 and 1940 was of being constantly uprooted: changing houses, changing schools, moving from London to a cottage in the New Forest, and then finally going to the United States.

My mother had chosen The Downs School because she thought I would be safer near the Malvern hills than in London. I did not at all relish going to boarding school. I much preferred Shirley as a companion to the boys I met there. The life of my parents hardly impinged on us, even though Shirley and I were constantly in their thoughts. I was not at the time fully aware of the extent to which my mother worried over everything and concerned herself with the minutiae of our régime, I just

134

accepted it as a fact of life. Interestingly enough, I do not think my mother ever enquired what we would like to do. She may have discussed what she had in mind and, when I was at school, I used to receive a stream of written advice and instruction but if, for instance, she ever asked me if I wanted to go to boarding school or even gave me her reasons for my going I have quite forgotten. What I do remember is my feeling of the essential unreasonableness of her decision. I was just presented with a fait accompli.

The Downs School had not been established very long by the time I arrived so it was not immersed in tradition. It had been founded on Quaker principles. The service or meeting on Sunday was not held in a school chapel, for there was none, but in the school hall. While I was at The Downs, W. H. Auden, who had recently been a master there, came to speak to us about his journey through China. Auden's poetry and plays were read in the school, one term we did *The Ascent of F6*. I was told that he liked boys to put buttercups in his mouth while he lay in the long grass, and that he was asked to leave the school because he used to wander naked round the school grounds in summer. Once, inadvertently, he had strayed too far and been apprehended by Colwall's one and only policeman.

Another visitor to the school was Herbert Read, the art critic. He had been on *The Realist*, and knew my father quite well. He published a book a few years after I left The Downs called *Education through Art* in which a self-portrait I had painted there appeared as one of the illustrations. I remember meeting him in 1943 when he inscribed for me a copy of his book on surrealism.

There was great emphasis at The Downs on fresh air and games against a background if not exactly of high thinking then at least of a certain strenuousness which seemed somehow consistent with my mother's outlook. What made a far deeper impression on me was reading James Hilton's *Lost Horizon*. I was determined to find my own Shangri-la. What appealed to me was the idea of an escape from world crises and disasters, of which I was always made so vividly aware from my parents' conversation. Shirley's response to and interpretation of these events was clearly different from mine. To her the world of action was the real world.

In the autumn of 1938 we spent six weeks in the same hotel opposite Columbia University in New York where my parents had stayed more than ten years before. As Shirley and I were eight and ten at the time, we clearly could not be left on our own, and my mother must have found our monopolisation of her time quite wearing. When I returned to The Downs at the beginning of 1939 I was looked on as something of a curiosity and with a new respect: a boy who had taken a term off to go to the United States without even the excuse of being ill. Anyone who could manage to get away with being away from school for six weeks was considered to have beaten the system.

By February my father was once more on his way back to America in order to lecture at the American University in Washington. The following month Hitler marched into Prague. The next day my mother joined Lord Ponsonby, who had been Under-Secretary at the Foreign Office in Ramsay MacDonald's first government, at a peace demonstration at the Brighton Pavilion.

While he was in Washington my father again tried to persuade my mother that we should all move to the United States, but though she reluctantly agreed that Shirley and I ought probably to go to America, she was determined herself to stay in England. She said that, although the Roman Empire was ending, life itself would go on and she wanted to take part in the new world that would be born. Her remarks were curiously prophetic in that the British Empire, the modern equivalent of the Roman one, was indeed coming to an end.

CHAPTER IX

WAR

IN April 1939 my mother had bought a cottage in the New Forest. It was the culmination of her dream of many years' standing of owning somewhere far from the commitments of London, and where she felt she would be able to achieve continuous concentration, if it was sufficiently secluded to deter uninvited visitors. It was unfortunate that she only acquired this cottage virtually at the outbreak of war, since if anything, its location was more dangerous than the middle of London. Soon, an anti-aircraft unit would be based at the big house, virtually next door to my mother's cottage; the gun itself being sited in the forest clearing in front. A wooden garden seat now acts as a memorial to the seventeen men of the unit who were killed when a bomb fell on the big house.

My father never cared for the country, where he felt cut off from what was happening at the centre of things, but Shirley and I were at least initially in our element. In the school holidays, we played in the forest, pretending that the larger fallen trees were submarines. Later, there seemed something inherently gloomy and strangely monotonous about the New Forest, with its endless pine-trees. When we lived there, and mains water was introduced, Allum Green became increasingly water-logged to a point where a walk through the forest could involve suddenly sinking six inches or more into an unexpected quagmire. Even my mother's mother, who had lived in or near the country in Staffordshire for many years, found the overhanging trees menacing. But perhaps the most off-putting characteristic of the forest, though I was probably not conscious of it as a child, was the almost permanently humid atmosphere which, in autumn particularly, caused an all-pervading smell of rotting vegetation. The weather in this part of Hampshire is generally mild. It is certainly the reverse of bracing. I found it increasingly difficult to keep awake, let alone alert.

137

FAMILY QUARTET

It was at the cottage in Allum Green that I heard Neville Chamberlain's broadcast after the invasion of Poland of September 3, 1939. This broadcast, like that in which Edward VIII announced his abdication, has remained clear in my mind. The significance of both was apparent to me from the tone of voice in which they were delivered. The Duke of Windsor and Chamberlain both sounded equally anxious, conscientious and resigned to defeat. You did not need to be either an historian or even an adult to realise that there was something seriously wrong, even if, as a child, I could not identify exactly what that might be.

Within a few days of Chamberlain's broadcast my mother received an invitation to devote her talents to the Ministry of Information. It was this which led her to decide to start her *Letters to Peace Lovers*, hardly a consequence which the Ministry could either have anticipated or indeed approved.

It seems extraordinary in retrospect that no serious attempt was made to utilise the services of either of my parents in promoting Anglo-American relations. They had been travelling back and forth between the two countries for more than a decade, my father for rather longer. He in particular had contacts at the highest level in the United States and could count President Roosevelt a close acquaintance. The answer was no doubt that officialdom was nervous of using the talents of anyone who had not spent the whole of their career in the corridors of power. And yet my mother's publisher was Harold Macmillan and they always maintained the most cordial relations. But then what was the standing of the future Prime Minister himself at this time? One wonders what Whitehall would have made of Disraeli in 1939 — let alone Churchill.

At the end of 1939 Winifred Holtby's mother, who had undergone an operation for appendicitis at the age of eighty, died in Yorkshire. At her funeral in Bridlington my mother reflected, rather pessimistically, that time betrays us all and that one day she would be defeated by me, Shirley and our friends. It is true that Shirley, like my father, was never a pacifist. It is equally true that I was a critic of my mother from the moment I could speak and most of my criticisms I made to her face. Nothing in this book would have come as a surprise to her. I could at least get her to laugh at herself, in itself quite an accomplishment. My father found it easier to enjoy himself but I think he would have been able to take a more detached view of the people with whom he came into contact if he had not accepted them at their own valuation. He had an exaggerated respect for anyone who held a position of power, however

138

modest. And if, say, you were Foreign Secretary, you must *ipso facto*, have something to say that was worth hearing.

The previous February my parents had had dinner in Los Angeles with Bertrand Russell. It was at this meeting that he explained to them why, in the face of Hitler, he could not adopt the pacifism which he had held in the First World War. If it was as a pacifist that my mother chiefly admired Russell, my father recalled that after reading one of Russell's books which he was reviewing he had written: 'Mind and heart are cheered by reading the work of so brilliant an intellect.' He added that Russeell did not regard himself as inferior to professional politicians but looked on them as junior to himself in the same political world; and that he was in the tradition of a great Whig nobleman who always displayed intelligence, wit, courtesy, some tolerance and an openminded respect for the opinions of the other person to whom he was talking. There was no one person for whom my father had greater regard than Bertrand Russell, and I feel that I inherited many of his values.

On her return from the United States in April 1940 my mother had a further meeting with Harold Macmillan. She gave him her impressions formed on the basis of her having by this time been to no less than forty-four states of the Union. Macmillan made the prophetic remark that if the Allies were to win the war it would take five years: my mother noted later that it was five years and twelve days.

In May the Nazis invaded Holland and Belgium. Increasingly my mother felt it was her duty not to leave England, although she was sure that she and my father would be at risk if the Nazis invaded. (She was right; after the war both my parents found their names on the Gestapo list of wanted people in Britain.) She felt an equal duty to send Shirley and me to the United States. So when she received a cable from one of her American admirers in St Paul, Minnesota, inviting us to go there, she decided to accept the offer. Mrs Ruth Gage Colby had met my mother on a lecture tour in 1934 and had been in touch with her ever since, not least in her capacity as Chairman of the Women's International League for Peace and Freedom in Minneapolis.

We left England a few weeks after the Dunkirk evacuation, at the most critical period of the war. Germany was expected to invade within a matter of weeks of our arrival at St Paul, on July 5, 1940. My mother undoubtedly came to regret that she ever sent us to the United States for three years. On the other hand if Shirley and I had suffered some terrible fate, whether England were invaded or not, she would never have forgiven herself. In fact our journey aboard the *Duchess of Atholl* in the submarine-infested waters of the Atlantic was probably the riskiest thing we could have undertaken. Shirley was just ten and I was twelve and a half. Apart from our long wait in the enormous station at Chicago what I remember best about the journey is that, just as we were getting into St Paul, Shirley decided to put some baked beans into her ice-cream. I felt strongly that this was definitely not the way to behave, that she was letting the side down, and I told her so.

Until Shirley and I had gone to boarding school, less than two years before we went to America, we had spent far more time together than we had with our parents. As she was with me in St Paul for two years, from my point of view, the essential nucleus of our family remained the same, for it consisted of her and me. I think both of us, but perhaps more particularly I, had regarded going to America as an adventure to look forward to rather than as the break-up of our family. Certainly I never felt homesick.

When Shirley and I went to our respective schools in St Paul, she, being more gregarious, soon made a number of friends with whom she spent much of her free time. I did not make any particularly close friend although I got on well with the other boys at my private school. This was the St Paul Military Academy. The headmaster was a very civilised man called Dequinteville Briggs, who had come from one of the Eastern seaboard states. We had to wear a uniform and there was drill on most days, but the school could not be described as intrinsically military and certainly not militaristic. It was just that throughout the United States at that time private schools for boys tended to seem military, based as they were on their better-known predecessors founded on the East coast.

Dr Colby's house was quite large, timber-built and painted white, with mosquito frames over the windows in summer. It was built on two floors with a large basement and attic. There was a reasonably large garden, chiefly grass, at the back, and a garage and drive behind the garden. On the ground floor there was a large sitting-room, dominated by a portrait of Mrs Colby painted in the 1920s, which was scarcely ever used. On the first floor were Dr Colby's own room, and also a library where I slept; the top floor Mrs Colby had converted an attic into a studio where Shirley slept.

I liked Dr Colby who was a man of few words and much common

sense. I never cared for Mrs Colby but find it hard to say why. It may be that I asserted my independence by being disagreeable and rebellious. I am not sure whether my mother paid for us to stay with the Colbys but, knowing her combination of keenness on independence and being able to control a situation, I imagine any contribution came from the royalties which my mother's books had earned in the United States at least up until the beginning of the war.

Although I did not get on particularly well with Mrs Colby, she certainly had a remarkable understanding of what I enjoyed. I soon started painting in the basement of their house. I had it largely to myself since the only other occupants were the wooden decoys which Dr Colby used during his annual pilgrimage to the lakes of northern Minnesota for duck-shooting.

My most creative period was my first two years in St Paul. This was probably due to the stimulating effect of the change which was more apparent in the earlier period than the latter part of my stay. By the third year I had almost given up painting and taken to writing poetry instead.

If the primary impulse of the artist is discontent and that discontent is the grain of sand in the oyster, then painting for me is a continual though not necessarily continuous effort to get back to an ideal world. If one is of a naturally discontented nature, the practice of art is the attempt to achieve equilibrium. I did not suffer from any inherent discontent so in order to continue to create I had to have a perpetually challenging and novel environment. I have only been restless to the point of discontent when I could not find the key to establishing a new and satisfying equilibrium.

Just as *Citizen Kane* was the movie which made the greatest impression on me during my three years in the States, so there was one book which had a profound effect — *The Early de Chirico*, by James Thrall Soby of the Museum of Modern Art in New York, which I bought when it first came out in 1941, when I was thirteen. The book contains a comprehensive if not exhaustive collection of photographs in black and white of de Chirico's work up to 1918 and also an extended essay by Soby in which he not only provides a biography of de Chirico, but also a psycho-analytical examination of each of the paintings illustrated. Its influence was so great that for many years my sole ambition was to do no more than produce paintings in the style of, and even with the subject matter of, these early works of de Chirico. It would not be true to say I copied them. It was more that I entered into their spirit. It took me more than twenty years to grow out of their influence, although in time I began to find them too literary in their inspiration. I do not say that de Chirico was the only artist I found stimulating. If anything, I found Picasso as a personality much more fascinating, and indeed attending his comprehensive exhibition in Minneapolis during my years in the States was a major experience; but I never had any desire to paint in the manner of Picasso.

As I came to find de Chirico too literary, so I began to prefer Seurat as an artist with whom I could in every way identify more completely. It was interesting to find that Soby, in his book on de Chirico, refers to the hypnotic figures of the girl with the hoop in the painting called *Melancholy and Mystery of a Street* and suggests that she was inspired, possibly unconsciously, by a similar figure who races through the background of Seurat's *La Grade Jatte*. Soby then goes on to make the point that Seurat's paintings, which had a considerable influence on avant-garde artists before the First World War, are the most enigmatic in the whole of nineteenth-century art. The frontispiece of Soby's book is a self-portrait by de Chirico entitled: *What Shall I Love Unless it be the Enigma?* From the first I found something profoundly appealing in this question. It has had an influence on me equivalent in force to the quotation from T. S. Eliot which I give at the front of this book.

For those brought up like myself in a conventional English middle- to upper-middle-class tradition, to be outrageously exhibitionist is either impossible or, alternatively, an act. The whole of a public school and Oxbridge education is devised to inhibit emotional display of any kind and to develop the intellect and intellectual control virtually to the exclusion of all other faculties. What would Bertrand Russell or Aldous Huxley have been like if they had been born in Spain or Italy? The advantage of the sort of education I received was the ability to maintain a completely conventional exterior and to be able to fade anonymously into the background. On many occasions this has proved extremely useful.

My life in St Paul was not entirely confined to the basement. My guardian was full of ideas on how I might spend my time. On one occasion during the summer we drove to an isolated shore of the Mississippi, perhaps fifty miles away, where we went to look at an early nineteenth-century clapboard house that belonged to her father's family. It had not been lived in for more than fifty years but, although there was no furniture, there were a number of old books, letters and pictures. I remember particularly some Gauday fashion prints of the 1880s. Mrs Colby allowed Shirley and me to remove what we wanted as souvenirs.

In 1941 I went to summer school in Stillwater, a small town on the Mississippi, where an 'art colony' was located. I enjoyed this so much that, when it was time for me to return to St Paul, I hid in the hope that I could not be found. Ultimately a compromise was reached and it was agreed that I could stay on for a further three weeks. Apart from painting, sculpture and music lessons, mostly organised by émigré practitioners from Europe, there was a play in which I took part. Whether because there were quite a number of English people in the art colony I do not recall, but the play, specially written for the occasion, called for portraits of Queen Victoria, Edward VII and George V, and I proudly produced these. I remember that I found it particularly difficult to make George V look significantly different from Edward VII.

The reason I was so unwilling to leave Stillwater in fact had little to do with the art colony or its activities, I wanted to say on because I had fallen madly in love with a local girl of seventeen, who to me, at the age of thirteen and a half, was the embodiment of all that was beautiful and sophisticated. Jean LeVine was at Duke University and I recall being very impressed. We both took part in the play so that I had numerous opportunities to be with her during the considerable number of rehearsals. Occasionally — the height of bliss — she would take me for drives in her parents' car. I did not see Jean again for a number of years, though we continued to write to each other. Up to the middle of 1941, my school work had achieved a good standard and it was thought that in due course I might go to Harvard, but after my brief summer encounter I ceased to concentrate and, under this highly-charged emotional experience, started to write poetry which expressed my feelings in a more direct way than I was able to show in painting.

In the last year of our stay in America, Shirley went to the East Coast to live with George Brett and his wife, but I stayed on in St Paul. I left the day school I had been at for two years, and went instead to a boarding school, Pillsbury Academy, named after the flour-making family. Pillsbury was another military school, but despite its uniforms and drill it contained a number of individualists. Among the masters there was Major Jones, who held his rank because of service in the United States Army in the First War. He taught English and I got on extremely well with him in class. On the parade ground he was a martinet. However, for my English literature exam he eccentrically awarded me *The Works of*

Oscar Wilde. There were also two expatriates from England who taught music. One of these, Arthur Johnson, played the piano with considerable skill. He worked himself up to a frenzy over the piano version of Ravel's *Bolero* and he relished the opportunities for virtuoso display which such composers as Albeniz provided. The second Englishman was a devotee of Chinoiserie and the first person I ever came across who burnt incense in his rooms and displayed bowls of rose leaves. These two were the last characters one would expect to find in a military school in Minnesota, but no doubt by this time all able-bodied younger American teachers had been called up. Perhaps Arty Johnson and his friend were conscientious objectors.

The school did not have a chapel and was of no particular Christian denomination. Nevertheless, we had church parade every Sunday morning and in true democratic style we attended a church of a different denomination every week, from the lowest of low to the Episcopalian Church in Owatona, the nearest town. We drew the line at the Catholic Church; perhaps the Pillsburys would not have approved. I noticed that the lower the denomination of the church the longer the sermon — or harangue.

Drill was not too onerous because all the rifles had been commandeered by the army. Ours were entirely of wood, except for a metal bolt which made it possible to carry out the regulation drill routine. For two of my three terms at Pillsbury I managed to have a room of my own. In my second term I removed all the furniture other than the bed, so as to reduce the amount of dusting and cleaning which I had to do myself. We used to have room-inspections two or three times a week. These made up for the lack of the real thing on the parade ground. Major Jones or one of his underlings would run his finger along the window ledge or other such places likely to remain undusted by the less obsessional cleaner. No objection was ever made to my having no furniture in my room, but no doubt this was a factor in my having to share in my last term.

In retrospect I see that I was able to bloom in a fairly uninhibited way while I was in the United States. I did not do anything too outrageous but I had never previously had such an unbridled opportunity to do what I liked over such a long period. An advantage of living with guardians rather than parents is they are not so emotionally involved, and if, as the Colbys were, they were also eminently sensible and responsible (Dr Colby was in fact a medical practitioner dealing exclusively with children) they also left me a good deal of latitude to be myself and develop as I chose. The only inhibition that I recall was that when Dr Colby had one of his migraine headaches we had to keep quiet. He also insisted on good table manners.

Shirley and I received a continuous stream of letters from my mother. Invariably the letters contained advice. My father was much given at this stage to quoting from the letters of Lord Chesterfield to his son. Whether this was wise I am not sure since Lord Chesterfield's son did not turn out particularly well; whether this was due to his taking the letters to heart or ignoring them, as I did my father's, I cannot say.

Both my parents had been having an adventurous time. Just before Christmas 1940 my father returned home from the United States on the *Western Prince*, which was torpedoed in the Atlantic just before dawn in bright moonlight between Ireland and Iceland. The alarm bells did not function and by the time my father got to the last lifeboat he was virtually the final passenger to leave the ship. A strong sea was running and there was intermittent rain accompanied by large waves so that my father spent much of the early part of his eight hours at sea baling out the water in the bottom of his lifeboat. About half an hour after the first torpedo the submarine reappeared and the survivors in the lifeboats thought their last hour had come. Fortunately the submarine merely took the opportunity to fire a second torpedo into the *Western Prince*. At the end of the day they were all rescued by a freighter.

My mother had discovered the impossibility of going abroad, either to the United States to lecture or, subsequently, to India, in view of the authorities' unfavourable attitude to her promotion of peace through her *Letters to Peace Lovers*. Although understandably, she found these spokes placed in her wheels extremely frustrating, I very much doubt whether she would have been allowed her campaign for peace in any other country which was at war. She received numerous poison-pen letters from those who considered her activities unpatriotic. Needless to say, while she found these disconcerting, they failed to deter her. Quite possibly she was only able to continue to publish her *Letters to Peace Lovers* because to have banned them would have turned her into a martyr. My mother's approach to peace was idealistic rather than subversive. It would have been difficult to show that she was trying to undermine the war effort even if she could not have been described as patriotic. From the remarks she made to me after I returned from America, I got the impression that she would have liked to have been sent to prison for expressing her views, as she fully realised that she would consequently drum up a good deal more publicity and support.

Sir Geoffrey Shakespeare, a relation of my mother's who was Under-Secretary for Dominion Affairs and Chairman of the Children's Overseas Reception Board from 1940 to 1942, must have found her a considerable embarrassment. It is an interesting question whether the fact that my mother was in touch with influential people in government circles helped or hindered her. On balance I think that it prevented her from petty harassment by minor officials. The office of my mother's *Peace Letter* was visited by the police from time to time but she had to admit that never was any attempt made to interfere with what she was doing.

My father did not share my mother's pacifism, and it says much for his tolerance that he supported her activities. However, in the longer term he was undoubtedly tarred with the brush of pacifism. This was remembered against him, whereas his efforts towards securing battle cruisers from the US Navy for Britain, an exercise which very nearly cost him his life at sea, was conveniently forgotten. As a result of his experiences at sea my father contracted jaundice which had a visibly ageing effect on him. When Shirley and I went to the United States just before my father's forty-fourth birthday, he did not look a day over thirty-five. When I returned from the States, before Shirley, in 1943, he was nearly forty-seven but by then looked, if anything, rather more than his age. His hair had gone quite grey.

In February 1941 my mother's book *England's Hour* appeared. It was castigated by the critics not only because it revealed the full devastation caused by air raids but also because it pleaded for values usually regarded as civilised but which had become unacceptable in wartime. My mother never agreed that values should be simply put to sleep for the duration of the war. Nor did she accept that Christian values were only an enlightened form of self-interest. She was no doubt surprised to hear from Shirley that she had read *England's Hour* and that she rather envied my mother her wartime experiences. The most significant point about Shirley reading the book, to my mind, is that it indicates her far greater interest than mine in what my parents were doing and what was happening in England. I looked on my arrival in America as a new beginning. Whether I consciously realised it or not, I think my attitude expressed my feeling that one must live in the here and now — wherever that may happen to be. Commitment to the present necessarily involves some lack of concern for both the past and the future.

My mother had not been allowed to go to the United States on a lecture tour in 1940, and in June 1941 she was not permitted to go to India. She even had a meeting with Leo Amery, Secretary of State for India, who explained that the Congress Party might make capital out of her pacifist views. It is relevant that at about the same time Gandhi made it plain to the Japanese that, while he hoped to rid India of British imperialism, he had no intention of helping the Japanese to substitute their version of rule for that of Britain.

In 1942 my mother published *Humiliation with Honour*, which was in the form of letters addressed to me, and which dealt with the theme that true understanding can only be achieved by the process of acquiring strength and dignity through the experience of humiliation and dishonour. I did not read the book although it was ostensibly addressed to me. I do not think my mother was terribly disturbed by this; no doubt she realised that the lessons of the book were quite beyond my experience. Perhaps she was also aware that children behave in the way they do to distance themselves from their parents and in this way create their own, independent, personalities. If I had been an admirer of my mother and her books at the age of fifteen I almost certainly would not have developed into someone in my own right. My mother was a great believer in developing one's own personality, for better or worse, and I was doing just that. Indeed I used to refer to my mother's many admirers as 'worshippers at the shrine'. She may even have been modestly amused by the description which was not entirely disparaging. After all, my mother liked being a shrine, even if I was not one of the worshippers.

My mother's decisions on what course to follow were always much influenced by the individuals who crossed her path at what were important junctures in her life. The fact that Roland Leighton had been a classicist had much to do with the efforts my mother made to read Latin and Greek in order to get to Oxford. Her meeting with Dick Sheppard had a tremendous influence on the energy and drive that she brought to pacifism and to the Peace Pledge Union. Now in 1943, her meeting with Corder Catchpool, member of a long-established Quaker family, did much to make my mother increasingly sympathetic to Quakerism; and indeed, under Catchpool's influence she very nearly became a Quaker. In the event, though, she never took this final step.

The austerity of the Quakers had always appealed to my mother, and undoubtedly a factor in my going to The Downs School was its Quaker orientation. At the same time, she thought there was a certain 'group-think' quality inherent in Quakerism that was not for her. She felt her rebellious spirit was not quite in tune with their 'quietist' approach to life, and that her concern for her appearance was a sign of vanity which would make her not wholly acceptable to other Quakers. My mother managed to combine an essential austerity of spirit with a wish to look attractive, and although the combination might be unusual each characteristic was as sincere as the other.

By the end of 1942, my parents were beginning to wonder how soon Shirley and I could come back to England. When this idea was put to me by my guardians I was far from enthusiastic. Had I been able to make decisions for myself I would undoubtedly have stayed in America. The pragmatic attitude to life which I encountered among Americans appealed to me enormously, and I also thought, rightly I still think, that the chances of my being able to do what I wanted, which at this stage was to paint, were much greater in the United States than in Britain. The fascination that my girl-friend from Stillwater still exercised over me, even though I had not seen her again, was a further reason for my wishing to stay in America. Early in 1943 the Colbys told me that I ought to write to my mother to say how much I was looking forward to coming home; in the end I was persuaded to do this — but not with a good grace. Mrs Colby told me that I would break my mother's heart if I did not return to England, and, of course, since I was only fifteen at the time I did not even consider making a reasoned and convincing appeal for being allowed to stay where I was.

In the freedom of the Mid-West I had in fact become what my parents had made me, but that is not to say that the result was exactly what they had hoped for. I had inherited my mother's strong will and strong feelings, largely exhibited in rebelliousness to authority, and with this I had also acquired my mother's ability to do things in my own way — but not without occasional opposition. From my father I had absorbed intellectual interests and an analytical approach, but also the desire to be reasonable, which tended to be in conflict with my more rebellious self.

By April 1943 the war had taken a turn for the better and my mother therefore reopened our house in Cheyne Walk. Complicated plans and much form-filling had gone into the preparation for my return, which involved sailing across the Atlantic to Portugal and then flying to England from Lisbon. Virtually at the last minute these plans were all but put aside because of the shooting down by the Germans of the plane on which Leslie Howard was travelling — on the identical route I was to take.

Following my parents' alarmed consultation with Lord Salisbury and Lord Ponsonby, who expressed the view that the downing of the plane was an event unlikely to be repeated, the plans for my return were adhered to, and on July 18, after only the briefest stay in Lisbon, I duly arrived back at an airfield near Bristol and took the train to Paddington, where my parents met me. My mother was disconcerted by my slightly American accent and the fact that I was now taller than she. And of course by this time my voice had broken. But these were only the outward changes for which she had not been prepared. In a rather adolescent way I had acquired a certain youthful sangfroid which she must have found unexpected if not disturbing. I was clearly not the same John who had sailed from Liverpool in the June of 1940. Before I even met my parents I had experienced feelings of malaise if not mild claustrophobia as we approached London through the south-western suburbs of London: row upon row, mile upon mile, of neat suburban houses with their gardens all laid out like minute fragments of a huge jigsaw puzzle in which, however, the individual pieces were virtually interchangeable. The contrast with the wide-open spaces of the Mid-West, where you could travel for hours and hardly see a house, let alone a town, could hardly have been more marked.

I had not been back home for more than a fortnight when I announced that I would have to get a job. Although plans were being made for me to go to school in the autumn there was still the best part of two months to go. After protracted discussion on the whys and wherefores, I made the point that in the United States it was quite common for boys of my age to take a job in the summer holidays, although in fact I had never taken one myself. I said that I would like to work in a bookshop, so my mother got in touch with Christina Foyle and within a matter of days I started work in the second-hand fiction, poetry and belles-lettres department of the famous bookshop in the Charing Cross Road. I had not anticipated the boredom of having to spend the whole day in one place doing the same thing over and over again. It proved a considerable strain on my self-discipline, but as it had been my idea to do the job in the first place I felt I must stick it out to the bitter end. In any case, it did have certain compensations. Apart from the fact that it provided an alternative to spending all my time idly at home with the danger that my mother or father might think of something 'useful' for me to do, I had by this time developed a love of second-hand books, partly based on the fact that we had more books at home than many small bookshops, and partly because I had spent much time in St Paul in a second-hand bookshop, where my last purchase had been a large illustrated history of the American Civil War in three volumes, published in 1870, but which I had had to abandon because of their combined weight.

My job had the advantage of enabling me to buy many first editions among the second-hand books. I was particularly keen on collecting first editions of Robert Browning, of which there seemed to be a number on the shelves. Where possible I tried to find a first edition which contained the signature or inscription of someone interesting in his own right. Thus, one of the editions of Browning that I bought bore the signature of the Edwardian composer, Granville Bantock. I never read the books. Although I was interested in the biographies of such poets I found their actual poetry unreadable. When I did start to read poetry it was the work of W. H. Auden and T. S. Eliot that I found had most meaning to me.

My wages were very modest but I took nearly all of them in the form of books, on which I was allowed a small discount. Sometimes I bought books in other shops in the Tottenham Court Road and of these Zwemmers was my favourite. Whether to soften the blow of my having to return to England I am not sure, but my guardian had sent me £50, quite a lot of money in 1943, and I was free to spend this as I thought fit. I bought a typewriter for £15; an edition of Longus's *Daphnis and Chloe* in two volumes, in one of which there were about twenty-five woodcuts by Aristide Maillol, all loose-leaf; and, also for £15, a silver-point of Picasso's *Deux Femmes sur un Arbre* signed by the artist. The typewriter served for about fifteen years, and the books and print proved to be a good investment. From that time on I became an inveterate collector of everything I could lay my hands on. Eventually I came to the conclusion that a passion for collecting, like one for listening to music, is a substitute for a satisfying human relationship. I became a collector of books chiefly because they were easy to handle and did not take up too much space. I very seldom spent more than £1 on a book. I hardly ever read the books I bought; often as not I was more interested in the pictures than in the text.

I only worked in Foyles for a few weeks. The serious business in hand, as far as my parents were concerned, was to find a suitable school for me. This should have presented no problem. When I was born, my name had been put down for Eton because the organist at Windsor at that time was a friend of my grandfather Catlin. It was, however, necessary for me to take an entrance exam which involved some simple Latin. I went down to Eton, where I saw my prospective housemaster and also the master at Gibbs' School with whom I had got on particularly well and who was now a master at Eton. My parents arranged for me to meet the art master and to see over the art school. Had I not insisted on doing a summer job I could easily have been coached for the basic Latin required. I claimed, however, that I would not have been able to do the Latin, and so I did not take the entrance exam at all. As in the previous stages of my education in England, my mother thought it would be a good idea to survey as much of the field as was possible in the time available. I remember I made the particular demand that whatever school I went to I must have a room of my own. I was more interested in this condition being met than any others.

At least one headmaster came to see us at Cheyne Walk so that in effect we were interviewing him rather than the other way round. After his departure we made various comments, chiefly adverse, on the inadequate basis that he had been particularly well-dressed and wore a rose in his buttonhole. The school was Stowe. I also went to see Harrow, which my mother liked because the gardens round the headmaster's house were particularly fine. Ralph Moore, the headmaster, was quite a young man who appealed to my mother, so it was decided that I should go to Harrow. I did not have to do an entrance exam and I got a room of my own. This was extremely small but at least it was exclusively mine.

I have often thought about the merits and otherwise of my having had so much say in the schools I went to. Because my parents quicky came to see that on my return from the States I was highly counter-suggestive, by allowing me a great deal of latitude and letting me make my own choice I could never subsequently blame them. Whether in the longer run it made much difference that I had had coaching in Latin and gone to Eton or worked in Foyle's and went to Harrow I very much doubt. At the time I definitely thought I had scored in that I had got my own way in due course. I regretted not having gone to Eton but really only in the abstract. Much to my mother's dismay, I enjoyed the two years I spent at the Headmaster's House at Harrow. She subsequently claimed that one of the reasons she had agreed to my going there was because she was sure I would react against it. In fact I never did. For a school with a strong military tradition and much devotion to games, Harrow allowed me a surprising amount of latitude. The fact that I had been an evacuee in America was not held against me unduly and, what is more, I was virtually the only boy in the school not to be in Army Corps, out of

151

deference to my mother's pacifism. I was never bullied or given a hard time because of this.

I did not, unfortunately, have a room of my own for long. In my second and third terms I shared with Marian Mikołajczyk, the son of the ex-Prime Minister of Poland who had made a hazardous escape to England after the Russians' take-over. For my second year, however, I again had a room to myself. Possibly he complained that I got up every morning at six o'clock. I did so in order to copy out the text and drawings from Leonardo da Vinci's Notebooks, which I found in the school library.

Shirley did not come back to England at the same time as me. Under Mrs Colby's influence, she had given much more attention to her appearance and clothes than she had ever done before in England. The result was that, by the time she was thirteen, Shirley looked very attractive. Her hair was still so fair that it seemed white, and she had large blue eyes. The only feature we had in common was rather heavy eyelids, but apart from our appearance we had more in common that I was aware of. We were certainly equally determined and, if not always outspoken, quite clear in our minds on virtually every subject, as we had been brought up to be. I was by no means as extrovert as Shirley but I never felt shy with those I did not know, and I always enjoyed meeting new people, even if I let them do most of the talking. I kept my thoughts to myself, but again we had been brought up to this: not to speak unless we had something significant to say. Shirley liked talking as much as my parents did; increasingly I came to feel that for my parents, if not for Shirley, discussion had become an end in itself. My parents had started to invite their friends and colleagues to the house again from early in 1943, but they scarcely ever included their friends' children. Since I had been away for three years I hardly knew anyone of my own age. The boys I got to know best at Harrow mostly lived in the country, while the ones I had known best before I went to the States I was no longer in touch with. Thus my holidays from school were immensely boring and lonely.

As I did not take part in the Corps activities at Harrow I had to run in the park in the afternoons. In this way I came across the school Chaplain, Philip Bryant, brother of the historian. He spent many afternoons a week sawing up the very large trees which had fallen in the school grounds. From their size many of them must have been at least two hundred years old. Cutting up the trees with a double-handed saw was a punishment meted out for various minor crimes, but I could see that I would get on well with the Chaplain so I volunteered. It provided an opportunity to get out of cricket and, in due course, football which for most boys occupied six afternoons a week in winter. The art of double-handed sawing is not to saw too quickly, but to develop a smooth, rather relaxed motion which, with a little practice, makes it possible to keep going for twenty minutes to half an hour at a time. I developed this ability and would then challenge much more athletic boys than myself to see who would last longer. I usually won. The Chaplain told me, when I got to know him better, that he sold some of the wood to local house-holders and he gave the money to war relief work. I liked Bryant who was a most unassuming man with an exaggerated respect for his brother. If I was an atypical Harrovian, he was certainly another. But then Winston Churchill and Nehru were hardly typical Harrovians either.

I also spent much time in the art school, where I had to draw from plaster casts. This was very good experience, because I had done very little disciplined drawing, and while I had painted in oils from the age of ten, my drawing was weak. It was possible to do art as a subject for School Certificate, so I incorporated my drawing into this objective, for which it was also necessary to study the history of painting in England from the late Middle Ages onwards. I also enjoyed English language and literature and history, and I won a number of prizes in these subjects. For one history prize I chose the *Odyssey* and *Iliad* of Homer which were bound in blue leather on the spine and on which the school's emblem was stamped in gold. When the Headmaster came to present me with these I noticed he was rather surprised, as he was well aware that I knew little Latin and no Greek. However, I had chosen these books because I liked them as objects in themselves — even though I could not read them.

When the buzz bombs began to fall on London shortly after I got back to England, there was a great concentration of them in the north of London, in and around the Harrow area. As a result, we had to sleep in the underground passages of our house. The school chapel, which faced the window of my room, was only fifty yards away when it was hit. I remember going to see what damage had been done and as a souvenir saved a small carved wooden leaf, probably from a damaged choir stall. At least on the basis of these experiences I could say quite truthfully that I had not wholly avoided the war.

I clearly remember the flying bombs fall; in fact I used to look out of my window and see them dropping. You could tell when they were going to fall because their engine would suddenly cut out and their noise would stop. Harrow being on a steep hill was an ideal place from which to see

153

them fall over a wide area of London — but it was not without its dangers. Perhaps Eton, being further away from central London, did not have the same hazards to face.

Once, at the end of term, I returned to London on the underground with my friend Eric Lubbock (the future Liberal MP after a spectacular by-election at Orpington) and we called at his parents' house in Lowndes Square. I was most impressed with how big the house was and also by the person who opened the front door whom I took to be the butler. In fact it was Lubbock's father suitably dressed to go to the City. Eric told me he was recording some jazz on glass discs, the like of which I had never seen before. Why I should have been so impressed by the Lubbock family house I am not sure as it was certainly no bigger than ours, but perhaps I had acquired my mother's self-deprecating modesty. I suppose, also, that one takes what one has for granted, whereas what others have comes as a surprise; perhaps I had even acquired from my father a tendency to be too easily impressed.

When Shirley returned from the United States in October 1943 she was keen not to go to a boarding school, but to stay at home in central London and attend a day school from there. St Paul's Girls School was selected. It was already becoming clear that Shirley, because she had always identified with the hopes and ambitions of our parents from the beginning, would eventually go into politics.

In my last year at Harrow I got a room of my own in the so-called 'new' wing of the Headmaster's House. It had a wonderful outlook over the park behind the school houses and was almost like being in the country. Here I achieved a sense of peace similar to what I had experienced in the wooden shed in the garden of Glebe Place and in the basement of my guardian's house in St Paul, Minnesota.

By February 1944, the bombing of London had become so bad that my mother decided once more to close Cheyne Walk and to open up her cottage in the New Forest. Shirley had to give up St Paul's School and went to a day school in Bournemouth instead. The Headmaster of Harrow offered all parents the opportunity of taking their boys away, but I was successful in persuading mine to let me stay on.

At this time my mother was completing *Seeds of Chaos*, a booklet in which she covered the development of obliteration tactics as part of the Allied bombing offensive. By now the British Government apparently accepted my mother's right to express her pacifist views, although these views were far from popular. Maybe she was fortunate that the Home

Secretary was Herbert Morrison who had been a conscientious objector in the First World War. Before making the move to Allum Green, my parents stayed for a few weeks with friends in a modern block of flats in Park Lane. One evening Herbert Morrison was a guest at dinner. My mother was apprehensive about seeing him, but Morrison was quite able to deal with the situation, making it clear that in his view my mother could say what she liked because anyway it would have no influence on what actually happened. Equally, if not more, important than my mother's conversation was Shirley's first meeting on the same occasion with Herbert Morrison. She went to see him in the House of Commons shortly afterwards. Her political career started then, when she was fourteen, even if this only meant sticking stamps on envelopes. Within slightly more than a year there was a General Election in which there was a massive swing to Labour. Shirley had been lucky in her timing. She had also been shrewd and practical enough to see that making a favourable impression on Herbert Morrison would make a good beginning. So it proved to be.

If *Seeds of Chaos* was not taken too seriously in Britain the extracts from it which were printed in a supplement to the magazine *Fellowship*, put out by the Fellowship of Reconciliation of New York, caused a sensation (it was re-titled *Massacre by Bombings* in the United States). Official reaction was extremely unfavourable. President Roosevelt's secretary issued a stinging rebuke, although my mother was not mentioned by name. The American press took this lead to suggest that my mother must be inspired by the Nazis. So, at the very time that criticism of my mother levelled off in Britain, it began in the United States. As a result the sale of her books there fell off significantly.

My father was working towards being selected as Labour Party candidate for the St Helen's constituency in Liverpool, a safe Labour seat. He was duly selected in the first instance, but it was then decided that the Labour candidate should be Hartley Shawcross because, as subsequently became clear, Attlee wanted him to be Attorney-General in the event of Labour winning the election. It is interesting to reflect why Shawcross was not presented with an alternative safe constituency. I suspect that Attlee did not support my father's candidacy not least because he regarded my parents as adherents of Herbert Morrison.

Not being selected to stand at St Helen's, my father turned his attention to the proposed international conference in San Francisco which had been provided for by the agreement reached at Yalta. My father arranged to go to San Francisco on behalf of Indian papers and for the English news magazine, *Cavalcade*. He left England in the middle of April 1945. In making his decision, my father had formed the view, on the basis of discussing the matter, as usual, with numerous friends and colleagues in the Labour Party, that there would not be an election until the autumn and that he would in fact have time to find another constituency which he might win. In fact Churchill resigned on May 23, scarcely a month after my father had gone to the United States.

How serious was my father about getting elected to Parliament? I think there are two answers. Firstly, he had many interests in the political field, both in practical politics and in its more academic aspects, quite apart from the possibility of being a Member of Parliament. His going to San Francisco was on a par with his visits before the war to Germany, Russia and Spain. Although the idea of being a Member of the House of Commons appealed he was by temperament and range of interests a more suitable candidate for the House of Lords. Despite his grasp of political issues, historical and current, my father did not have an instinctive feel for how to go about the struggle for power, an instinct which can guide highly educated politicians like Bismarck or uneducated ones like Hitler. If he had possessed a greater grasp of the necessary techniques he might have depended less on the advice and guidance of others and more on his knowledge of human nature. But this, I would say, was not particularly well developed. If my father was naïve, I think it also true that he lacked the unwavering determination of the less brilliant and the less imaginative. He had many intellectual qualities which my mother did not possess, but he lacked her perseverance and concentration on one objective at the time. I believe Shirley acquired from my mother this practical ability to put things in an order of priority and to this she added a similar determination applied to the fighting of elections. Although brought up in a politically-orientated household I think Shirley learnt more in six months from Herbert Morrison than she ever learnt at home. By contrast, my father was so dependent on what others thought he did not develop his own undoubted powers of intuition. Nor did he develop the ability to decide quickly what, at any particular juncture, was the right course of action. Being by nature too cautious to be wholly practical, he did not seize the many opportunities that experience offers for acting on one's own intuition. I have said my parents loved discussion for its own sake and this became an end in itself, particularly in the case of my father. My mother, it is true, liked discussion in order to clarify her own thoughts, particularly on political matters in which, however, she had no personal involvement. Throughout her life, although considerably influenced by those whose example was important to her, I do not think she was influenced by discussion except on points of detail. My father, however, allowed himself to be talked out of those decisions at which he had arrived by himself, but which he held more tentatively than did my mother. He was, in any case, too much influenced by my mother who could afford to hold unpopular beliefs; she was not aiming to secure election in a democracy. By the promotion of unpopular beliefs she succeeded in getting her name well-known; and, in any case, what is unpopular today, pacifism for example, may be popular tomorrow. But, for a prospective politician, what is not popular today will certainly not get you elected today.

Shirley fought three elections before she got into Parliament, but the three elections she fought were over a ten-year period and even at the end of this time she was still only thirty-four. By the time of the election in July, 1945 my father was nearly fifty.

While my father was sailing across the Atlantic, the death of President Roosevelt was announced — on Friday, April 13. Within three weeks, not only Roosevelt but Hitler and Mussolini were dead. Within six weeks of the President's death, Parliament in Britain was dissolved. For someone with parliamentary ambitions this was clearly no time to be abroad.

To my mother VE Day, in May 1945, was significant personally because she experienced if not a religious conversion certainly a religious conviction that was new to her: that the sorrow and suffering of the world were the result of men refusing to obey God's laws, and that the way of suffering, as opposed to the way of self-interest, was the only means to raise men up from the edge of the abyss. Perhaps this experience was my mother's response to her personal humiliation first in Britain and second in the United States as a result of her pacifist beliefs and the actions she had taken in support of them. In undergoing this conversion, my mother now accepted the suffering she had experienced during her life as a necessary means of salvation, as opposed to her previous rebellion against what she had regarded as completely pointless grief and sacrifice. From the most pragmatic point of view, and quite apart from the concept of religious conversion, if you regard suffering as a means to a good end it is likely to be so, whereas if you regard it as pointless you gain nothing from the experience and so will not be able to turn a negative experience into a positive one.

The end of the war found my mother with an overwhelming feeling of inertia. Undoubtedly her continuous campaign as a pacifist in the various forms it took — the books she published during the war, the campaign for greater famine relief, and the reduction in obliteration bombing — left her in a vacuum. Although always strong and energetic in the face of opposition, she had temporarily exhausted her inner resources and was in need of a rest. One of the signs of this exhaustion was her lack of interest in the General Election in which Shirley for the first time took a hard-working if minor part. My mother had now to believe that personal salvation was a more worthwhile quest than any political victory and that in any case no political party, however well-intentioned, would ever produce the millennium.

CHAPTER X

JOHN AND SHIRLEY

IN September 1945 I started at the school of the Architectural Association in Bedford Square, an area already well-known to me because of its nearness to the Tottenham Court Road — and to Foyles. The first months I found extremely difficult for, apart from the sketching that was required and of which I had experience, the work involved a great deal of detailed drawing, for which I had no training. A considerable amount of mathematics was also involved, and although I had got a Credit in my School Certificate exam for maths, this was more by luck than because of any real proficiency. My previous educational experience had been almost entirely in the use of words and I could always express myself quickly on paper. Detailed drawing was another matter. It used a totally fresh part of my mind and I found the work excruciating, monotonous and dull. I have never had to work such long hours with so little to show for it. The chief benefit I derived from my first term was that I became a friend of the Leverhulme scholar of my year, John Godwin. With him I went on many happy bicycle rides at weekends and in the holidays. His father was himself an architect and so John was prepared for the kind of work which a first-year student had to endure, in a way which I was emphatically not.

So, when my call-up came at the end of my first term towards the end of 1945, conscription still being in force, I was only too happy to give up my studies, and in the following January I found myself in the RAF. My mother never put any objections in my way. My one ambition was to go abroad. To this end I did not apply for officer-training since, had I been successful, I would have had to spend many more months in England. By volunteering for overseas service and by remaining in the ranks I was able to get overseas on the completion of my basic training and within four months of my joining up.

By the time I reached Port Said in Egypt in May 1946 it was exactly

159

three years since I had returned to England from Minnesota. In retrospect I can see that it was in those three years that I was most at loggerheads with my family. I had not wanted to come back to England, for the positive reason that while in America I had been finding my feet and for the negative reason that I felt sure that my parents would want to take part in deciding my future. I was in a particularly vulnerable position because I had not in fact made up my mind exactly what it was I wanted to do. I was therefore open, if resistant, to every form of pressure and influence my parents might exert. Essentially, the explanation of the situation in which I found myself was quite simple: my parents really wanted me to continue on my return to England from the point where I had left when I had gone to America in 1940. But I was no longer twelve and I wanted to develop from the point I had reached in 1943.

I simplified this situation by claiming that I wanted to devote my time to painting, but this was an over-simplification. I had done very little painting in my last year in the United States, and I spent very little time doing so in my own time on my return to England. I did a lot of drawing, to good effect, at Harrow; but this was essentially a form of self-discipline rather than a creative activity. I was very much like a plant that had been removed to a favourable climate only to be pulled up again and put back in the less propitious soil in which it had originally been grown. I am sure that I appeared very negative to my parents in that I had a clearer idea of what I did not want to do. Unless one has a strong sense of vocation at an early age one is at the mercy of those who have a clearer picture of what one's vocation should be than one has oneself. Shirley was fortunate in that virtually from the date of her return from America she took to politics. It is true that this was not her sole interest. She also liked acting, which was to take up an increasing part of her time when she got to Oxford. (She was short-listed for the major role in the film of *National Velvet*, the part ultimately taken by Elizabeth Taylor.) Although she took to politics, that is not to say that Shirley agreed with everything my parents said or did, but at least she was on the same wave-length.

I made it clear that my intention was to return to America and, had it not been for conscription, I would undoubtedly have done so earlier than I ultimately did. By the time I did go back in 1948 the momentum which I had previously established had been lost. In the meantime I was in Egypt, a country which appealed to me because in my last months at school I had become fascinated by Lawrence of Arabia. I was to remain

Aircraftsman Catlin in the tradition of Aircraftsman Shaw. Like Winifred's friend Harry Pearson, and perhaps like Lawrence too, I was trying to get away from the establishment atmosphere in England and the persons of power and importance whom I met at home.

My posting was to a small embarkation unit in Port Said of less than thirty men, based on the docks. I do not recall there being more than four officers in all. By remaining with the rank of AC/2 (aircraftsman-under-training) I could not enter any club for officers in Egypt, although I might perhaps have done so in England, and my social life was distinctly limited. I got on well enough with my other-rank compères but basically there was no one to talk to, and I doubt whether I would have found any of the officers particularly stimulating either: they had flown during the Desert War and were now waiting to be posted back to England as a preliminary to being demobbed.

I cannot say I have ever felt the need for continuous 'profound' conversation, but the talk of those without any formal education tends to become somewhat limited not to say repetitive, on longer acquaintance. It was in this situation that I came across the local RAF Catholic Chaplain, Father Quigley, whom I met on his routine visit to our unit, one of the many he made in the geographical area covered by Middle East Command. I prolonged our meetings and their frequency in order to have someone to talk to and someone from whom I could borrow books. The Chaplain was an intelligent, well-informed and amusing Irishman and we at once got on well together.

Taking a course of religious instruction was one of the very few ways in which I could legitimately take time off from my unit, even if only for a couple of hours at a time. So it came about that I began to be instructed in the Roman Catholic faith. As I have said, Fr Quigley was able to get me books to read and I see from the notebooks I kept at the time that he provided a number which had no relevance to Catholicism in particular or indeed to religion in general. In addition to reading G. K. Chesterton's *Francis of Assisi* and Helen Waddell's *Peter Abelard* and two books entitled *Our Faith* by Bishop Shine and Bernard Kelly, I also read R. B. Cattel's *Psychology and the Religious Quest*, *The Way of All Flesh* by Samuel Butler, and Freud's *Totem and Taboo* from which I quoted into my notebook: 'The unconscious mental activity which is made up of repressed infantile material forever tries to express itself'. This was not in fact the first of Freud's books I had read. While still at Harrow I had got hold of a copy of *The Ego and the Id*. All that I can remember about it is

161

that I lent it to a boy in my house, who took it home for the holidays. His father, who was a general practitioner, telephoned to ask me if I had really read it and didn't I think I was too young? He was much taken aback, judging the book quite unsuitable for his son who was aged about sixteen.

I could not read books in my embarkation unit office partly because it was so small that anyone passing through would have seen that I was not attending to my duties (which were hardly onerous) and also because it gave on to the commanding officer's room. I had plenty of time, however, for writing poems and essays which, as I had learned to type in America, I could copy out on the office typewriter. I had the sole use of it because, although I only held the rank of the lowest form of life, I acted as assistant adjutant and in this capacity completed the numerous forms, with the required number of copies, which had to be filled in weekly, monthly or quarterly. Though my opportunity for conversation of a stimulating kind was limited I could at least express myself in writing.

In Port Said I reached the height of my adolescent idealism which culminated in what I would now call my first Catholic phase. But I had not entirely turned to religion or even psychology. I was still under the spell of de Chirico's paintings. I noted down the findings of a fortune-teller whom I consulted in June 1946, when I was sitting drinking coffee at a café. I remember the occasion well. Someone came up to me in a rather bedraggled Arab costume. At first I took him to be a beggar, but he spoke to me in reasonably good English and said that if I crossed his palm with silver he would tell my fortune. I has occurred to me since that if I had crossed his palm with more silver his predictions might have been more encouraging. He looked first to the past. He told me that the summer would be the end of an eight-year cycle; that I would be making a change from my former occupation; that in school I had been obstinate and lazy. Looking to the future he said that I should obey my parents' will; that something important would be happening that summer as a result of which I would be going home; that I should keep my secret thoughts to myself; that one girl thought about me but there would be no hasty marriage: and that I would not live to a great age. Against all these points I eventually made my own entries, but not for another four months. The following October, I noted that as far as the eight-year cycle was concerned I had gone to New York in October 1938 — eight years before — as the start of my extensive travels abroad. I was certainly to change my occupation, not for the first time, and in fact I returned home far sooner than I had expected at the time of the hand-reading. I had to agree that I was obstinate and, although less willing to admit it, lazy too. As far as obeying my parents' will was concerned, if the soothsayer meant that I would be doing what my parents wanted then he proved to be right however unlikely this seemed at the time. Other prognostications were to prove equally accurate.

In June, after I had been in Port Said for a month or so, I heard from my father that Lord Stansgate, the Secretary of State for Air, was coming to Egypt and that he would be at the Antoniades Palace outside Alexandria. As Stansgate was a long-time friend of my father's, he suggested I write a suitably respectful letter asking if I might call on him while he was in Egypt. I ended my letter: 'I have the honour to be, my Lord, your respectful servant, J. Brittain-Catlin (AC/2).' In due course I got an invitation to appear for dinner at the Antoniades Palace and permission from my astounded commanding officer to go to Alexandria. I went by train which, although the distance from Port Said is only about a hundred miles as the crow flies, involves a long roundabout journey. I was met at the station by a chauffeur and I insisted on being saluted by him, although in rank we were of the same low standing. The thought of myself as Aircraftsman being chauffeur-driven to meet the Secretary of State was not lost on me and I think I was more interested in being saluted so as to extract the maximum entertainment from my visit than from any desire to tyrannise over the driver.

I was only away for one night. Nevertheless, it did not take me long to discover on my return that my rank of AC/2 was regarded as cover, and that I was thought to be some eager-beaver representative of the powers that be; maybe my job was to investigate the large-scale pilfering on the docks.

The most unfortunate repercussion of my dinner at the Antoniades Palace, however, was that I had been tempted to eat the fruit and vegetables which in Port Said we did not have and against which we had been rightly warned as being the cause of the dreaded and debilitating 'Gypo Tummy' or dysentery. Our diet was spartan but, if you could see the weevils baked into the bread, at least you knew that they were well and truly baked. I rapidly lost weight and within a few weeks of my return from Alexandria I had to go to Ismailia for a check-up.

In the meantime I had heard again from my father, that he would shortly be in Rome on his way to India to which, as I later found out, he had been invited by the President of the Indian Congress in view of imminent Indian independence. He suggested that I apply for leave and join him in Rome. To obtain leave outside one's Command, I was told, was virtually impossible, although it could occasionally be obtained on compassionate grounds. I made my application and to my surprise it was granted. I boarded the next troopship to Sicily and proceeded on to Rome by train.

It was little more than a year after the end of the war in Europe, but we were able to eat in some very good restaurants, known to my father's friends, Princess Beatrice Pignatelli, and Contessa Simonetta di Visconti, who was only a few years older than I. She shocked me by giving the steak off her plate to her dog; of course it might have been horsemeat. My father and I were also invited to dinner at the residence of the American Chargé d'Affaires, David Key, who lived in a castle in the Alban Hills and from which I could see in the middle distance the lights winking in the Pope's summer residence at Gandolfo. It was at this dinner that, for the first time in my life, I was waited on by servants in white gloves.

My father had to leave Rome the day before I was due to return to Port Said and on my last day I decided to revisit, on my own, the basement restaurant where we had had our most notable meal. I told the proprietor exactly how much money I had left, which was in fact very little, and that I would like the best meal he could provide for this sum. The proprietor spoke English well himself so I assumed he understood what I meant, and, moreover, that I meant what I said. I got a marvellous meal and some superb dry white wine. He then presented me with a bill for a sum about three or four times what I had in my pocket. I explained the position, and the propietor to my surprise accepted what I told him. Whether he did not want to antagonise my father's Roman aristocratic friends or whether he planned to recover the balance from them I cannot say and in any case I was probably too drunk to care. The restaurant was down a steepish staircase and I now had to climb up it. My RAF regulation boots with thick heels did not help. My dignity was preserved, but only just.

When I got back to Port Said I discovered that my new-found friend Fr Quigley, had been posted to Greece. My instruction in the Catholic faith, therefore, came to an abrupt end. No more conversation and no more books. I decided, reluctantly, that to counter the boredom of Port Said, where I had now been for very nearly six months, I would apply for a commission and so undergo officer-training. This would at least provide some novelty. The first step was to have a complete medical examination, including an X-ray. As I have said I had lost quite a lot of weight as a result of my indulgence in the forbidden fruits of Alexandria although I had got over my dysentery before going to Rome. I was told that the X-ray examination showed I had a spot on my lung, which meant that I must have tuberculosis, and I was immediately admitted to the 19th General Hospital in Ismailia.

When I arrived there it was October. Before the end of the year I travelled by train to Haifa, in what was then Palestine, and then by ambulance to Jerusalem, where there was a much larger hospital. Travel by ambulance had become dangerous because the terrorists claimed the British were using them to transport arms and ammunition (I later learnt that an ambulance following the same route the day before my journey had been blown up).

The hospital in which I now found myself was just outside Jerusalem on the Mount of Olives and from my bed I had a marvellous view towards the Dead Sea. At night the landscape, which reminded me of Holman Hunt's painting *The Prodigal*, was occasionally seared by the white light of tracer bullets.

My most memorable experience indeed was when, on one occasion, I achieved what can only be described as a heightened sense of reality while looking towards the Dead Sea as the sun was setting; I am quite unable to explain the immediate cause, but it was akin to the hero Larry's experience in Somerset Maugham's *The Razor's Edge*, which I had read before I went to Palestine.

Both in Egypt and in Palestine, the morale was very high in the hospitals even when one knew that someone was dying. When we got back to England this atmosphere totally disappeared. First of all I was at the RAF Hospital at Barry in South Wales, and then at the Edward VII Sanatorium near Godalming in Surrey. The arrival of the patients' relations caused the change. It was inevitable that we should all be thinking about home. Our joint lives in the Air Force were to all intents and purposes over. The appearance of relations gave to each man a social class which had not existed before. The awareness of these social differences soon broke down the goodwill that had existed before and destroyed solidarity.

In March 1947 my father made a second visit to India. He saw Gandhi three times, once when the Mahatma was having his bath. My father also had discussions with Lord Mountbatten and advised him that

165

Gandhi would be amenable to the British plans if he, Mountbatten, were to listen to what Gandhi had to say, which really meant enduring his life story. My father said that Gandhi was essentially pro-British and would go along with what the Viceroy had in mind. My father went on to China but, on his return, stayed with Mountbatten, who told him: 'Well, I took your advice. It was quite true that we had to listen to the whole of his life story, but in the end we got the agreement we wanted.' My father was particularly pleased that Mountbatten had given him credit for his suggestion. Nothing did he enjoy more than the sensation that he was at the centre of great affairs, and that he was advising those who wielded great power. He admired Mountbatten rather as he had previously admired President Roosevelt: both were prepared to listen to him.

By the time I got back to Cheyne Walk in the summer of 1947 it was clear to me that I would have to make a definite decision about what to do next. I had already decided while I was in the RAF that I would not be returning to the architectural school. I was still writing a lot of poetry but had put my painting aside for the time being. My interest in psychology had been revived and I had begun to take an interest in philosophy too.

After much discussion with my parents it was agreed that I would sit for the entrance exam to Oxford. Once this was decided, and in view of my having got an honourable discharge from the RAF, I was able to get permission to take sufficient money out of the country for a six-week holiday in Switzerland. My mother came with me. She spent the mornings working and I read the required books for my entrance exam. The small hotel where we stayed in Wilderswil, just below the Jungfrau, was extremely comfortable and the food was marvellous, but owing to the high altitude I never felt really hungry. What with having no appetite and spending most of my time in academic reading, I began to cordially dislike Wilderswil. I also felt exasperated by my mother, whose idea it had been to go to Switzerland, and on one occasion I tried to push her down a hill.

I was now told that even if I passed my entrance exam I would not be able to go up to Oxford for another year. After a couple of months — doing very little on our return from Switzerland I went back to Foyles. I had two decisions to make: what was I going to read? and for which college should I put my name down? I discovered that there was a Psychology School at Oxford, of comparatively recent origin, and that with Psychology one could either study physiology and then read medicine before, in due course, becoming a psychiatrist or one could read

166

philosophy. I also found out that the Psychology School only took twelve undergraduates a year so that there was a very good chance that I might not be accepted at all.

As far as which college to apply for was concerned I was interviewed by Warden Smith of New College. I then put my name down for Balliol, chiefly I think because my father seemed to have been impressed by Benjamin Jowett, who had been Master there. I explained this to my father but I could see that he was very disturbed that I had not done the right thing. In view of the fact that my father had never received any recognition from Oxford in general or from New College in particular, I could not see why he was so upset. Perhaps, eternal optimist that he was, he thought my choice of college would prejudice his chances of being favourably considered there.

My mother had started work on her book *In the Steps of John Bunyan*, with whom she identified herself. She felt that both she and Bunyan were conscientious objectors to orthodoxy and oppression; perhaps at the time she included me among the oppressors rather than the oppressed. In October 1947, much to my surprise, I got a place in the Psychology School, subject to my reading Philosophy, Politics and Economics for my first year. I was also accepted by New College.

My father thought I should continue my instruction in Catholicism. Although my mother was certainly not a Catholic, she was not opposed to the faith, perhaps because Roland Leighton had in fact been received into the Catholic Church some months before he died. My parents, when they married at the Catholic Church of St James's, Spanish Place, must both have vowed to bring up any children of the marriage in the faith, but oddly enough neither Shirley nor I had been baptised.

In *Testament of Youth*, my mother wrote that my father had assured her, when he proposed marriage, that 'he offered as free a marriage as any man could propose'. She then went on to quote from a letter: 'I ask you to give what you want to give, no more.' These were very generous terms and my mother never forgot them. Whatever she may have said or agreed to say when she did marry my father, my mother always took the view that as soon as Shirley and I were old enough to do so we must make up our own minds about everything, including religion. In taking this view did my mother appreciate that a child is not brought up in a vacuum, and that it will respond to and inevitably be influenced by the environment in which it finds itself and the people by whom it first knows? The child's outlook on life will largely be determined by these factors which will have begun to be influential long before the child has even become conscious of them. Although Shirley appeared to fit into the pattern established by my parents and I rebelled against them, we both abosrbed our home environment and acted in accordance with it. In due course Shirley became a Catholic and took to Labour Party politics. I reacted against my parents but ended up leaving the United States, going to Harrow and Oxford, and becoming a Catholic, all of which would once have seemed extremely unlikely if not inconceivable.

I cannot remember when I became aware that my father was a Catholic and my mother was not. My mother was deeply aware of moral issues and was moved by a moral imperative in nearly all aspects of life. Perhaps my mother was too sceptical by nature to believe in divine revelation and for at least thirty years after the First World War she doubted, even denied, the very existence of God. Not until the very end of the Second War did she experience a kind of personal revelation that suffering and grief, both her own and that of others, were to some purpose.

My earliest awareness of religion was when, at the age of four or five, I found a small chest of drawers, significantly placed next to my bed, a large crucifix, a rosary, one or two religious books, a black beret and a gown not unlike those worn by a commoner at Oxford or Cambridge on a ceremonial occasion or when dining in college. These may have belonged to my grandfather Catlin who moved, theologically speaking, in ever higher circles of religious belief during the course of his life: starting as a non-conformist minister and eventually becoming a minister in the Church of England. Or they may have belonged to my father. I used to look into this drawer as something of a secret rite and I do not think I ever mentioned the contents to anyone. I may have told Shirley, but certainly I did not talk about them to any grown-up.

In due course, my father began to look to my sister to realise his political ambitions and to me to realise his very real but unfulfilled ambition in the Church of Rome. He sugared the pill of persuasion by saying that I might well become a bishop by the time I was forty-five. Apart from the fact that, at the age of nineteen, forty-five seemed immensely old, I had no more wish to become a bishop than I had to become a cabinet minister. My father credited me with his own worldly ambitions, and he was certainly determined to set me on a course of which he would be proud even if it had no appeal to me. However, I agreed to continue my religious instruction, which had come to an abrupt conclusion a year before, and he arranged for me to see Fr James Bevan at the Brompton Oratory.

Fr Bevan used to receive me in his rather gloomy study and always insisted on my sitting in an armchair while he sat on a hard-backed chair. As he was very tall, thin and tubercular-looking (by this time I had achieved an almost professional capacity to recognise the symptoms) he must have found the chair particularly comfortable. Perhaps to him it was a modern version of the hair shirt. On more than one occasion I tried, without success, to get him to move to the armchair, not least because in its depths I was both more relaxed and more vulnerable to suggestion. I would be able to exert more control over the situation by sitting on the hard chair which provided in every sense a more elevated level from which to conduct our interviews.

I decided to try and score a more subtle point. Fr Bevan was an inveterate smoker. Although I did not smoke myself I bought a packet of cigarettes in order to be able to offer him one. Some of these I put in the gold cigarette case which I had bought for about £25 from the pay which I had been able to save up in the RAF as a result of being in hospital. Addicted smoker that he was, Fr Bevan could not resist the offer of a cigarette but I did not fail to see that, in taking one out of the proffered case, he had the look of one who had fallen for the blandishments of the devil.

Fr Bevan was otherwise an extremely austere man and I am sure a good one. However, he lacked the human touch and I could not strike up the same rapport with him as I had with Fr Quigley, who disguised the fact that he was a man of some considerable learning under his Irish bonhomie. I expect Fr Bevan found me tiresome because I preferred to raise difficult points over tenets of belief rather than accept them as a matter of faith, but I enjoyed the occasional philosophical argument. In due course I felt it was unfair of me to dispute endlessly with him and after some months I abandoned the exercise. I professed faith in the Church and I was baptised. I did not see Fr Bevan again. I was not wrong, however, about his health. He died of tuberculosis in 1958.

My father gave much thought to the choice of my godfather and produced a short list of two: the Archduke Robert of Austria and Sir Francis Rose, baronet and artist. In 1947 the stock of the House of Hapsburg was not high, but I nevertheless thought it would be pretentious of me to choose the Archduke. At this time he was in his early thirties. Immensely tall and thin, and with the family's prominent lower jaw, he was always very amiable. I later found out that he had established good relations with Winston Churchill and had talked to him about the possible formation of a free Austria after the war. However, I believe Anthony Eden was against the idea of the restoration of the Hapsburgs because it would undoubtedly not have been popular in Czechoslovakia and Hungary who had no love for the Austro-Hungarian Empire. The Archduke Robert always appeared imperturbable; and he was a man of great courtesy even though his position must have been a difficult one. I maintained a good if not close relationship with him and met him about fifteen years later, in Paris, in quite different circumstances. He did not seem to mind that he had not been made my godfather.

In deciding in favour of Sir Francis Rose I undoubtedly made what was to prove a less worldly choice. Francis himself was thrilled since to him it was an event of real importance. Although he was only six years older than the Archduke, who had been born in 1915, he seemed considerably more. I felt that my godfather must be of a fatherly appearance. To me Francis appeared truly middle-aged although he was less than twenty years older than I.

Francis liked telling stories in which it was hard to distinguish between fact and imagination, or perhaps wishful thinking. He had had considerable expectations in the years up to the Wall Street crash of 1929, when, so he told me, the family fortunes had been embezzled by the distinguished stockbroker who had been one of his trustees, Francis's father having died when he was only six. His trustee was no doubt making a sincere if desperate bid to avoid disaster for himself, quite apart from his clients. When he failed he took the only step open to him and jumped to his death from a window of his office on Wall Street.

Francis was the grandson of the man who had built the Canadian Pacific Railway. One of his many regrets was that, although his grandfather had apparently given Edward VII the gates to Sandringham, the monarch had died on the day he was to sign the documents that would have created the entrepreneurial Rose an earl. Francis therefore had to bear the cross of being a penniless baronet rather than a penniless earl. In fact he was not completely indigent, but until the loss of his fortune he had owned houses in London, Scotland and the south of France and enough cash to lead a thoroughly self-indulgent life. He never got used to making ends meet and quite often they did not, or so it appeared to me. Nevertheless he had a perfectly presentable flat in Flood Street and a studio nearby. He was the kind of person who, even if he had not lost his

170

capital, would still have brooded over the fact that he ought to have been an earl. As it was he had more pressing problems on his mind.

In the period immediately after the war when the excitement was over and 'reconstruction', let alone inflation, had not begun, there were many who looked on life as Francis did. For them the great days were always in the past — whether those days had been in the war itself or before the war. In comparing my prospective godfathers it must be said that the Archduke Robert, who lost an inheritance much greater than that ever dreamed of by Francis Rose, had a dignity, modesty, and lack of self-pity which Francis regrettably did not possess. The Archduke clearly did not live in the past. Francis lacked the character to live in the present, and perhaps he is best summed up in one of his own stories which, to his credit, he told against himself. He had prevailed on Queen Mary to visit his studio in Cheyne Row. Francis did not keep this newsworthy item to himself and so, when the appointed day arrived, unknown to him, some of his confidantes were waiting in the room above the studio with pails of water. Queen Mary duly arrived, and Francis displayed his paintings. Suddenly water began dripping from the ceiling: first a few drops only, then an increasing flood. One may assume that the Royal Personage was not amused, and after all the anxious planning Francis did not even have the opportunity to give one of his pictures away.

Christina Foyle had plans to extend her bookshop so I did not spend more than a month or two with my old friends, the second-hand novels. I suggested the idea that we promote the sale of second-hand or 'rare' books to the United States. I spent several months setting this up and became so enthusiastic about the prospects that I felt I ought to go over to New York myself. In any case I had long wanted to get back to the United States.

My first step was to go and work in the bookshop of the Macmillan Company in New York. My pay was very modest, but fortunately in the bookshop I met Ellen O'Donnell, who was working there, and she took me to meet Mrs Van Rensaeler Wyatt. Mrs Wyatt was a very grand lady, as she pointed out to me, because one of the New York telephone exchanges, Van Rensaeler, was named after her family. When she got to know me better she also told me that her husband had come unstuck in the 1929 crash and had committed suicide. Mrs Wyatt took on respectable lodgers to live in her tall and narrow early nineteenth-century house and, as she had a high regard for Ellen O'Donnell's judgment, I was included on the basis of a small weekly rental. I soon discovered that my new friend from the Macmillan bookshop was one of the most extrovert people I had ever met or was likely to meet, and she had a wider range of acquaintance even than my parents. Much later she told me that her father had been in charge of the Port of New York, one of the great sinecures in the days when it was run by a Catholic-Democratic political combine. Without knowing anything about her background, I appointed her as my godmother, although she was only four years older.

From the Macmillan bookshop I moved to reading manuscripts, mostly historical novels, but I did not enjoy this nearly so much as the shop because I felt unable to express any critical judgment or make any practical assessment of the books. I was quite unable to evaluate what demand, if any, there might be for them.

I had come over to the United States with my father and I saw him from time to time. On one occasion we went to stay with the Duchesse de Talleyrand, whose father had been Jay Gould, the railway financier. The name of the house, or mansion, was 'Lyndhurst', which made a great impression on my father, since my mother's cottage in the New Forest was near the village in Hampshire called Lyndhurst. This was also the second time I had seen the waiters, or perhaps more correctly footmen, wearing white gloves when waiting at table. I had not realised before the dinner started that there would be so many courses and also that a different wine would be served with each. I found that I was in a race against time, not so much as far as the food was concerned, because the helpings were small, but I had scarcely got started on one glass of wine before another one was filled. I felt that I must finish them all. There could not have been more than six or eight people at table, but it seemed exceptionaly crowded because of the cutlery for each of the courses and all the wine glasses. My father was in his element.

We also stayed with Mrs Roosevelt at Hyde Park; three years after the President's death, she still lived in considerable style, but it was style of a restrained variety. When we arrived, Mrs Roosevelt opened the front door herself. To my considerable amazement she was wearing a bathing dress.

I returned to England and continued working for Foyles, but I soon realised that there was no future in the firm for outsiders. Nevertheless I had identified an important area for future development in the second-hand book trade.

As soon as the war was over my mother was able to resume her travels. In September 1945 she made a ten-day visit to Holland. This was quicky followed by a six-week tour under the auspices of the Save Europe Now and Women's International League for Peace and Freedom organisations, to Denmark, Norway and Sweden.

By 1946 my mother was once more able to give a lecture tour in the United States and she went there under the auspices of the Quaker Friends in support of their food conservation programme. In August she attended the annual meeting of the Women's International League in Luxembourg. She had discontinued her *Letters to Peace Lovers*, since the emphasis of what she had begun to do, once peace was achieved, was on reconciliation and reconstruction. On her return from the United States, she was soon off to Germany; she discussed her proposed visit with the Foreign Office who advised her on the text of the three lectures she proposed to give on her extensive tour: travelling from Hamburg to Kiel, and on to Hanover and Cologne which she had previously visited in 1924 and 1936. Then she visited the Ruhr, Münster and Berlin. She was now viewed with official favour.

At the end of 1947 Shirley was able to leave St Paul's Girls School because she had got an open History Scholarship to Somerville College, Oxford, although she was only seventeen at the time. In discussing the state of the world with the Principal of the College, Dr Janet Vaughan, Shirley had undoubtedly been able to make clear that she knew a great deal about what was happening politically and no doubt the Principal saw a glittering future for her.

Shirley spent the best part of the year after leaving school in various jobs that gave her a width of experience and enabled her to say, once she made her start in politics, that she had earned her own living. First of all she went to work on the community farm in Frating, Essex, which was run by J. H. Watson, who, shortly after Shirley's arrival, became part-time political agent for the Labour Party in Harwich. While Morris Janis was the Labour candidate there Shirley worked for him and then, when he moved to another constituency, she took his place. In due course, at the age of twenty-two, she was elected as Labour candidate for Harwich the year after she came down from Oxford. Shirley did not spend the whole of 1948 working on a farm. She also attended a Labour League of Youth conference in Bavaria. Then, to widen her experience further, she had six weeks as a housemaid in a hotel near Newcastle-upon-Tyne. Finally, before

173

going up to Oxford, she worked at the Cherry Blossom shoe-polish factory in Chiswick.

When she was still living at home, Shirley used to go in and out of our house in Cheyne Walk by the basement entrance. She gave the impression to those who did not know her well that the housekeeper and her husband were her parents. No doubt she had acquired her democratic ideas, as had I, from three years in the United States. Whether she felt guilty about our parents appearing well-off and living in an impressive house, or whether she regarded the basement entrance to our house as the door into the Labour Party I am not quite certain. I am not saying that she was either priggish or doctrinaire. Her great characteristics then and later were her enormous energy and vitality and her generally optimistic outlook. I was more priggish than she. We had been exceptionally close in the years between 1930 and 1942, but after that it was not just different interests that engrossed us but the literal fact that we were scarcely ever together; even when we happened to be at Oxford at the same time I doubt whether Shirley and I saw each other more than half a dozen times over the three years. Shirley followed in the direction indicated by our parents; I was totally uninvolved in English politics.

EPILOGUE

By the time Shirley and I went up to Oxford in the autumn term of 1948 the major work of both my parents was completed. It is true that my mother published books after this date, and of these *Testament of Experience*, the successor to *Testament of Youth* is the most important. However, it cannot be said that it achieved either the acclaim or the sales of its predecessor. *Testament of Experience* was first published in 1957 and is based largely on my mother's diaries for the years 1925 to 1950; but well before 1950 my mother had ceased to keep a diary in any detail.

My mother devoted an increasing amount of her time from 1947 onwards to corresponding with her admirers. These people, whether they admired her books, her feminism or her pacifism, were always important to her because her name was never so well known before her death in 1970 as it subsequently became after the television serialisation of *Testament of Youth*. Her books had perhaps been read by, say, 100,000, but the TV series , starring Cheryl Campbell and Jeremy Irons, was shown twice in Britain and throughout the English-speaking world. The fame which she achieved during her lifetime exceeded her expectations but she would have been both astounded and pleased by the reception which the serialisation of *Testament of Youth* achieved.

By 1948 my father had also made his main contribution to political science. It is true that after this date he continued to publish books, particularly on Anglo-American relations and unity, however this was not a new field of endeavour; it has been a major concern of his from the early 1920s when he first went to Cornell. After the war my father held academic posts in Canada, India and in the United States, but he did not really add to his reputation after 1948. He was ever-hopeful that he would go to the House of Lords but my father did not approach this objective in a realistic way. In due course he was knighted. Long before Shirley became a Member of Parliament in 1964 he had been compelled

175

to realise that, despite his experience and connections in Britain and the United States, he would never achieve eminence in the political world. As Shirley climbed the slopes of the political mountain, my father was on the way down. His reaction combined a complex mixture of admiration and jealousy. To a greater extent than my mother, he had been responsible, directly and indirectly, for Shirley's career. She had learnt from him and applied his own lessons more successfully.

Both my parents, then, had conscious ambitions which they were determined to fulfil, my mother with more and my father with less determination. But they also had less worldly values and interests which were an important part of their make-up although these were not and could not have been important to anyone except Shirley and myself. Shirley was influenced by their more obvious ambitions; I was influenced by the less obvious ones. Shirley and I have acquired important but different characteristics. She acquired the desire for success in a political career; for succeses in the Establishment world. I gained my mother's more rebellious approach along with my father's philosophical leanings, and the creative or cultural interests of both.

I believe that Shirley quantifies her success by the number of votes she gets in parliamentary elections and, more importantly, by her relative position in the inner circle of the party of which she is a member. She looks to the applause of the multitude and undoubtedly has always aimed to be among those holding the most important official positions in the country. I believe that Shirley would only regard herself as totally successful if she were to become Prime Minister. Paradoxically, I believe that I have succeeded to a greater extent than she in the sense that I have always been quite clear what I wanted to achieve; my objectives have been many, and for the most part I have achieved what I set out to do. But my success has not been dependent on what most other people thought of me and I do not greatly care for their evaluation of whether I have succeeded or not.

Both Shirley and I were converted to Catholicism. Shirley likes to see herself as a leading if not the leading Catholic laywoman in Britain. Her home in the country is not far from the retreat of the Archbishop of Westminster, and she enjoys being invited to an exchange of views with Cardinal Hume. When the Pope came to England and visited Canterbury, Shirley was in his retinue along with prominent Catholics, clerical and lay. It so happens that on the route to the cathedral my present wife, Barbara, who is Polish, was in the waiting crowd, and she called out a

Polish greeting to the Pope. He came over to where she was standing and replied in Polish; then he moved on and one of his Chaplains gave her a signed photograph. She told me that Shirley noticed what was going on and looked most disconcerted. Perhaps she was worried that Barbara would tell the Pope that she was Shirley's sister-in-law.

I cannot say that I expect to be received by the Cardinal Archbishop or by the Pope. I take the view that the Catholic Church in England sits on the fence on important political and social issues; at the same time it does not respresent a powerful spiritual force. The public image of the Pope is extremely strong but what he believes is wholly out of touch with the real problems of the capitalist world of the West. I realise that in Poland, which is virtually untouched by Western economic forces, the Pope was and remains a force for good, but he appears to have no message which extends to the corruptions of the capitalist world. The moral issues arising out of earning a living in a highly competitive society such as England are not a subject which I have ever heard raised or discussed from the pulpit.

The appeal to me of the Catholic Church is solely as a means of communication with God, but I often wonder whether the Church is as much concerned with bringing people to God as it is in getting more subscribing members. The Church should be more than an organisation for collecting money. If it cannot bring a spiritual message to its congregation which is relevant to the times in which we live it might as well cease to exist. Indeed, if it cannot take up as effective a stance as either Western capitalism, primarily making an appeal to greed, or to communism, primarily speaking to envy and fear, it must cease to exist. The Catholic Church is as self-interested an organisation as a political party or a trade union: self-preservation at all costs and never mind the real interests of the members.

Towards the end of my second year at Oxford I met Jennifer Manasseh who had arrived at Somerville from St Paul's Girls School. We married shortly after I took my degree in 1951. A major motivation for marriage was the need to distance myself from my parents. I looked forward to a degree of domesticity which I had never known, except in the years I was evacuated to America during the war, and which I no doubt idealised in my imagination. What I did not appreciate before I got married and indeed for many years afterwards was that, at the age of twenty-four, I was a quite unsuitable candidate for married life. I was totally un-prepared for and quite unwilling to face the major demand of marriage: to consider the interests of one's wife and of one's children. I reacted against the non-domestic character of my early life, but it is altogether too easy to imitate exactly what one's parents did — even though in childhood one has so detested their behaviour. To take a minor example: my mother spent virtually every morning of the week, when she was in London, at her typewriter. I came to regard her typewriter as my chief rival for her attention and indeed affection. I was more jealous of her typewriter than I ever was either of my sister or my father. But with time, and no doubt as a result of this very influence, I gradually became a compulsive typist myself.

I do not know enough about Shirley's private life to be able to say exactly why she divorced Bernard Williams, the Provost of King's Col-lege, Cambridge. But Shirley was undoubtedly subject to exactly the same highly self-centred orientation of both our parents as I am. I can think of no childhood less likely to produce a model of domesticity or of self-sacrifice in the interest of one's husband and children.

Shirley has few friends, as indeed she herself has said, and she tends to prefer those who not only agree with her but who also do what she wants. In making this comment about her I would be the first to agree that it equally applies to me. Here again the influence of my parents is para-mount. My mother was not dependent on having friends and my father was constantly adjuring us to 'cultivate' those who might be useful.

When I married I did not find the domestic bliss which I had sought and which had existed only in my imagination. Of course I blamed my wife for this. I rapidly came to the conclusion that, if I looked elsewhere, I might be able to find someone with whom I could not only establish a much more satisfying relationship but with whom I would be more able to realise all that I felt I had previously been missing. I do not think my first marriage was unsatisfactory just because I was either too young or too immature. I did not appreciate the importance of parents giving sufficient time to their chidren, showing them affection, even though I was by training a psychologist, until I became a magistrate in the Inner London Juvenile courts many years later. Only with this experience did I fully appreciate that a paramount cause of juvenile crime is parents' lack of interest in or affection for their children, irrespective of whether they come from well-off or deprived homes.

Of all Shirley's boy-friends I always liked Peter Parker the most.

Shirley got to know him when they were both at Oxford and then acting together in the United States. He was, and is, not only a man of considerable charm, but, much rarer, also of great humanity. My father never cared for him and indeed felt jealous of him as indeed he did of anyone of whom Shirley was fond. He certainly did not like Bernard Williams, not least I think because Bernard had been elected a Fellow of All Souls. It seems to me that Shirley has been particularly drawn to academic men: those who are lecturers or tutors or who have become professors.

When I met my second wife, Elaine Drakeford, she was undoubtedly the personification of my dreams and, due to her, I experienced a degree of personal happiness which I had not previously felt, except for very short periods, since the death of Winifred Holtby. With this greater happiness I also felt a new degree of personal ambition. At the age of twenty-nine she died of cancer, almost exactly ten years after I had first met her. After her death my ambitions evaporated and I had for the first time in my life to put the interests of others above my own since we had had two children. Larissa was eight when her mother died. My son, Alexander, had his fourth birthday about three weeks before her death.

I have often been asked whether I see Shirley frequently and whether we get on well or not. The answers to these questions are quite simple. When you have known someone for fifty years or more you do not have to see them all the time in order to understand their point of view or to know what they think. I see Shirley about once a year, not least because she is always busy and in any case our fields of interest are entirely different. Nevertheless, I find that we agree on most points of principle and our outlook is surprisingly similar. We have nearly always felt the same about most things.

Many of the people I meet immediately assume that I must feel jealous of Shirley. In this they project their own feelings on to me. I might be jealous of Shirley if I had pursued an unsuccessful career in politics. But I have never had political aspirations. I am very interested in political events both in Britain and elsewhere; and indeed as a management consultant working on the marketing side, I have to be in touch with what is going on both politically and economically. I set out to please myself and achieve my own ambitions; my aim has never been to please the electorate since I am not looking for votes. Even in my painting, which has been my most consistent occupation from the time I was at school, but in which I have achieved no success in the sense that I have not sold many

179

pictures, I have, within the last few years, obtained the results which I have been working towards all my life. The art dealer, Clovis Whitfield, asked me a few years ago whether I painted to please myself or other people. This was a more profoundly relevant question than I appreciated at the time, and I told him that I had always painted for myself. Indeed, I had never asked myself the question he asked me; subsequently I realised why my pictures did not sell. Again, more recently, Godfrey Pilkington, the proprietor of the Piccadilly Gallery, told me that if I wanted to sell my paintings I would have to change my style. I have not been willing to do this because the style I use is an essential part of my expressing what I have to say. In selling my services as a management consultant I am selling a service for which there is a certain demand at a certain fee, but to sell my services I am offering something for which there is a demand: this is not true of my painting.

What does Shirley think of me? I have the impression that she would prefer me to work in an organisation such as the BBC or, better still, the Treasury where I would have to be extremely careful about what I said about anyone or anything. The person who works for the State, particularly the increasingly totalitarian state in which we are now living, whether they are politicians or civil servants, is not free to express personal views except to a very limited extent. As someone who is self-employed I believe that I enjoy a degree of freedom which is not found in organisations run and financed by the State. As I have no political ambitions so I would lose nothing by making highly critical remarks about Shirley — had I any such comments to make.

On a superficial level Shirley and I are about as different as we could be, at least as far as our personal interests and habits are concerned. For as long as I can remember Shirley liked to stay up very late. I, on the other hand, have always preferred getting up early. I have gradually risen earlier and earlier so that it is rare for me now to stay in bed after six in the morning. On the other hand, I like to go to bed early. I would not have been a good Member of Parliament because I would have found it very difficult to stay up late night after night. Shirley has always been extremely untidy and she appears to be disorganised, although I think this disorganisation is more apparent than real and is due to her doing so many things at once. I have always been punctilious, not to say meticulous, and I like order in all things. I like to organise my time and to plan everything well in advance. I am obsessional like my mother while Shirley appears to be free of this characteristic. I think I am much more domesticated than she, perhaps because I have had five children. I like to do the shopping and to buy the food. I enjoy cooking although I am not a gourmet and prefer simple food.

I do not think Shirley has much imagination, any more than my mother had. Nor are the arts very important to her although she likes listening to music. Her musical tastes seem to be the same as my mother's: Elgar and Verdi. Like most English people (by contrast with the French, for example) Shirley is basically a philistine. It is extraordinary to me how many Secretaries of State for Education have so little appreciation of science and even less of the arts. The arts in England are totally cut off from the majority of the population. The arts are regarded as a form of escapism and, in the case of antiques and works of art, only as a form of financial investment.

Shirley's interests have always been confined to a far more limited sphere than mine. Apart from acting at Oxford I do not think she has any real interests other than politics. Perhaps that is a major reason for her success. Most of those who succeed tend to do so by continuous concentration on one field of activity.

Although painting has been my prime interest, I made original contributions in market research, particularly in attitude and motivational research during the formative days of the 1950s. This was a practical application of my studies at the Institute of Experimental Psychology at Oxford. As a market researcher and as a marketing man, and even more as a management consultant, I have had to deal with a wide variety of clients in virtually all types of industrial and consumer products and of consumer services both in this country and on the continent. I have already referred to my experience as a magistrate in the Juvenile Courts and I found this one of my most valuable experiences, not least because it involves learning to listen carefully without comment for considerable periods of time. The job demands the ability to make rapid decisions on the basis of an abundance of evidence, both verbal and written in the form of reports, and much of this material is contradictory. I acquired from my father a degree of detachment, and from him I also gained an interest in philosophical speculation.

That Shirley acquired all my mother's determination and ambition can be seen in the progress of her career. She contested three parliamentary seats; unsuccessfully in 1954 when she was only twenty-four, also in 1955 and in 1959. It was not until 1964, when she was thirty-three that she won Hitchin for Labour. She held this seat until 1974 after

181

which date she became Member for the Hertford and Stevenage Division until 1979. Within two years of her first election to Parliament she was appointed PPS to the Ministry of Health. Subsequently she became Minister of State in two Departments and then Secretary of State in two Departments; in 1979 she became Paymaster General.

Shirley's leaving Labour to be co-founder of the Social Democratic Party is proof of her high principles. As one of the senior members of the Parliamentary Labour Party she had everything to gain by remaining. Had she been dedicated to success at all costs she would, I think, have remained. Had she done so when her fellow founders of the SDP left she would have been by now that much nearer to the summit of the Labour Party.

On behalf of the SDP she won a spectacular by-election in the Crosby Division of Liverpool and she held this seat for two years. It is possible that the Liberals and SDP will become a big political battalion. They are not so as yet. Although she might not herself agree, I feel that Shirley would only regard her career as a success if she became Prime Minister. This is what she was brought up to be from the earliest possible age. Whether this ambition will have been thwarted by her leaving the Labour Party only time will tell. For her sake I hope she achieves the top of the greasy pole.

I have deliberately ended this book before my parents died. Anything after 1948 would be an anti-climax. Their triumphs and failures were in the past. Mine and Shirley's lay in the future.

INDEX

1914 57; gives up university for nursing 63, 65, 68–9; effect of Roland Leighton's death, 1915 70; friendship with brother Edward's friends 67, 68, 70, 71, 72, 94; posted to Malta, 1916 72–3; returns to England, 1917 73; posted to France 73–4; gives up nursing to look after parents 74; effect of brother Edward's death 74–5; returns to nursing 75; returns to Oxford, 1919 75, 76; graduates, 1921 79; visits Edward's and Roland's graves, 1921 79–80; settles in London with Winifred Holtby, 1922 80–1; teaches 81; becomes speaker for League of Nations 81, 82; meets famous writers 81–2; scars of First World War 84; publishes first novel, 1923 86; E. European tour with Winifred Holtby, 1924 88, 89; joins Labour Party 89; becomes engaged to George Catlin, 1924 88; marriage 38, 89, 100, 101; goes to Cornell with husband 89; visits Geneva with Winifred Holtby, 1926 93; in US with husband, 1925–6 101–2, 103; birth of son, 1927 53, 54–5, 107, 109; inheritance from father, 1935 122, 133; attracted to George Brett 123–5; blow of father's suicide and Winifred's death, 1935 126–7; marital tension 127; work in 1935 election 128; visits Nazi Germany 131; lecture of US 133; inheritance from Aunt Florence 133; buys New Forest cottage, 1939 137; conducts peace campaign throughout Second World War 145–6, 147; gains religious conviction, 1945 157, 168; holidays with son in Switzerland, 1947 166; post-war foreign tours 173
marriage terms 98–100, 104, 167
memorial 6
opulent life-style 11–12
pacifism 10, 12, 85, 131–2, 134, 139, 145, 157, 158
pacifist books 2
physical strength 15
promotion of causes 2, 12, 85, 86, 132, 133

romanticism 10, 11, 15, 94
Seeds of Chaos 154, 155
study 111
style of writing 25–6, 94
Testament of Experience 175
Testament of Friendship 44, 78, 79, 81, 94, 97
Testament of Youth ix, xi, 1, 4, 6, 12, 14, 15, 16, 28, 56, 61, 64, 70, 78, 82, 84, 93, 94, 97, 104, 109, 118, 124, 126, 129, 132, 167, 175
unconventionality 11
uses Mrs Gaskell as literary guide 94
youthful appearance 3, 11, 13
Bryant, Philip 152, 153
Buchan, John 82
Buxton, Charles Roden 108
Buzz bombs 153–4

Catchpool, Corder 147
Catlin, Alexander (son) 179
Catlin, Barbara (wife) 176–7
Catlin, Elaine (wife) 179
Catlin family 39–42
Catlin, George (father) ix, x, 3, 22, 52, 53, 62, 70, 138
ambitions for son 168–9
appearance of snobbery 27
books published, 1922–74 27
contribution to political science 105–7, 134, 175
failure of ambitions 28, 36
famous friends 113–18
girl friends 27
History of Political Philosophers 131, 133
identification with Anglo-American cooperation 25, 134, 138, 175
intellectual versatility 26–7
interest in philosophy 31
jealousy 27, 176
lack of political acumen 156–7
life and career: birth 28; quarrelling parents 29–30; scholarly ability 30; Civil Service job 30, 31; rejected by Army until 1918 30, 31; enjoyment of Army life 32; university years 32–3, 34–5, 36; post at Sheffield University 37; posts at Cornell University 37–8, 88, 89; courtship and marriage 38, 89, 95–8, 100, 101; conversion to Catholicism 35, 95; honeymoon 101;